New York Real Estate License Exam Prep

All-in-One Review and Testing to Pass New York's Real Estate Exam

First Edition

Stephen Mettling
Jane Somers
Ryan Mettling

Performance Programs Company
6810 190th Street East
Bradenton, FL 34211
www.performanceprogramscompany.com

Material in this book is not intended to represent legal advice and should not be so construed. Readers should consult legal counsel for advice regarding points of law.

ISBN 978-1955919258

Contents

Introduction

Welcome licensee candidates and future real estate professionals!

We know you have worked hard just to get here – you've completed or nearly completed your pre-license curricula, and now all you have to do is pass the state license exam. But easier said than done – and that's where we come in. We know the exam can be tough, and very nerve-wracking to prepare for. That's why we created New York Real Estate License Exam Prep (NY-RELEP) the way we did. Since we have been managing real estate schools and developing curriculum for forty years, we know how all this works – or fails to work. Let us assure you – you made the right decision buying this publication to prepare for your New York exam. Here's why.

First, NY-RELEP is comprehensive. It contains both extensive content review as well as testing practice. And the text review, unlike most competing books, is New York-specific – not just simplistic national content, but terse, relevant and accurate state and national laws and regulations presented as a set of 'key point reviews' ideal for pre-test memorization. NY-RELEP precisely follows the official New York salesperson syllabus topic by topic in the correct ordered sequence. Consequently, the material serves as a more user-friendly review for students who have taken pre-license courses throughout New York containing this required content and organization. Finally, our review content and question selection is tailored to follow the state testing outline promulgated by the state of New York. As such, the breadth and depth of the law reviews and test questions reflect the topic emphasis of New York's license exam.

A word about the tests. The NY-RELEP's test questions are designed to cover the content covered by the law reviews – which reinforces your learning of the total body of information tested by the state of New York. The questions are direct, to the point, and designed to test your understanding. When you have completed a given test, you can check your answers against the answer key in the appendix. You may also note that each question's answer is accompanied by a brief explanation to further reinforce your understanding.

Your particular study and testing practice strategy using NY-RELEP is up to you. But to fully exploit its comprehensive content coverage, you should try to review and memorize the key point reviews as much as possible. Then you should make every effort to take each exam, review your mistakes, and re-read the key point reviews that cover your weaker areas.

In the end, as you know, it's all up to you. Unlike other publications, we are not going to tell you that using this book will guarantee that you pass the New York state exam. It still takes hard work and study to pass. But we have done our best here to get you ready. Following that, the most we can do is wish you the best of success in taking and passing your state exam. So good luck!!

About the authors

For nearly fifty years, Stephen Mettling has been actively engaged in real estate education. Beginning with Dearborn in 1972, then called Real Estate Education Company, Mr. Mettling managed the company's textbook division and author acquisitions. Subsequently he built up the company's real estate school division which eventually became the country's largest real estate, insurance and securities school network in the country. In 1978, Mr. Mettling founded Performance Programs Company, a custom training program publishing and development company specializing in commercial, industrial, and corporate real estate. Over time, Performance Programs Company narrowed its focus to real estate textbook and exam prep publishing. Currently the Company's texts and prelicense resources are used in hundreds of schools in over 48 states. Mr. Mettling has authored over 100 textbooks, real estate programs and exam prep manuals.

Jane Somers has been a writer and educator for more than 30 years. She has directed the academic programs for a multi-campus college and has in recent years become an accomplished developer of online and classroom real estate curricula for a national real estate licensing organization, specializing in state licensing laws. Ms. Somers is also active in condominium association management and has served as president of a condominium owners association for ten years.

Ryan Mettling, partner and currently publisher of Performance Programs, is an accomplished online curriculum designer, author and course developer. His other principal publication is Real Estate Math Express. Mr. Mettling graduated Valedictorian from the University of Central Florida's College of Business Administration.

Section I: New York Principles & Law Key Point Review

UNIT ONE: LICENSE LAW AND REGULATIONS

Licensing

❑ **Purpose**

- To protect general public's welfare, safety, and health;

- To prevent economic loss resulting from dishonest and incompetent brokerage practices for a fee or other valuable consideration;

- To maintain high professional standards.

❑ **License Types**

- Broker – any person, firm, LLC, or corporation who, for another and for a fee or other compensation, lists, sells, exchanges, buys, rents, negotiates, relocates tenants, or offers to perform any of these actions, or who collects rent or relocates tenants

- Associate broker – a licensed broker who chooses to work under the name and supervision of a sponsoring licensed broker who is licensed under a partnership, trade name, limited liability company or corporation

- Salesperson – person who performs real estate activities under the direct supervision of a sponsoring licensed broker

❑ **Licensee Responsibilities**

- Broker

  o fair and honest dealings with public

  o accountability for escrow funds belonging to others

  o seller agent's limited disclosure of material facts affecting property value and/or buyer agent's limited disclosure of buyer's ability to financially complete purchase

  o supervision, guidance, training of affiliated licensees

  o records maintenance of affiliated salespersons' listings and transactions; submission of records to Department of State as needed

- Salesperson and associate broker

  o perform all business in affiliated broker's name

  o perform all business in alliance with other licensees and appropriate laws

  o fair and honest dealings with public

  o accountability for escrow funds belonging to others

  o seller agent's limited disclosure of material facts affecting property value and/or buyer agent's limited disclosure of buyer's ability to financially complete purchase

7

❑ **License Requirements**

  ▪ Salesperson

    o at least 18 years old

    o submit application and fee

    o complete 77-hour salesperson education course

    o pass end-of-course exams

    o pass state examination and pay exam fee

    o obtain sponsorship of NY licensed broker

    o possess NY photo driver's license or ID card

    o no criminal or sexual offense conviction unless secretary deems there is no bar to licensure

  ▪ Broker

    o at least 20 years old

    o 2 years' experience as licensed salesperson or 3 years' experience in general real estate field or combination of both

    o submit application and fee

    o complete 152-hour broker education course (77-hour salesperson course plus 75-hour broker course)

    o pass end-of-course exams

    o pass state examination and pay exam fee

    o possess NY photo driver's license or ID card

    o no criminal or sexual offense conviction unless secretary deems there is no bar to licensure

❑ **Licensed Activities**

  ▪ When performed for another and for a fee or other compensation,

    o negotiating sale, exchange, rental of real property

    o collecting rent

    o negotiating commercial loans secured by a mortgage

    o representing self as or acting as licensed broker or salesperson

❑ **Licensure Exemptions**

  • Public officers performing official duties

  • Executors, guardians, referees, receivers, administrators acting under court order

  • NY licensed attorneys who are not acting as broker with supervision over salespersons

  • Resident manager who is employed by one owner to manage rental property, to lease units, and/or to collect rent

  • Tenant associations and not-for-profit corporations who enforce the NY City housing maintenance code for residential property owned by the city

- ❑ **Maintaining the License**
  - ▪ Change of business address
    - ○ broker to notify Department of State (DOS) with fee for each license
    - ○ new license and pocket card mailed to broker and licensees
  - ▪ Change of status or name
    - ○ licensee to file notice of change with fee online
  - ▪ Who holds
    - ○ broker to hold licenses
    - ○ licensees to hold pocket cards
- ❑ **Change of Association**
  - ▪ Salesperson not to perform real estate acts until associated with new broker
  - ▪ Salesperson termination
    - ○ broker to notify DOS
  - ▪ Salesperson change of broker
    - ○ current broker to return license to salesperson
    - ○ current broker to file termination notice with DOS
    - ○ salesperson to give all client and listing information, agency agreements, transaction documents to broker when ending affiliation with broker
    - ○ new broker to file change of association notice with DOS
- ❑ **Nonresident Licensure**
  - ▪ Reciprocity
    - ○ licensing agreement between states with similar licensure requirements
    - ○ no additional education or testing required for licensure in reciprocal state
    - ○ family members of armed forces members may qualify for NY licensure even when from state with no reciprocity agreement if currently licensed in home state
  - ▪ Mutual recognition
    - ○ no reciprocity agreement with other state
    - ○ state recognizes licensee's education and experience in another state
    - ○ additional education may be required to compensate for fewer education hours in home state; may need to pass law section of state's licensing exam
  - ▪ Nonresident licensees
    - ○ must meet NY licensing requirements
    - ○ if no exam is required in home state, then nonresident must meet NY exam requirements
    - ○ do not need to maintain place of business in NY if maintain place of business in home state
    - ○ must file irrevocable consent form
    - ○ nonresident license not to be granted to residents of states that do not permit NY licensees to become nonresident licensees in that state

- ❑ **Dual Licensure** – broker/salesperson
  - Broker holds multiple NY licenses
  - Salesperson holds licenses under multiple brokers
- ❑ **Renewals and Continuing Education Requirements**
  - Continuing education (CE) requirements
    - 22 ½ hours approved continuing education every 2-year licensure period
    - CE to include 3 hours of fair housing or discrimination, or both in sale of, rental of, or interest in real property
    - completed in classroom (minimum 90% attendance), distance learning (online), or combination of both
    - completion deadline may be extended for hardship by filing waiver request and evidence of hardship
    - attorneys with broker license exempt from CE completion
    - full-time brokers licensed before July 1, 2008, who practiced at least 15 years exempt from CE
  - Renewal requirements
    - must renew every 2 years
    - must file online, pay renewal fee, complete CE requirements
    - failure to renew within 2 years of expiration date results in retaking state licensure exam
  - Sponsoring broker requirements
    - sponsoring broker license to be displayed in place of business
    - if sponsored licensees' licenses are displayed, broker, associate broker, salesperson licenses to be separated
    - broker to keep licenses; licensees to keep pocket card
    - current sponsoring broker to file termination notice with DOS
    - with change of broker association, broker to return license to licensee and to file termination of association with DOS; new broker to file change of association notice and pay fee
    - suspension or revocation of sponsoring broker's license results in suspension of sponsored licensees' licenses until affiliated with new broker
- ❑ **Promulgated Regulations**
  - Secretary of State to promulgate rules that establish method, content, setting, and supervision requirements for CE courses
  - Secretary to permit alternatives to content and presentation method for CE courses
  - Real estate board is not to promulgate rules, regulation, or guidance for CE courses
- ❑ **Branch Office Requirements**
  - Must be approved by Secretary of State
  - Separate license required
  - Owned, maintained, operated, supervised by branch office licensed broker
  - Broker owner to pay all related expenses

- Associate broker with office manager license may operate branch office with broker owner's supervision
- Salesperson never to operate branch office

❑ **Advertising Guidelines**
- All ads must identify advertiser as real estate broker; blind ads prohibited
- Ads must include name of brokerage
- Internet ads to include link to brokerage website with broker supervising salespersons' websites
- Licensees' individual websites to have link to Fair Housing Notice
- Logos, nicknames, team names allowed
  - team names to include team members' names or include "at/of (full name of the brokerage)"
  - must include "team" in the name
  - must identify licensed and unlicensed team members when names are included
- Must be clear, honest, accurate, and not confuse public
- Must have property owner's approval to place for sale sign on property or on any website
  - must include listing brokerage name on sign
- Advertise another broker's exclusive listing only with consent of other broker;
  - must include other broker's name conspicuously on advertisement,
  - must include words to identify other broker as listing broker
- Initial email to include all required information; not necessary on subsequent emails
- Violations of advertising regulations result in license revocation or suspension, fines and restitution

❑ **Common License Law Violations**
- Violations
  - noncompliance with license law provisions (Article 12-A Real Property Law)
  - noncompliance with Rules of Secretary of State (Section 442-H)
  - material misstatement within licensure application
  - fraud or fraudulent practices
  - dishonest or misleading advertising
  - untrustworthiness or incompetency
    - misrepresentation
    - false promises
    - failing to account for money belonging to others
    - failing to make required disclosures
    - interfering with another licensee's agency relationship
    - providing legal opinions when not an attorney
    - failure to comply with nondiscrimination laws

- ◆ entering into net listing relationship with seller
  - o failure to comply with child support summons, subpoena, warrant
  - o accepting compensation for real estate activities when unlicensed
  - o offering compensation for real estate activities to unlicensed individual
  - o paying or accepting compensation or referral fees without full disclosure and informed consent
  - o salesperson accepting compensation from someone other than sponsoring broker
  - o receiving or offering kickbacks
  - o failure to disclose licensee's ownership or purchasing interest in self-listed property
  - o failure to present all purchase offers to seller
  - o failure to comply with advertising regulations
- ▪ Penalties
  - o license suspension or revocation
  - o fine up to $1,000
  - o reprimand
  - o restitution and/or damages
  - o imprisonment (criminal violations)

❑ **Unlicensed Assistants**
- ▪ May perform any of the following without a license:
  - o answer phones and take messages
  - o arrange appointments for licensees
  - o obtain loan status reports
  - o assemble closing documents
  - o write and place broker-approved ads and promotional materials
  - o compute commission checks
  - o place and remove signs from property
  - o order repair items as directed by broker
  - o gather information for market analyses and appraisals
  - o monitor licensed and personnel files
  - o perform general clerical duties
- ▪ Duties discharged under supervision of broker
- ▪ Paid hourly or salaried by either broker or salesperson
- ▪ If paid per transaction, assistant must be licensed

❑ **Property Condition Disclosure Act**
- ▪ Residential property sellers required to complete a property condition disclosure statement to buyer prior to buyer signing contract for purchase of the property
- ▪ Statement to be signed by both seller and buyer; attached to purchase contract

12

- Regardless of disclosures in the statement, buyer and seller may still enter into purchase agreement for property "as is"
- Disclosure is not warranty or replacement for property inspection
- Seller's agent required to inform seller of disclosure obligation
- Failure to provide disclosure statement can result in seller's liability and buyer receiving $500 credit toward purchase price
- Transactions exempted from disclosure requirement
  - court-ordered transfers
  - property transfers to lender
  - transfers to beneficiaries of estate or trust
  - transfers related to guardianship or conservatorship
  - transfers to co-owner or relative
  - settlement transfers
  - transfer to government entity
  - transfer of never-occupied new construction
  - transfer by sheriff

❏ Gas Well Disclosure

- Per NY Real Property Law,
  - property sellers must disclose the existence of any uncapped natural gas wells on the property
  - seller must inform buyer prior to entering into a purchase contract

UNIT TWO: LAW OF AGENCY AND DISCLOSURE

Agency

❑ **Basic Roles**

- Principal (client)

    o party who hires the agent; may be seller, buyer, landlord, or tenant

- Agent

    o fiduciary of principal; works for the client; hired to perform authorized work; bound to fulfill fiduciary duties; must be licensed broker

- Customer or prospect

    o third party in transaction; not represented by agent, but agent works with a customer in fulfilling client's objectives; may be seller, buyer, landlord, or tenant; third party potential customer is a prospect

❑ **Types of Agency**

- Universal agency

    o wherein principal utilizes a power of attorney to empower the agent to perform any and all actions legally delegated to an agency representative

- General agency

    o wherein principal delegates ongoing tasks and duties to the agent within a particular business or enterprise; may include authority to enter into contracts

- Special or limited agency

    o wherein principal enters into special agency agreement to delegate authority to allow the agent to conduct a specific activity; when activity is completed, the agency relationship terminates; special agents typically may not bind principal to a contract

    o real estate brokerage typically based on special agency wherein principal hires broker to procure a buyer or seller; relationship terminates when the objective is achieved

❑ **Agency Creation**

- Written or oral agreement

    o most common is written or oral listing agreement wherein an agency is established for specified transaction with a designated expiration date; agreement sets authorizations, duties, and requirements for compensation

- Implied agency

    o intentionally or unintentionally establishes agency by implication wherein the parties behave as though there is an agreement even though one has not been specifically discussed; obligates agent to fiduciary duties and standards of care for which agent can be held liable for failure to fulfill

❑ **Types of Agent**

- Seller's agent

    o engaged by seller to find buyer for seller's home at price and terms acceptable to seller; puts seller's interests above others

14

- Buyer's agent
    - engaged by buyer to find a home and negotiate the price and terms acceptable to the buyer; puts the buyer's interests above others
- Broker's agent
    - agent who works for firm other than listing agent's firm or buyer's agent's firm but cooperates or is engaged by either agent to assist in finding property for either agent's client to buy or sell; no direct relationship with client; no directions or instructions directly from client
- Dual agent
    - represents both buyer and seller if both provide written informed consent; no full fiduciary duties to either client but subject to provisions included in agency agreement; no undivided loyalty to either client
- Designated sales agents
    - individual sales agents working for same broker engaged in consented dual agency, each agent designated to represent either the buyer or seller as a single agent, providing undivided loyalty

❑ **Fiduciary Duties**
- Agent to client
    - skill, care, diligence – agent to do job with diligence and competence (level of real estate marketing skills and knowledge), using care to observe the agent's limited scope of authority
    - loyalty – client's interest above all others
    - obedience – comply with client's legal instructions
    - confidentiality – hold client's personal and business information in confidence during agency relationship; duty extends after termination of agency agreement
    - accounting – safeguard and account for all funds and property received from client or customer
    - full disclosure – inform client of all material facts and rumors that agent knows or should know that might affect the client's interest in the property transaction; no duty to disclose information protected under anti-discrimination laws as that information is immaterial to the transaction
- Agent to customer
    - honesty and fair dealing – no deceit, defraud, or taking advantage of customer
    - reasonable care and skill – agent held to certain standard of knowledge, expertise, ethics; failure to live up to standards may result in agent's liability for negligence, fraud, or violation of license laws
    - proper disclosure – disclose agency, property condition, environmental hazards
- Principal to agent
    - availability – principal to be available for consultation, direction, and decision-making, especially in special agency relationship
    - information – provide agent with sufficient information to perform desired activity
    - compensation – if agency agreement includes compensation to agent, principal must provide the compensation when the agent performs according to the agreement

- Breach of duty
  - agents held liable for breaching duty to client or customer
  - breach may result in
    - recission of listing agreement with potential loss of compensation
    - forfeiture of earned compensation
    - disciplinary sanctions against agent
    - lawsuit against agent for damages

❑ **Termination of Agency**
- Reasons for termination
  - full performance of all obligations by parties to the agreement
  - involved parties' mutual agreement at any time
  - agreement's expiration
  - either party's death or incapacity
  - agent's abandonment
  - subject property's condemnation or destruction
  - agent renunciation
  - client revocation
  - either party's breach of contract
  - either party's bankruptcy
  - agent's license revocation

❑ **Misrepresentation**
- Intentional misrepresentation
  - defrauding buyer by misrepresenting or concealing facts
- Negligent misrepresentation
  - failing to disclose facts agent is unaware of if agent should have known such facts
- Misrepresentation of expertise
  - agent held accountable for acting or speaking outside the agent's area of expertise

❑ **Antitrust Laws**
- Sherman Antitrust Act, 1890
  - prohibits restrictions on interstate commerce and competition in the marketplace; empowers federal government to act against antitrust violators
- Clayton Act, 1914
  - prohibits practices that create monopolies, such as price discrimination against competing companies, conditioning sales on exclusive dealing, mergers and acquisitions that reduce competition, serving on board of directors for competing companies; legalizes certain labor strikes and boycotts
- Antitrust violations
  - Group boycotting – when two or more competitors join together and agree to boycott an

additional brokerage competitor

- o Price fixing – when two or more competitors conspire to set like commissions or fees regardless of market conditions or competition, resulting in a restraint of trade

- o Market allocation – when competing firms agree to divide a market area and restrict their competitive activities to their own designated market area

- o Tie-in Agreements – when the sale of one product or service is tied to the sale of another, less desirable product or service, thus restricting competition and limiting the consumer's freedom

- Penalties for violations by individuals
  - o fines up to $350,000
  - o prison up to 3 years
  - o both fines and prison
  - o other penalties as imposed by the DOJ and the FTC

- Penalties for violations by business entities
  - o fines up to $10,000,000
  - o separate DOJ fines
  - o both types of fines

❑ **Agency Alternatives/Relationships**

- Cooperative brokerage / selling
  - o when brokers and salespersons cooperate with listing broker to find buyers or tenants for a share of listing broker's commission
  - o can be seller's subagent, buyer's agent, or broker's agent
  - o includes use of MLS

- Subagency
  - o agent of the broker who is agent of the client
  - o includes cooperating licensed broker (from another firm) and/or that broker's licensed salespeople as well as listing broker's licensed salespeople, all working for listing broker on behalf of client

- Brokerage without subagency
  - o listing broker splits commission with broker who provides buyer without subagency relationship, thereby eliminating seller's liability for agent's actions
  - o in NYC, other broker is automatically buyer's agent

- Single agency
  - o agent represents one party in a transaction
  - o client may be seller or buyer, landlord or tenant

❑ **Dual Agency**

- Broker represents both principal parties in the same transaction
- Legal relationship in NY
- Can be created unintentionally by behavior

- Results in conflict of interest
- Duties
    - no fiduciary duties of full disclosure and undivided loyalty
    - each party's pricing strategy and other designated information to remain confidential
- Requirements
    - must have informed voluntary written consent by all parties; can use disclosure form
        - failure to disclose dual agency to all parties results in sanctions against agent
    - agent must disclose agency to all involved parties
- In-house sales
    - listing broker's salesperson finds and represents buyer, resulting in dual agency
    - can involve same salesperson representing both seller and buyer or different salespersons in same brokerage with one representing seller and other representing buyer
- Company policy on dual agency
    - must inform client of possible dual agency resulting from in-house sales
- Designated agent
    - within dual agency, broker assigns one agent to seller and another agent to buyer
    - broker is dual agent; designated agents are each single agents with undivided loyalty to their clients

❑ Seller Agency and Agreements

- listing agreement defines relationship between seller and agent
- buyer broker agency agreement defines relationship between buyer and agent

❑ Types of Listings

- Exclusive right-to-sell
    - permitted in NY
    - most commonly used type of listing
    - seller contracts with one exclusive broker to procure buyer and sell property
    - broker paid commission if buyer procured prior to listing expiration, regardless of who actually procures the buyer
    - gives broker greatest assurance of compensation for marketing efforts
- Exclusive right-to-lease
    - permitted in NY
    - similar to exclusive right-to-sell
    - owner/landlord contracts with one exclusive broker to act as leasing agent to procure tenant
    - broker is paid commission or fee regardless of who actually procures the tenant
- Exclusive agency
    - permitted in NY
    - broker is paid commission if property is sold by any agent prior to listing expiration

18

- seller may sell property without broker's help and without owing broker commission
- Open listing
    - permitted in NY
    - seller may contract with multiple brokers
    - only broker who actually procures ready, willing, ad able buyer is paid commission
    - seller may sell property without any broker's help and without owing broker commission
    - may be written or oral agreement
    - not favored by brokers due to no assurance of compensation for marketing efforts
    - can cause commission disputes
- Multiple listing (MLS)
    - listing broker and cooperating brokers must be members of specific MLS
    - not a listing contract
    - provision in exclusive right-to-sell or exclusive agency contract
    - allows broker to place listing in multiple listing service to share listing information with other brokers
    - listing must be placed in MLS within designated time frame
    - allows multiple brokers to cooperate in the property sale in exchange for share of commission
    - cooperating brokers are subagents
- Net listing
    - not permitted in NY
    - owner sets minimum sale price
    - broker may sell at any price above the minimum and keep the difference as commission
    - creates conflict of interest between broker and seller
    - violates broker's fiduciary duties to client by failing to put client's interests first

❑ **Listing agreement requirements**
- Listing agent to confirm property is owned by seller
- Listing agent to obtain zoning classification, lot size, and yearly tax information
- Listing agent to inform buyer that property tax is for current year only
- Term of broker's employment; NY prohibits automatic extension clauses in exclusive listings
- Must include
    - name and address of property owner
    - property description, including lot size, room number and size, square footage, construction and age of structure
    - neighborhood information
    - current taxes
    - existing financing and any seller financing
    - utilities

- o included appliances and fixtures
- o occupancy/possession date
- o listing agreement beginning and ending dates

❑ **Listing agreement termination**
- Reasons for termination
  - o sale of property
  - o cancellation by broker and/or involved parties
  - o listing time period expiration
  - o either party's death or incapacity
  - o agent's abandonment and/or lack of effort
  - o subject property's condemnation or destruction
  - o seller revocation
  - o either party's bankruptcy
  - o outside entity changes allowed use of property

Disclosures

❑ **New York Agency Disclosure Requirements**
- NY brokers and licensees required to disclose their role and who they represent in a real estate transaction
- Disclosure must be in writing and signed by all involved parties
- Buyers and sellers must sign acknowledgement form confirming they have read the disclosure and understand the agent's role
- Agency disclosure form must be presented to prospective clients or customers upon the first substantive meeting
- Agency disclosure form describes the roles of all types of agents
- Disclosure form required for
  - o sale or lease of residential property with four or fewer units
  - o any transaction involving a condominium or cooperative, including buildings with more than four units
- Broker cannot accept compensation from more than one party unless all parties consent
- Current disclosure form allows clients to give advance consent to dual agency
- Written consent to dual agency must also be obtained when the agency is created
  - o failure to obtain dual agency consent upon creation of the relationship results in violation of agent's fiduciary duties to client
- Client may sign an advance consent to dual agency with designated sales agent
- Listing broker must comply with agency disclosure and acknowledgement requirements with buyers at their first substantive meeting with principals; buyers' agents must comply with same requirements

- Disclosure and acknowledgement form must be maintained with transaction records for at least 3 years
- If seller or buyer refuses to sign the disclosure or acknowledgement, broker must note the refusal on the form and maintain it with transaction records

❑ **Seller-Landlord Disclosures**

- Property condition disclosure statement (aforementioned)
  - NY residential property sellers required to provide buyer with property condition disclosure statement
    - ◆ disclosure to be delivered prior to contract signing
    - ◆ disclosure to be signed by seller and buyer and attached to purchase contract
    - ◆ failure to provide disclosure results in buyer receiving $500 credit towards purchase price
  - Agent is not to help seller complete the disclosure form
- Lead
  - sellers and landlords of homes built before 1978 must disclose the presence of lead-based paint
  - disclosure to be made at time of listing and again before closing or lease signing
  - NYC requires landlords to annually inspect for lead hazards when children under 6 years are residents
- Truth-in-heating law
  - when requested in writing, seller is to provide buyer with 2-years' heating and cooling statements for one or two-family properties
  - seller to provide statement regarding the property's insulation
- Bedbug disclosure
  - landlord must provide prospective tenants with a bedbug infestation history for the prior year, using state-required form

UNIT THREE: ESTATES AND INTERESTS

Rights

❑ **Bundle of rights**

- **"PUTEE":**
    - **P** ossession
    - **U** se
    - **T** ransfer
    - **E** xclusion
    - **E** ncumberable

❑ **Land; real estate; real property**

- Land: surface, all *natural things* attached to it, subsurface, and air above the surface.
- Real estate: land + manmade permanent attachments
- Real property: real estate + bundle of rights
- Constitution guarantees private ownership of real property.

❑ **Real vs. personal property**

- Real property
    - land
    - fixtures
    - attachments
- Personal property
    - chattels
    - trade fixtures
    - emblements
- Differentiation criteria: item is real or personal property depending on why, how item is attached to the real estate. Depends on the owners'
    - intention; adaptation; functionality; relationship of parties; contract provisions
- Trade fixtures
    - personal property items temporarily attached to real estate in order to conduct business
- Emblements
    - plants or crops that are considered personal property despite being attached to land
- Conversion
    - real to personal property referred to as severance
    - personal to real property referred to as affixing

- Factory-built housing – mobile homes and manufactured homes
  - units are real or personal property: real if permanently affixed to ground; otherwise personal

❑ **Property Characteristics**
- property is either real or personal
- property is either tangible or intangible
- Immobility
  - land cannot be moved from one site to another; its location is forever fixed
- Indestructibility
  - land is permanent and cannot be destroyed since by definition it extends below ground and into the sky
  - since land is permanent, it does not depreciate
  - only improvements depreciate and are insurable
- Non-homogeneity
  - land is non-homogeneous; no two parcels of land are exactly the same since they have a different location

❑ **Real Property Rights**
- Airspace = air rights
- Surface (of the earth) = surface rights
- Subsurface = subsurface or mineral rights

❑ **Water Rights**
- Doctrine of Prior Appropriation
  - state controls water usage
  - state grants usage permits
- Riparian rights (rivers and streams)
  - applies to rivers and streams
  - if waterway is navigable: owners own land to water's edge
  - if waterway is not navigable: owners own land to midpoint of waterway
- Littoral rights (lakes and seas)
  - applies to seas and lakes
  - abutting property owners own to high water mark
  - state owns underlying land

  Memory Tip: **R**: River – Riparian   **L**: Lake – Littoral

❑ **Rights Not Recognized in NY**
- Dower –wife's interest in deceased husband's real estate
- Curtsey –husband's interest in deceased wife's real estate
- Community property – husband and wife's equal interest in property obtained during the marriage

- Homestead – owner's special rights in property used as family home; NY defines homestead as an owner occupant's interest in the primary residence; state law requires homestead to be residential property

Estates & Interests

- ❑ **Estates in Land**
    - Include right of possession
    - Leasehold = limited duration
    - Freehold: duration is not limited

- ❑ **Freehold Estates** (Own)
    - Fee simple
        - o *not limited* by one's lifetime
        - o absolute: *highest* form of ownership interest
        - o defeasible: *reverts* to previous owner per conditions
    - Life estates
        - o passes *to another* on death of named party
        - o remainder: *named party* to receive estate
        - o reversion: *previous owner* to receive estate
    - Conventional life estate
        - o *limited* to lifetime of life tenant/ named party
        - o ordinary: estate passes to remainderman or previous owner when life tenant dies
        - o pur autre vie: limited to lifetime of another, passes to remainderman or previous owner
    - Legal life estate
        - o created by operation of state law as opposed to a property owner's agreement
        - o designed to protect family survivors

- ❑ **Leasehold Estates** (Lease)
    - Estate for years
        - o specific, *stated duration*, per lease; expires at end of term
    - Periodic
        - o lease term *renews automatically* upon acceptance of rent; renews indefinitely if landlord accepts rent
    - Estate at will
        - o for *indefinite period* subject to rent payment; cancelable with notice
    - Estate at sufferance
        - o tenancy *against landlord's will* and without an agreement

- ❑ **Forms of Ownership**
    - Tenancy in severalty

- *sole* ownership of a freehold estate; passes to heirs
- Tenancy in common
  - co-tenants individually own undivided interests
  - *any ownership share possible*
  - no survivorship
  - can convey to outside parties
- Joint tenancy
  - equal undivided interest jointly owned
  - survivorship (may require express provision)
  - requires *four unities* to create: time, title, interest, possession
    1. *P*ossession: acquire same possessory rights
    2. *I*nterest: acquire equal, undivided interests
    3. *T*ime: acquire interests at same time
    4. *T*itle: acquire interests with same deed
- Tenancy by the entireties
  - *husband and wife* own equal undivided interest
  - now applies to same-sex couples
- Community property
  - *joint ownership* by spouses of property acquired during the marriage
  - *separate ownership of property acquired prior to marriage, as gift or inheritance, with separate-property funds, or income from separate property*
- Termination of joint tenancy or tenancy in common
  - by partition suit – one owner's interest legally disposed of by division of physical property
  - by foreclosure or bankruptcy

❑ **Trusts – created by deed, will, or trust agreement**
- *Trustor (fee owner, grantor)* gives title, deed, trust agreement to trustee (fiduciary)
- *Trustee* renders fiduciary duties to trustor and beneficiary to maintain property condition and value
- *Beneficiary* receives ownership benefits
- Living trust – trustor conveys real or personal property to trustee during trustor's lifetime for benefit of third party
- Testamentary trust – same as living trust but takes effect after trustor dies as established by trustor's will
- Land trust – trustor conveys fee estate (real property) to trustee and names trustor as beneficiary
  - trustee holds legal title with fiduciary duties
  - beneficiary controls property use and proceeds
  - beneficiary controls trustee's power to sell or encumber the property
  - beneficiary's name not on public records
  - trust term is limited and must be renewed or trustee must sell the property and distribute

the proceeds

- ❑ **Ownership by Business Entities**
  - ▪ Corporation
    - o owned by stockholders
    - o elected board of directors oversees business
    - o officers and managers conduct daily business activities
    - o officers and directors held liable for corporation's actions
    - o may own real property in severalty or as tenants in common
  - ▪ Partnership
    - o two or more individuals work together and share profits
    - o may own real property
    - o *general partnership* – not a distinct legal entity; partners share full liability for debts and obligations
    - o *limited partnership* – one or more partners as general partners who run the business with liability for debts; others as limited partners with liability based on investment in the partnership
  - ▪ Limited liability company
    - o offers members limited liability with income passed directly to members and taxed as individual income
    - o management structure is flexible
    - o may own real property

UNIT FOUR: LIENS AND EASEMENTS

Liens

❑ **Lien Types and Characteristics**

- Lien types

    - voluntary / involuntary – mortgage lien / tax lien

    - general / specific – against any & all assets / against car or house

    - superior / junior – paid before juniors / paid after superiors by date of recording

- Characteristics

    - encumbrance affecting ownership, value, transfer

    - claims attaching to real and personal property as security for debt

    - recorded on title effectively reducing equity in the amount of the lien

    - does not convey ownership unless a mortgage in a title theory state

    - lien attaches to the property

    - property can be encumbered by multiple liens

    - lien terminates upon payment of debt, recording of satisfaction documents

❑ **Lien Priority**

    - order in which liens against a property are satisfied

    - determined by superior v junior class and by date of recordation

    - the highest priority lien is paid by foreclosure proceeds before any other lien

- Superior liens by rank (not by date of recordation; paid before junior liens)

    - real estate tax liens

    - special assessment liens

    - federal estate tax liens

    - state inheritance tax liens

- Junior/inferior/subordinate liens (by date of recording)

    - federal income tax liens – on real and personal property for failure to pay income tax

    - judgment liens – on real and personal property from money judgment issued by court

    - mortgage liens – secure loans on real property in lien-theory states (i.e., NY)

    - vendors' liens – secure seller's loan to finance buyer's purchase of property

    - mechanics' liens (priority by date work performed) – secure costs of labor, materials, and supplies for repair or construction of real property improvements

- Subordination

    - Lienor changes priority of junior lien by voluntarily agreeing to lower the lien's position

❑ **Deed restrictions**

- Encumbrance affecting use

- Conditions, covenants imposed on property by deed or subdivision plat

    o *condition* only created within transfer or ownership; violation may result in ownership reverting to previous owner

    o *covenant* created by mutual agreement; breaches may result in injunction to force compliance or payment of compensatory damages

- May apply to single property or entire subdivision

- Goes with the property upon transfer

- Established to control quality, standards of a subdivision

- Apply to land use, type of structure, setbacks, minimum house size, etc.

- Take precedence over zoning ordinances if more restrictive

Easements & Encroachments

❑ **Easements**

- Characteristics

    o encumbrance affecting use

    o rights to use portions of another's property

    o must involve easement landowner and another non-owning party

    o pertains to defined physical area within property boundaries

    o benefited party – receiver of easement right

    o burdened party – giver of easement right

    o affirmative easement: allows a use

    o negative easement: prohibits a use

- Appurtenant

    o *attaches* to the estate

    o *dominant* tenement's *right to use* or restrict adjacent *servient* tenement

    o *by necessity*, to *landlocked* owners

    o party wall easement in a shared structure: to not damage or destroy

- In gross

    o *does not attach* to the estate

    o personal-- not transferrable, ends upon death of easement holder

    o commercial-- transferrable, granted to a business

- By prescription

    o property used without permission; can come to exist regardless of owner's consent

    o obtainable through *continuous, open, adverse use* over a period of time which varies by state

28

- Creation
  - by voluntary action of owner or reserved right expressed in deed
  - by necessary or prescriptive operation of law when used by non-owner without owner's permission for statutory period of time and under specified conditions
  - by government power of eminent domain
- License
  - *personal* right to use a property
  - does not attach
  - non-transferrable
  - revocable
  - ceases upon death of owner

❑ Encroachments

- Encumbrance affecting use
- Unauthorized intrusions of one owner's real property into that of another
- May diminish property's value
- May require survey to detect
- May not appear on property title records
- Owner may sue for encroachment removal or compensation for damages
- May become prescriptive easements if not remedied over prescription period

UNIT FIVE: DEEDS AND CONVEYANCES

Titles

❑ **Transferring and Recording Title**

- Legal vs. equitable title

    o Legal title: owner enjoys full bundle of rights

    o Equitable title: party can obtain legal title subject to agreements with creditors

- Notice

    o how ownership is evidenced to the public

- Actual notice

    o *knowledge acquired directly* through demonstrable evidence, e.g., presenting or inspecting a deed, visiting a party in possession

- Constructive notice (legal notice)

    o *knowledge one could have obtained*, as presumed by law; imparted by recording in public records "for all to see"

- Transfer = Alienation

    o conveyance – when written instrument is used for title transfer

- Voluntary title transfer

    o deed

    o will

    o public grant

- Involuntary title transfer

    o descent (without will, with heirs)

    o escheat (without will nor heirs)

    o foreclosure (loan default)

    o eminent domain (public good)

    o adverse possession (hostile, open use)

    - ♦ "unwanted owner" may claim ownership to a property

    - ♦ must show "claim of right" as reason

    - ♦ must be notorious possession (unconcealed)

    - ♦ must be hostile (possessor claims ownership)

    - ♦ must be continuous for a statutory period of time

Deeds

- **Deeds of Conveyance**
  - Definition
    - legal instrument used by an owner (grantor) to transfer title to real estate voluntarily to another party (grantee)
  - For title to pass
    - grantee must receive and accept deed; physical possession of deed or record
    - grantor must be competent and intend to deliver deed beyond act of physical delivery

- **Deed Validity**
  - Requirements
    - grantor
    - grantee
    - in writing
    - legal description
    - granting clause
    - consideration
    - grantor's signature
    - acknowledgement (notarized)
    - delivery and acceptance

- **Deed Clauses**
  - Conveyance clauses
    - Granting or premises – only required clause; includes intentions, parties, property, consideration
    - Habendum – type of estate
    - Reddendum or reserving – restrictions and limitations to estate
    - Tenendum – property conveyed besides land
  - Covenant or warrant clauses
    - Warrant of seisin – grantor's ownership assurance
    - Warrant of quiet enjoyment – grantee's non-disturbance by third party assurance
    - Warrant of further assurance – grantor to assist in clearing title
    - Warranty forever – grantee to receive good title; grantor to defend contrary claims
    - Warrant of encumbrances – only expressly named encumbrances exist
    - Warranty against grantor's acts – trustee's assurance no title impairments

- **Deed Types**
  - Bargain and Sale – "I own but won't defend."
  - General Warranty – "I own and will defend."

- Special Warranty – "I own and will defend against my acts only."
- Quitclaim – used to clear title, not convey – "I may or may not own, and I won't defend."

❑ **Special Purpose Deeds** – Tailored to requirements of specific parties, properties, and purposes
- Personal Representative's deed – executor to convey decedent's estate
- Guardian's deed – court-appointed guardian to transfer property of minor or mentally incompetent person
- Sheriff's deed – convey foreclosed property at auction
- Deed of trust – convey to third party trustee as collateral for loan
- Deed in trust – convey to trustee of a land trust
- Master deed – convey land to condominium developer
- Partition deed – convey co-owner property per court order
- Patent deed – transfer government property to private parties
- Tax deed – convey property sold at tax sale

❑ **Transfer Tax**
- Documentary stamp tax: tax on conveyance of real property based on price of property conveyed
- Facilitates ad valorem assessment
- Payment evidenced on deed
- Exemptions
    - transfer within immediate family
    - consideration less than designated amount
    - transfer between government entities or non-profit organizations
    - trust deed transfer and reconveyance
    - tax deed

❑ **Last Will and Testament**
- Voluntary conveyance after death
- Maker = owner; devisor or testator
- Heir = beneficiary or devisee
- Types
    - Witnessed – in writing and witnessed by two people
    - Holographic – handwritten, dated, signed
    - Nuncupative – oral but written down by witness; not legal for property transfer
- Validity
    - legal age; mentally competent; entitled "last will & testament;" signed, witnessed, voluntary
- Probate objectives
    - settle decedent's estate with or without a will
    - validate existing will

- o identify and settle claims and outstanding debts
- o distribute remainder of estate to rightful heirs
- Testate (with will) with heirs
  - o first to creditors
  - o then to homestead
  - o then to heirs by will
- Intestate (without will) with heirs
  - o first to creditors
  - o then to homestead
  - o then to heirs by laws of descent
- Intestate (without will) without heirs
  - o first to creditors
  - o then to state by escheat

UNIT SIX: TITLE CLOSING AND COSTS

Title Closing, Costs, Records

❑ **Title Closing**

- Process
  - o buyer and seller verify sales contract terms are fulfilled
  - o seller proves marketability of title (via title insurance)
  - o seller removes encumbrances prior to title transfer
  - o buyer has survey and property inspection performed
  - o lender provides seller's mortgage payoff statement
  - o buyer provides escrow funds (earnest money, loan funds)
  - o escrow officer disburses funds as appropriate when conditions are met
    - ◆ conditions include survey, inspection, hazard insurance, title insurance, tax and insurance reserve account, private mortgage insurance

❑ **Real Estate Settlement Procedures Act (RESPA)**

- Purpose
  - o to clarify, disclose costs
  - o to eliminate kickbacks and undisclosed fees
- Applicability
  - o applies to residential property
  - o applies to federally-related mortgages, including VA and FHA
  - o regulated by Consumer Financial Protection Bureau (CFPB)
- Information booklet
  - o requires lenders to provide CFPB booklet, "Your Home Loan Toolkit"
- Loan estimate
  - o requires lenders to provide CFPB's H-24 Loan Estimate of settlement costs within 3 days of loan application
- Closing disclosure
  - o requires lenders to use CFPB's H-25 Closing Disclosure
- Referral fees and kickbacks
  - o prohibits payment of referral fees and kickbacks
  - o requires disclosure of business relationships between firms involved in the transaction

❑ **Settlement Process**

- Identify selling terms & costs
- Determine non-prorated debits and credits

- Complete prorated debits and credits
- Complete closing statement
- Disburse funds

❑ **Closing Costs**

- Costs and payors identified in sales contract
- Costs include brokerage fees, mortgage-related fees, title-related expenses, real estate taxes, settlement of buyer and seller debits and credits, prorated and non-prorated items
- Prorated items
    - items seller or buyer paid in advance, such as property utilities
    - items paid in arrears
- Buyer's non-prorated items
    - mortgage recording fees
    - document stamp tax
    - intangible tax on mortgage
    - mortgage fees – appraisal, credit, survey, loan
    - impound reserves – insurance, taxes
    - attorney fees
- Seller's non-prorated items
    - stamp tax on deed
    - title insurance
    - brokerage fee
    - inspection fees
    - title-related expenses
    - attorney fees

❑ **30-Day 12-Month Proration**

- Formula:
    - monthly amount = (annual amount ÷ 12)
    - daily amount = (monthly amount ÷ 30)
    - proration = (monthly amount x no. of months) + (daily amount x no. of days)

❑ **365-Day Method**

- Formula:
    - daily amount = annual amount ÷ 365 days; or
    - daily amount = monthly amount ÷ no. of days in month
    - proration = (daily amount x no. of days)

❑ **Truth-in-Lending Integrated Disclosures Rule (TRID/TILA)**

- Key points
    - combines financial disclosure requirements of RESPA & Truth-in-Lending Act (TILA)
    - replaces "Good Faith Estimate" and HUD-1 forms

- o uses new "Loan Estimate" form" and "Closing Disclosure" form
  - Forms and procedures required
    - o "Your Home Loan Toolkit" booklet at loan application
    - o loan estimate form: 3 business days after loan application
    - o closing disclosure: 3 business days before consummation
    - o forms to use same general terms
  - Good faith
    - o loan estimate costs based on best information available
    - o closing disclosure costs equal estimate costs within certain tolerances
  - Types of charges
    - o no limitation on increase over estimate
    - o 10% tolerance charges
    - o 0 tolerance charges
  - Applicable transactions
    - o most closed-end consumer mortgages, including: construction loans, loans secured by vacant land, loans to trusts
    - o not covered: home equity loans, reverse mortgages, loans on mobile homes, loans by small lenders (no more than 5 loans per year)
  - H-25 Form
    - o 5 pages, variable by loan type

❏ **Title Records**
  - Key terms
    - o title records – public records that contain a history of every parcel of real estate
    - o chain of title – successive property owners from original grant to present
    - o cloud on title – unrecorded claims
    - o suit to quiet title – lawsuit to settle claims
    - o abstract of title – written chronology of recorded owners, transfers, encumbrances
    - o title plant – duplicate set of property records maintained by private company
  - Features
    - o instruments affecting title must be recorded
    - o gives public constructive notice of ownership, condition of title
    - o determines property marketability
    - o protects lienholders; establishes lien priority
  - Evidence of title
    - o to assure the owner's identity, lack of defects, claims, or undisclosed encumbrances
    - o title insurance policy
    - o attorney's opinion of the title abstract
    - o title certificate

36

UNIT SEVEN: CONTRACT OF SALE AND LEASES

Leases

❑ **Leases**

- Definition – both an instrument of conveyance and contract between tenant (renter) and landlord (owner) to uphold certain covenants and obligations; document that conveys **temporary, exclusive** use of premises in exchange for rent and right of reversion

- Types of leasehold estates
  - o estate for years – specific lease term
  - o estate from period-to-period – lease term automatically renews
  - o estate at will – no specified lease term
  - o estate at sufferance – tenancy without consent

- Types of leases
  - o gross lease (full service) – landlord pays operating expenses; tenant pays only rent which is higher than in net lease; common for office, industrial, and residential with tenant paying utilities
  - o net lease – tenant pays some or all expenses in addition to rent; common for office, industrial, and sometimes for single-family homes
  - o percentage lease – tenant's rent is paid as percentage of income generated from use of property or gross sales; can be
    - ◆ fixed percent of gross revenue with no minimum rent
    - ◆ fixed minimum rent plus additional percent of gross sales
    - ◆ percentage rent or minimum rent, whichever is greater
  - o residential lease – net or gross with landlord paying expenses such as repairs and improvements with tenant paying utilities; differs from other leases by
    - ◆ shorter lease terms
    - ◆ standard lease clauses to comply with landlord-tenant laws
    - ◆ non-negotiable lease clauses to provide uniform leases
  - o commercial lease – complex net, gross, or percentage lease with
    - ◆ long lease terms
    - ◆ requirements for tenant improvements as needed for use
    - ◆ negotiable lease clauses
    - ◆ precise lease clauses to cover financial consequences of default
  - o ground lease (land lease) – tenant has leasehold interest in land only; used primarily for
    - ◆ raw land leased for agricultural or mining interest
    - ◆ unimproved property to be developed with land ownership staying with owner

37

- ♦ improved property where owner sells interest in improvements but retains ownership of the land
  - o proprietary lease – for cooperative unit owners with no stipulated rent or lease term; lease is assigned to new owner when unit is sold
  - o rights lease – for rights other than occupancy and possession; used for water rights, air rights, and mineral rights
- Standard provisions
  - o lead paint notice – tenant to be given lead paint hazard brochure prior to signing lease for residential property built before 1978, with some exceptions
  - o use of premises – residential or commercial; may restrict type of business; must allow disabled persons to make reasonable and necessary alterations
  - o lease term – starting and ending dates with length of term included; may include option to renew or extend
  - o rent and security deposit – date, place, manner, and amount of rent; may include grace period and late payment penalties; amount of security deposit collected for protection against property damage by tenant; in NY must be held in interest-bearing trust and not commingled with other personal or business funds; may be required to notify tenants where funds are held; NY Emergency Tenant Protection Act stabilizes rent in some apartments and limits security deposits to one month's rent
  - o repairs and maintenance – identifies who is responsible for repairs and maintenance expenses
  - o subletting and assignment – transfers portion or all of leasehold interest to third party with original tenant liable for lease unless landlord agrees otherwise
  - o rules and regulations – spells out usage restrictions
  - o improvements and alterations – identifies permissions and procedures for making improvements and who owns the improvements
    - ♦ NY leases contain implied warranty of habitability with landlord responsible for maintaining livable conditions
    - ♦ NY leases entitle tenants to quiet enjoyment, right to no disturbance by other parties
  - o options – gives tenant option to choose course of action in the future under identified terms, such as buy the property, lease additional space
  - o damage and destruction – defines rights and obligations of each party in case of property damage or destruction
- Lease termination causes
  - o expiration of lease term
  - o voluntary agreement
  - o default or breach of lease
  - o notice by either party
  - o death of either party
  - o property destruction
  - o property condemnation or eminent domain

- foreclosure
- abandonment under certain conditions
- constructive eviction

Contracts

- ❑ **General Contract Law**
  - Contract defined
    - an agreement between two or more parties who have a "meeting of the minds," and have pledged to perform (or refrain from performing) some act
    - *valid* contract – legally enforceable by meeting certain requirements of contract law
    - *invalid* contract – requirements not met; contract parties cannot have court of law enforce contract provisions
  - Contract status
    - valid – meets all requirements
    - valid but unenforceable – certain oral contracts; cannot change outcome if contract is performed
    - void – not valid; unenforceable
    - voidable – may be rescinded due to subsequent discoveries: cannot change outcome if contract is performed
  - Contract validity
    - competent parties – legal age, mental competency, legitimate authority
    - mutual consent – clear and unequivocal offer and acceptance with an underlying meeting of the minds
    - valuable consideration – exchange of valuable consideration for performance by the other party; not "love and affection"
    - legal purpose – promise, intent and content must be lawful; if illegal, contract is void – cannot contract to break the law
    - voluntary act of good faith – no duress; coercion, fraud, or misrepresentation
  - Conveyance contract requirements
    - must be in writing
    - must contain legal description
    - must be signed by one or more parties
    - *exception: per Statute of Frauds*, leases for 1 year or less may be verbal and still be enforceable
  - Contract assignment
    - assignable unless expressly prohibited or contract is a personal service contract (listings)
  - Contract preparation
    - restricted unless licensed as attorney or a party to the contract

39

- licensees must be aware of contract preparation restrictions in the states where they operate
- Contract classifications
    - oral vs. written
        - oral, or parol, contract may not be enforceable
    - express vs. implied
        - express – all terms expressly agreed to
        - implied – unintentional agreement deemed to exist due to terms implied by actions
    - bilateral vs. unilateral
        - bilateral – both parties promise to perform
        - unilateral – one party performs only if other party performs
    - executed vs. executory
        - executed – fully performed
        - executory – performance yet to be completed
- Contract termination causes
    - performance
    - infeasibility
    - mutual agreement
    - cooling-period rescission
    - revocation
    - abandonment
    - lapse of time
    - invalidity of contract
    - breach of contract
- Contract breach and remedies
    - rescission – cancel contract; return deposits
    - forfeiture – defaulting party gives up something according to contract terms
    - liquidated damages – damages due a damaged party as stated in contract
    - suit for damages – civil suit for money damages not covered by contract
    - specific performance – suit to force party to fulfill contract promises

Sales Contracts

❑ **Key Characteristics**

- binding, bilateral contract for purchase and sale

- the enforceable "blueprint" for closing

- contract is executory, or to be fulfilled

- expires upon closing

- must be in writing

- for validity, must

    o contain valuable consideration

    o identify property

    o be signed by all

❑ **Sales Contract Creation**

- Creation

    o created by unqualified acceptance of an offer

    o gives buyer equitable title and power to force specific performance

- Offer

    o intention to enter into contract

    o must contain all intended terms

    o must be in writing

    o expires in "reasonable time" or date and time specified

- Deposit or earnest money escrow

    o secures contract validity and buyer's equitable interest

    o varies in amount

    o deposit controlled by disinterested party who must act according to escrow instructions

- Contingencies

    o conditions that must be met for the contract to be enforceable

    o must be clear

    o have expiration date

    o require diligence to satisfy

- Buyer default

    o seller can cancel, claim liquidated damages or sue for specific performance (i.e., buyer's deposit)

- Seller default

    o buyer can cancel or sue for damages or specific performance

- Termination

    o acceptance; rejection; revocation; expiration; counteroffer; death or insanity of either party

41

❑ **Primary Clauses**

- parties
- consideration
- legal description
- price and terms
- loan approval provisions
- earnest money
- escrow
- closing and possession dates
- conveyed interest

- type of deed
- title evidence
- property condition warranty/disclosures
- closing costs
- damage and destruction
- default
- broker's agency disclosure and who pays commission
- seller's representations: property condition, marketable title

❑ **Contract for Deed**

- Essentials
  - purchase price is paid over time in installments
  - seller retains title, buyer takes possession, equitable title
  - at end of period, buyer pays balance, gets legal title

- Interests and rights
  - seller may encumber or assign interest
  - seller remains liable for underlying mortgage
  - buyer may use, possess, or profit
  - buyer must make periodic payments, maintain the property, and purchase at the end of the term

- Default and recourse
  - buyer may sue for cancellation and damages or specific performance
  - seller may sue for specific performance or damages, or may need to foreclose

❑ **Option-to-Buy**

- Essentials
  - optionor gives option to optionee to buy at a given time and price; optionee must pay for option right
  - unilateral contract: seller must perform, buyer need not
  - if option is exercised, option becomes bilateral sale contract
  - options are assignable

- Requirements
  - non-refundable consideration for the option right
  - price and terms of the sale
  - option period expiration date
  - legal description
  - must be in writing
  - must meet contract validity requirements
  - option should be recorded

42

- Common clause provisions
  - how to exercise option
  - terms of option money forfeiture
  - how option money will be applied to purchase price

❑ **Statute of Frauds**

- Requires certain contracts to be in writing to be enforceable
  - real estate contracts; contracts that convey interest in real property
  - 1-year or less lease exempt; may be oral
- Concerns contract's enforceability, not its validity
- May not be used to rescind contracts

UNIT EIGHT: REAL ESTATE FINANCE

Mortgages

❑ **Mortgage Transaction**

- Elements
  - o promissory note: promise to repay loan
  - o mortgage: pledge of property as collateral for loan
- Mechanics
  - o borrower gives lender promissory note and mortgage
  - o lender gives borrower funds and records a lien
- Hypothecation
  - o use of real property as collateral for a mortgage loan
- Financial components
  - o original principal: capital amount borrowed on which interest payments are calculated
  - o loan balance: remaining unpaid principal at any point in the life of the loan
  - o interest: charge for the use of money; rate fixed or variable
  - o Annual Percentage Rate (APR) includes interest and all other finance charges; lender must disclose on residential properties
  - o point: one percent of the loan amount
  - o loan origination fee: charged by lender at origination to obtain required return
  - o term: period of time for repayment of interest and principal
  - o payment: the periodic payment of interest and/or principal
  - o down payment: borrower's cash payment applied to the purchase price
  - o loan-to-value ratio: the loan's share of the total value of the property
  - o equity: at closing, the borrower's cash invested in the property; thereafter, the difference between the market value and the loan balance

❑ **Mortgage Clauses**

- Payment of principal and interest – prepayment and late charges
  - o borrower must make timely payments according to the terms of the note
  - o late payments or early payoffs may trigger penalties
- Funds for taxes and insurance
  - o borrower must make monthly payments to cover taxes and hazard insurance
  - o borrower may also have to pay flood insurance and mortgage insurance premiums
  - o **escrow account:** reserve account for periodic payments of taxes and insurance.
  - o Real Estate Settlement Procedures Act (RESPA) limits funds the lender can require for

44

this purpose.

- PITI (Principal, Interest, Taxes, Insurance)
  - principal and interest (P&I) – borrower's monthly payment for principal and interest
  - PITI – the amount which includes the escrow payment
- Charges and liens
  - borrower liable for paying any charges, liens, or other expenses with priority over the mortgage or trust instrument
- Hazard or property insurance
  - borrower required to keep property insured as the lender requires
- Occupancy, preservation, maintenance, and protection of the property
  - borrower required to take and maintain occupancy as the borrower's principal residence
  - borrower required not to abuse or neglect the property, including using for illegal purposes, creating hazardous waste on the property, or destroying the improvements
- Protection of lender's rights in the property
  - lender may take actions to protect its rights in the property if the borrower jeopardizes the property's value, with costs of these actions charged to the borrower
- Mortgage insurance
  - lender may require private mortgage insurance, or PMI which protects the lender against loss from borrower default
  - applies to loans that are not backed by the Federal Housing Administration (FHA) or Veterans Administration (VA) and that have a down payment of less than 20% of the property value
- Inspection
  - lender may inspect the property with reasonable cause to fear damage to the collateral
- Condemnation
  - if the property is condemned or taken by eminent domain, lender reserves a claim on any resulting proceeds
- Transfer of the property or a beneficial interest in borrower
  - if borrower sells the property without the lender's approval, the lender may demand immediate repayment of the loan balance. This alienation clause, aka a due-on-sale clause, allows lender to prevent unapproved loan assumptions
  - the requirement to repay the loan before the scheduled due date is called **acceleration**.
- Borrower's right to reinstate
  - if lender holds borrower in default, borrower has right to reinstatement by performing certain actions, usually paying overdue payments plus expenses to the lender
  - called a redemption clause
  - gives the borrower time to satisfy obligations and prevent a forced sale
- Release

- o agreement to release the lien obligation when borrower has paid off the loan
- o release clause, aka defeasance clause, may require lender to execute a satisfaction of mortgage, aka release of mortgage
- o if deed of trust, lender directs trustee to execute a release deed or deed of reconveyance to the borrower as trustor.
- o release deed or satisfaction should be recorded as necessary
- Escalation clause
  - o allows lender to increase the loan's interest rate

❑ **Loan Qualification**

- Equal Credit Opportunity Act (ECOA)
  - o lender must evaluate applicant according to applicant's own income and credit information
  - o lender cannot deny credit based on
    - ♦ discounted income from part-time work
    - ♦ future plans to have family
    - ♦ locational factors
    - ♦ protected classes
- Income qualification
  - o income ratio and debt ratio qualify borrower's income
  - o income ratio applied to gross income determines housing expense maximum
    - ♦ annual gross income x income ratio percent ÷ 12 months = monthly allowable housing expense
  - o debt ratio takes revolving debt into account
  - o income ratios: 25-28% conventional; 31% FHA-insured
  - o debt ratios: 36% conventional; 43% FHA and 41% VA
- Cash qualification
  - o lender verifies applicant's sources of cash for down payment; extra cash enhances income qualification evaluation
- Net worth
  - o extent to which applicant's assets exceed liabilities as a further source of reserves
- Credit evaluation
  - o lender obtains credit reports to evaluate applicant's payment behavior

- Loan commitment
  - o written pledge by lender to grant loan under specific terms; firm, lock-in, conditional, take-out
- Loan-to-value ratio (LTV)
  - o relationship of loan amount to property value

46

- o expressed as a percentage
- o 80% LTV = loan is 80% of property value

- ❑ **Mortgage Laws**
  - ▪ Truth-in-Lending and Regulation Z
    - o Reg Z implements Truth-in-Lending Simplification and Reform Act and Consumer Credit Protection Act
      - ◆ lender must disclose finance charges and APR prior to closing
      - ◆ borrower has limited right of rescission, but excludes primary residence
      - ◆ lender must follow **advertising requirements** for full disclosure of costs, loan mechanics
  - ▪ Equal Credit Opportunity Act (ECOA)
    - o prohibits discrimination in lending based on
      - ◆ race or color
      - ◆ religion
      - ◆ national origin
      - ◆ sex
      - ◆ marital status
      - ◆ age
      - ◆ dependency upon public assistance
    - o licensees assisting in qualifying must also comply
    - o denied applicants must get notice within 30 days
  - ▪ Real Estate Settlement Procedures Act (RESPA)
    - o standardizes settlement practices & ensures buyers understand settlement costs
    - o lender must:
      - ◆ provide CFPB booklet explaining loans, settlement costs and procedures
      - ◆ provide CFPB Loan Estimate of settlement costs within 3 days of application
      - ◆ provide CFPB Closing Disclosure 3 days before loan consummation
  - ▪ National Flood Insurance Act
    - o borrowers of "federally-related loans" must obtain flood insurance if property is in designated flood-hazard area
    - o flood zone maps indicate where homeowners must obtain insurance

- ❑ **Mortgage Market**
  - ▪ Supply and demand for money
    - o relationship between supply and demand for money affects interest rates, consumer prices, availability of mortgage money; regulated by Federal Reserve
  - ▪ Federal reserve control of money supply among banks
    - o sells T-bills to reduce money supply and increase interest rates; buys T-bills to increase supply and decrease rates

47

- sets the reserve requirement for member banks
- increase reserves to tighten money and raise interest rates
- decrease reserves to loosen money and lower interest rates
- sets the discount rate for member banks
- increase rate to tighten money
- decrease rate to increase money supply

- Federal Home Loan Bank System (FHLBS)
  - counterpart to the Fed for savings and loan associations
- Federal Deposit Insurance Corporation (FDIC)
  - insures deposits up to $250,000 per depositor, per insured bank, for each account ownership category
- The primary mortgage market
  - originates mortgage loans directly to borrowers;
  - includes savings and loans, commercial banks, mutual savings banks, life insurance companies, mortgage bankers, credit unions
- The secondary mortgage market
  - buys existing loans to provide liquidity to primary lenders; Fannie Mae, Ginnie Mae, Freddie Mac, investment firms, life insurance companies, pension funds
- Role of FNMA, GNMA, and FHLMC
  - FNMA buys conventional, FHA- and VA-backed loans and pooled mortgages; guarantees payment on mortgage-backed securities
  - GNMA guarantees payment on certain types of loans
  - FHLMC buys and pools mortgages; sells mortgage-backed securities
- Mortgage loan originator v. lender/banker v. broker
  - mortgage loan originator: solicits, negotiates mortgage loans; requires MLO license
  - mortgage broker: an intermediary who brings mortgage borrowers and mortgage lenders together, but does not use its own funds to originate mortgages
  - mortgage banker: person or entity who funds or services loans for others and/or who sells mortgages to the secondary market

❑ **Types of Mortgages**
- Conventional mortgages
  - originated by banks and private financial institutions
  - no government-related insurance or guarantees as with FHA or VA
  - typically require 20% down payments; smaller down payments may require PMI
  - assumptions require approval
- Government loan programs
  - FHA – federally insured loan programs
    - insures loans from approved lenders

- ♦ operates under HUD
- ♦ FHA 203(b) – most used FHA amortized loan; 1-4 family residences
- ♦ sets limits on loans based on area of NY
- ♦ down payment required
- ♦ appraisals by FHA-approved appraiser
- ♦ MIP required
    - o VA – federally guaranteed loan programs
        - ♦ guarantees against loss on mortgage loans to eligible veterans
        - ♦ no down payment required; can offer 100% financing
        - ♦ limits amount guaranteed but not amount borrowed
        - ♦ only veteran/owner-occupied 1-4 family residences
- ▪ Amortized Fixed-Rate V Adjustable Loans
    - o amortized: payments include increasing increments of principal which retire loan balance over loan term
    - o fixed rate: interest rate does not change – can have for amortized or interest-only loans
    - o adjustable loans: interest rate fluctuates up or down with an index; payments may also vary

❑ Predatory Lending

- ▪ Unfair and deceptive lending practices
- ▪ Loans with high interest rates, large closing costs, hidden fees
- ▪ Subprime loans

❑ Sale of Mortgaged Property

- ▪ Subject to a mortgage
    - o buyer does not assume note and mortgage, no obligation to lender
    - o seller remains liable to lender for loan repayment, even with foreclosure sale
- ▪ Assumption of mortgage
    - o buyer purchases subject to mortgage, assumes mortgage, agrees to pay debt
    - o buyer becomes liable to lender for loan repayment
    - o both buyer and seller liable for repayment if funds from foreclosure sale are insufficient to pay off loan unless seller obtained release from lender
- ▪ Alienation clause (aka due-on-sale clause)
    - o upon sale of property, allows lender to choose between entire debt being immediately due or buyer assuming the loan
    - o NY mortgages are assumable unless loan document includes alienation clause
- ▪ Assignment of mortgage
    - o mortgage sold to third party investor (secondary mortgage market)
    - o note and mortgage must contain assignment clause
    - o estoppel certificate signed by borrower verifies amount owed and interest rate

❑ **Recording and Satisfaction**

- Mortgage document to be recorded in county recorder's office; serves as constructive notice and lien priority

- First mortgage has priority over second mortgages or home equity loans

- Satisfaction of mortgage document recorded to remove lien; NY requires recording within 45 days of request or noncompliance penalties incur

UNIT NINE: LAND USE REGULATIONS

Land Use

❑ **Land Use Definitions**

- Building code – a standard of construction of an improved property established by local government officials

- Certificate of occupancy – a document confirming that a newly constructed or renovated property has fully complied with all building codes and is ready for occupancy

- Concurrency – a planning policy that requires developers to correct foreseen negative impacts of a development during the construction period of the project itself rather than afterward

- Condemnation –

  o a decree that a parcel of private property is to be taken for public use under the power of eminent domain

  o a government order that a is no longer fit for use and must be demolished

- Deed restriction – a provision in a deed that limits or places rules on how the deeded property may be used or improved

- Eminent domain – a power of a government entity to force the sale of private property for subsequent public use

- Land use control – regulation of how individual owners use property in a municipality or planning district. Control patterns are in accordance with a master plan

- Master plan - an amalgamated land use plan for a municipality, county, or region which incorporates community opinion, the results of intensive research, and the various land use guidelines and regulations of the state. Acts as a blueprint for subsequent zoning ordinances and rulings

- Non-conforming use – a legal or illegal land use that is not consistent with the current zoning ordinance

- Police power – a government's legal authority to create, regulate, tax, and condemn real property in the interest of the public's health, safety, and welfare

- Restriction – a limitation on the use of a property imposed by deed, zoning, state statute, or public regulation

- Special exception – a land use in conflict with current zoning that is authorized because of its perceived benefit to the public welfare

- Variance – a land use that conflicts with current zoning but is authorized for certain reasons, including undue hardship to comply and minimal negative impact to leave it alone

- Zoning ordinance – a municipal land use regulation

❑ **Land Use Planning**

- Goals of land use control

  o preserve property values; promote highest and best use; safeguard public health, safety and welfare; control growth; incorporate community consensus

51

- o process: develop plan; create administration; authorize controls
  - The master plan
    - o long term growth and usage strategies; often required by state law
    - o local plans fuse municipal goals and needs with state and regional laws
  - Planning objectives
    - o control growth rates: how much growth will occur and at what rate
    - o control growth patterns: type of growth desired, where it should be located
    - o accommodate demand for services and infrastructure
  - Plan development
    - o research trends and conditions; blend local and state objectives into master plan
  - Planning management
    - o planning commission makes rules, approves permits, codes, and development plans

- ❑ **Public Land Use Controls**
  - Zoning
    - o "police power" granted by state-level enabling acts; zoning ordinance: creates zones, usage restrictions, regulations, requirements
    - o through enabling acts, enables urban land managers to create separate land uses that do not conflict with one another nor create incompatible adjacencies
    - o zoning ordinance – regulation enacted by local government; vehicle for zoning city or county; specifies land usage for every parcel within the jurisdiction; addresses
      - ♦ nature of land use
      - ♦ size and configuration of building site
      - ♦ site development procedures
      - ♦ construction and design methods and materials
      - ♦ use of space within buildings
      - ♦ signage
    - o ordinance validity – ordinances to be
      - ♦ clear in import
      - ♦ apply to all parties equally
      - ♦ promote community health, safety, and welfare in reasonable manner
    - o building permits issued for improvements, repairs, or refurbishments; project to comply with ordinances and codes
  - Types of zones
    - o residential
      - ♦ restricts land use to private, non-commercial dwellings
      - ♦ sub-zones stipulate types of residences allowed
      - ♦ regulates density – limits number and size of dwellings and lots

52

- values and aesthetics – limits type of residences; adopts buffer zones between residential and commercial or industrial zones
  - commercial
    - regulates location of office and retail land usage
    - limits area of store or office per site area
    - intensity regulation achieved by minimum parking requirements, setbacks, and building height restrictions
  - Industrial
    - intensity of usage
    - type of industrial activity
    - environmental consequences
  - agricultural
    - restricts land usage to farming, ranching, and other agricultural enterprises
  - public
    - land usage restricted to public services and recreation, e.g., parks, post offices, schools, etc.
- Zoning administration
  - zoning board of adjustment or zoning appeals board rules on interpretation of zoning ordinances regarding specific land use cases
  - conducts hearings and renders official decisions
- Zoning appeals
  - legal nonconforming use – use that differs from current zoning, resulting from zoning change causing existing properties to be in violation of new ordinance; zoning board allows use to continue either
    - indefinitely
    - until destruction of property structures
    - only while the same use continues, or
    - sale of property
  - illegal nonconforming use – use that conflicts with ordinances in place prior to use commencement
  - variance – use allowed for justifiable reasons:
    - compliance to cause unreasonable hardship
    - use not to change essential character of area
    - use not to conflict with ordinance's general intent

    variance may be unconditional or may require conditions to be fulfilled

  - special exception – use not consistent with ordinance allowed to continue if clearly beneficial or essential to public welfare and does not materially impair other uses in the same zone
  - amendment – property owner may petition zoning board for zoning change; can have economic and social impact; often involves public hearings

53

- Eminent domain
    - allows a government or public entity to purchase a fee, leasehold, or easement interest in privately owned real property for the public good and for public use in exchange for "just compensation" regardless of owner's desire to sell
    - entity adopts formal resolution to acquire property (resolution of necessity)
    - resolution adopted at formal hearing where owner can voice opinion
    - entity initiates condemnation suit
        - must show project is necessary
        - must show property is necessary for project
        - must show location offers greatest public benefit with least detriment
        - must accord with due process of law so as not to violate individual property rights
    - title transferred in exchange for just compensation
    - title transfer extinguishes all existing encumbrances
    - tenants may or may not receive compensation
- Planned Unit Development (PUD)
    - PUD zoning restricts use to development of whole tracts for residential, commercial, industrial, or any combination
    - design purpose is to achieve optimum space efficiency and maximize open space
- Subdivision regulation
    - Developer to obtain subdivision plat approval prior to starting project
    - Requirements regulate
        - location, grading, alignment, surfacing, street width, highways
        - sewers and water mains
        - lot and block dimensions
        - building and setback lines
        - public use dedications
        - utility easements
        - ground percolation
        - environmental impact report
        - zoned density
    - concurrency – policy holding developers responsible for impact of projects on local infrastructure; developer to make accommodations concurrently with project development, not afterwards
    - FHA requirements – adequate level of construction quality, aesthetics, and infrastructure services to meet qualifications for FHA financing
- Building codes
    - protect public against hazards caused by unregulated construction

54

- o establish standards for every aspect of construction project
- o new development to be inspected for code compliance; certificate of occupancy issued to clear property for use

❑ **Environmental Restriction**

- Federal and state laws in place to conserve and protect environment

- Air quality – threats include asbestos, carbon monoxide, formaldehyde, lead, mold, and radon

- Soil and water – threats include dioxins, lead and mercury, MTBE gasoline additive, PCB electrical insulation, underground storage tanks, wetlands development and use, electromagnetic fields from powerlines, noise, earthquake and flood hazards

- Major legislation

    - o National Environmental Policy Act – standards for land use planning and environmental impact surveys

    - o Clean Air Amendment – air quality standards for industrial land uses and auto and airplane emissions

    - o Water Quality Improvement Act, Water Pollution Control Act amendment, Clean Water Act amendment – standards to control water pollution and industrial waste

    - o Lead-based paint ban, Residential Lead-based Paint Hazard Reduction Act – banned lead in paint and established disclosure requirements and remediation guidelines

    - o CERCLA, Superfund – solid and toxic wastes disposal; clean-up charges

❑ **Private Land Use Controls**

- Deed restrictions – covenants, conditions, and restrictions limit use of property; may not be discriminatory; can be terminated by quitclaim deed

- Declaration restriction – private use restrictions; attaches to rights in property; cannot be extinguished by private party agreement or quitclaim deed

    - o can be enforced by court injunction

- Deed condition – restricts certain uses of property; violation can result in grantor re-taking possession of property and filing suit for legal title

UNIT TEN: CONSTRUCTION AND ENVIRONMENTAL ISSUES

Construction

❑ **Construction Regulation**

- Regulated construction process
    - documents
        - ◆ plans and blueprints – scale drawings of building and components
        - ◆ specifications – written narratives of materials and techniques; impact construction costs
    - building permits
        - ◆ plans, specifications, permit fee submitted
        - ◆ plans reviewed for compliance with building codes
        - ◆ separate permits may be required for major systems and environmental concerns
    - inspections
        - ◆ approvals issued when in compliance
        - ◆ final approval qualifies for certificate of occupancy (building in compliance and ready for occupancy)

❑ **New York Statutes**

- New York Construction Law
    - covers all construction concerns, including contracts, site conditions, insurance, professional's role and liability, construction safety, environmental problems, damages, remedies, dispute resolution, and more

- National Electric Code
    - national standard for electricity installation and service; renewed every 3 years

- New York Home Improvement Law
    - applies to improvements, goods, services costing more than $500
    - contractors to provide written contract for home improvement work
    - contractor to deposit customer payments into escrow account or bond to guarantee funds are used only for the contracted work
    - penalties for non-compliance include fines up to $1000 for first offense, $2500 for second offense, $5000 for subsequent offenses

- New York New Home Warranty
    - called Housing Merchant Implied Warranty
    - provides exclusive warranty for all new construction home sales
    - implied, not required to be in writing

56

- applies to single family houses and units in multi-unit residential buildings of five stories or less

- provides 1-year warranty for construction defects; 2-year warranty for plumbing, electrical, heating, cooling, and ventilation systems; 6-year warranty for material defects

- warranty claims to be filed in writing no later than 30 days after warranty expiration

- contractor to be given reasonable opportunity to repair defect

- NY State Energy Code

  - sets minimum energy efficiency requirements for building design and construction

- New York Smoke Detector Law

  - smoke alarms required in all homes, to be hardwired or powered by 10-year sealed battery

  - new home construction requires hardwired smoke alarms with battery backup

  - all smoke detectors for sale must be either hardwired or powered by 10-year non-removable, non-replaceable battery

- Amanda's Law

  - carbon monoxide alarms required in all one- and two-family dwellings, townhouses, condominiums, cooperatives, multiple dwellings regardless of construction date or sale date

- 2020 Fire Code of New York State

  - sprinklers are to be installed in buildings meeting the square footage and occupancy requirements

  - installing contractor is to provide written statement to the fire code official confirming installation

❑ **New York Site Requirements**

- Site definition – parcel of land with legal development entitlements assembled

- Site preparation – clearing and grading land, providing drainage and building location for construction of legal improvement with landscaping considerations

- Considerations to be included for

  - access

  - utilities

  - on-site well and sanitary waste system to meet established standards

  - HVAC system

  - electrical systems to meet set standards

- Compliance with zoning regulations for site and structure

- Compliance with NY State Energy Code regulations for building envelopes (roof, walls, doors, windows, foundation)

❑ **Construction Components**

- Doors

  - types – bifold, Dutch, French, hollow core, raised panel, sidelight, solid core, steel

  - parts – jamb, threshold, hardware

57

- Windows
  - types – awning (swings out at bottom), bay, bow, casement, double-hung, eyebrow (arched), fanlight, French, hopper (hinged on bottom), jalousie (horizontal glass slats), oriel, transom
  - parts – casing, light, louver, mullion, muntin, rail, sash, sill, stile, stool
- Electrical
  - amperage – measure of overall capability of household supply; modern minimum standard is 100 amp
  - circuit breaker – interrupts circuit when an overload or fault occurs on the line; is then reset
  - conduit – metal piping for carrying flexible wiring
  - fuse – interrupts circuit when an overload or fault occurs; is then replaced
  - junction box – contains wire splices or cable connections
  - outlet box – protects wire connections; holds switch or receptacle
  - rheostat – dimmer switch
  - service entrance panel – main control box for electrical system
- Exterior coverings
  - beveled siding (horizontal), board and batten (vertical boards), brick, clapboard (smooth beveled siding), redwood siding (weather resistant), shingle, shiplap, siding, stucco (cement based), tongue and groove
- Foundations and parts
  - brick, cement block, poured concrete, slab, stone, footing (base for foundation)
- Heating and cooling
  - central air, duct work, forced air, heat pump (recirculates air), register (wall or floor grate), window unit
  - sources or fuels for heat and cool: electric, gas, oil, solar, steam
- Insulation
  - asbestos (unsafe), batting, blown, fiberglass, firestop, foam, foam board, R-factor (measure of insulation efficiency, vapor barrier (waterproof)
- Plumbing
  - types of pipes – cast iron, copper, lead, PVC
  - parts – cleanout, soil stack, soil pipe, sump pump, trap, vent pipe, vent stack, well and septic (waste removal)
- Roof
  - types – asphalt shingle, cross gable, built-up, flat, gable, gambrel, Gothic mansard, pitched, shed, tile
  - elements – decking, felt, hip, membrane, rafter, rake, ridge, roll roofing, roofing paper, shake, slate, truss, valley
- General structure
  - framing – balloon frame, basement, beam, bearing wall, bridging, crawl space, deck, dormer, eave, flashing, girder, half-timber, joist, knee wall, lath, lintel, masonry, plate,

platform frame, post, rafter, sole plate, stringer, stud, subfloor, top plate, underlayment

- o structural elements and materials – bay, blueboard, building paper, casing, downspout, drain tile, drywall, facade, fascia, greenboard, gutter, gypsum board, partition, plaster, rise, riser, run, sheathing, sheetrock, shoe, sill, soffit, suspended ceiling, termite shield, terrazzo, tread, trim, wallboard

Environmental Issues

- ❑ **Environmental Issues**
  - Fresh water wells
    - o water should be tested for contamination
    - o Private Well Water Testing Law in Westchester County requires testing of well water when property for sale or lease and for new wells
  - Waste disposal
    - o water and soil contaminated by poorly built and maintained landfills
    - o poorly handled radioactive waste can cause cancer
  - Septic
    - o underground tanks can release contaminants into soil and water
    - o should inspect periodically and prior to any conveyance
  - Termites
    - o live in the ground; eat and destroy wood foundations and structures
    - o when constructing new homes, only treated wood should touch the ground
    - o extermination and damage repair to be done by NY State Department of Environmental Conservation licensed professional
  - Asbestos
    - o used as insulation for homes and plumbing
    - o harmless if left undisturbed
    - o when disturbed, asbestos dust can cause lung disease and cancer; must be removed by experts to prevent contamination
    - o manufacture banned in 1989
  - Lead, lead disclosure
    - o banned in paint in 1978
    - o if property built before 1978, must disclose possible lead-based paint hazard
    - o use form "Protect Your Family from Lead in Your Home"
    - o NY City requires lead dust testing when occupants have children under 7 years
    - o also found in water pipes; water testing
  - Radon
    - o detectable radioactive ground gas that can cause lung cancer
    - o enters homes through foundation cracks and floor drains

- o removed from home and water through filtration and ventilation systems
- Mold
    - o must be disclosed if present in home
    - o may cause allergy problems
    - o caused by moisture or water damage in home
- Underground storage tanks
    - o found mostly on-site at gas stations
    - o leaking tanks contaminate surrounding ground and ground water
    - o potential for fire and explosion
- Polychlorinated Biphenyls
    - o man-made organic chemicals used in electrical and hydraulic equipment, plastics and paints
    - o manufacture banned in 1979
    - o Toxic Substances Control Act of 1976 provides EPA authority to require reporting, testing, and restrictions
    - o can cause cancer, neurological problems, and other health issues
- Chlorofluorocarbons
    - o gases used in solvents, refrigerants, and aerosol sprays
    - o deplete earth's ozone layer; adds to greenhouse effect
    - o use and import banned in some areas
- Urea formaldehyde
    - o used in foam insulation, adhesives, and pressed wood products, e.g., particle board
    - o respiratory and cancer health dangers occur when formaldehyde is released into the air and air concentrations rise

❑ **Comprehensive Environmental Response, Compensation, and Liability Act (CERCLA)**
- Established Superfund for cleaning up uncontrolled hazardous waste dumps and spills
- Holds current and previous landowners responsible for contamination and cleanup
- Real estate licensee may also be liable for improper disclosure
- If tenant operations linked to contamination, tenant can be held liable for cleanup costs
- Property for sale – Phase I audit identifies prior users, presence of hazardous materials
- Phase II audit – chemical analysis to find hazardous substances
- Phase III audit – remediation, cleanup, follow-up monitoring

❑ **Superfund Amendments and Reauthorization Act of 1986 (SARA)**
- Reauthorized Superfund that expired in 1985
- Stricter standards for contamination cleanup; higher funding than CERCLA
- Removed liability from innocent landowners with no link to or knowledge of cause of contamination

❑ **Environmental Laws**

Legislation	Date	Regulated
Solid Waste Disposal Act (later part of RCRA)	1965 (1976, 1999, 2002)	landfills
Air Quality Act, Clean Air Act	1967 (1970)	air quality standards
National Environmental Policy Act (NEPA)	1969 (1970)	created EPA
Flood Control Act	amended 1969	building in flood zones; flood insurance
Resource Conservation and Recovery Act	1970	solid waste disposal
Water Quality Improvement Act	1970	dumping in navigable waters; wetlands
Water Pollution Control Act amendment	1972	dumping in navigable waters; wetlands
Clean Water Act	1972 (1977)	dumping in navigable waters; wetlands
Lead-based paint ban (US Consumer Product Safety Commission rule)	1978	lead-based paint in residences
PCB ban (EPA rule)	1979	polychlorinated biphenyls
RCRA amendment	1984	underground storage tanks
Comprehensive Environmental Response, Compensation and Liability Act (CERCLA)	1980	hazardous waste disposal
Superfund Amendment and Reauthorization Act	1986	hazardous waste cleanup costs
Asbestos ban (EPA rule)	1989	asbestos in building materials
Residential Lead-based Paint Hazard Reduction Act (EPA and HUD rule)	1992 (1996)	lead-based paint disclosure and treatment
Flood Insurance Reform Act	1994	flood insurance in flood zones
Brownfields legislation	2002	industrial site cleanup

UNIT ELEVEN: VALUATION PROCESS AND PRICING PROPERTIES

Value and Price

❑ **Concepts and Principles of Value**

- Supply and demand

    o when demand exceeds supply, scarcity exists, values rise.

    o when supply exceeds demand, surplus exists, values decline.

    o when supply and demand are equal, the market is in balance, values stabilize.

- Utility

    o a property's use in the marketplace contributes to the demand for it.

- Transferability

    o how readily or easily title or rights to real estate can be transferred affects the property's value.

- Anticipation

    o the benefits a buyer expects to derive from a property over a holding period influence what the buyer is willing to pay for it.

- Substitution

    o a buyer will pay no more for a property than the buyer would have to pay for an equally desirable and available substitute property.

- Contribution

    o the contribution to value of an improvement is equal to the change in market value that the addition of the improvement causes.

- Change

    o market conditions affect the benefits that can arise from the property.

- Highest and best use

    o a property achieves its maximum value when it is put to whichever use generates the greatest income and return. The highest and best use must be legally permissible, physically possible, financially feasible, and maximally productive.

- Conformity

    o a property's maximal value is attained when its form and use are consonant with surrounding properties and uses.

- Progression and regression

    o the value of a property is influenced by the values of neighboring properties.

- Assemblage

    o conjoining adjacent properties can create a combined value in excess of the values of the unassembled properties. This excess value is called **plottage value.**

62

- Subdivision
  - the division of a single property into smaller properties can result in a higher total value.

❑ **Types of Value**

- Market value
  - an estimate of the price at which a property will sell at a particular time; this type of value is the one generally sought in appraisals and used in brokers' estimates of value

- Insured value
  - the face amount a casualty or hazard insurance policy will pay in case a property is rendered unusable

- Reproduction value
  - the value based on the cost of constructing a precise duplicate of the subject property's improvements, assuming current construction costs

- Replacement value
  - the value based on the cost of constructing a functional equivalent of the subject property's improvements, assuming current construction costs

- Salvage value
  - the nominal value of a property that has reached the end of its economic life; also an estimate of the price at which a structure will sell if it is dismantled and moved

- Assessed value
  - the value of a property as estimated by a taxing authority as the basis for ad valorem taxation

- Depreciated value
  - a value established by subtracting accumulated depreciation from the purchase price of a property

- Book value
  - the value of the property as carried on the accounts of the owner; the value is generally equal to the acquisition price plus capital improvements minus accumulated depreciation

- Investment value
  - the value of an income property as indicated by the capitalized value of the cash flow the property generates

❑ **Supply and Demand**

- Supply – the quantity of a product or service available for sale, lease, or trade at any given time
- Demand – the quantity of a product or service that is desired for purchase, lease, or trade at any given time
- Supply / Demand / Price
  - real estate supply – property available for sale or lease; measured in dwelling units, square feet, acres
  - real estate demand – property buyers and tenants wishing to acquire; measured in households, square feet, acres
  - interaction – if supply increases relative to demand, price decreases; if demand increases relative to supply, price increases

63

- Supply-Demand Cycle

unmet demand →
    construction adds supply →
        market equilibrium →
            construction adds more supply →
                oversupply →
                    construction stops →
                        market equilibrium →
                            demand absorbs supply →
                                unmet demand →
                                    cycle repeats

- Factors influencing supply and demand
  - cost, availability of financing
  - availability of developable land
  - construction costs
  - capacity of infrastructure
  - governmental regulation and police powers
  - changes in the economic base
  - in- and out-migrations of major employers
  - labor availability
  - land availability

❑ Market Value Requirements

- Market value – an estimate of the price at which a property will sell at a particular time; this type of value is the one generally sought in appraisals and used in brokers' estimates of value

- The price willing buyer and seller would agree on given:
  - a cash transaction
  - reasonable market exposure
  - parties have market and property use information
  - there is no pressure to complete the transaction
  - transaction is arm's length: parties are not related
  - marketable title
  - no hidden influences

❑ Sales Comparison Approach

- Takes into account subject property's specific amenities in relation to competing properties and incorporates present market realities
- Steps

1. identify comparable sales

   ♦ resemble the subject in size, shape, design, utility, location

   ♦ sold within 6 months of appraisal

   ♦ sold in arm's-length transaction

2. compare comps to the subject and make adjustments to the comparables

   ♦ if comparable better than subject, deduct from comparable

   ♦ if comparable worse than subject, add to comparable

   ♦ do not adjust the subject

   ♦ factors for adjustments – time of sale, location, and physical characteristics

3. weight values indicated by adjusted comparables for the final value estimate of the subject

   ♦ fewest and smallest adjustments and less total adjustment, the more reliable the comparable

❑ **Depreciation**

- Depreciation

  o **loss of value** from deterioration, functional obsolescence, or economic obsolescence

- Deterioration

  o **wear and tear** from use and aging

- Functional obsolescence

  o **outmoded** physical or design **features**: curable or incurable

- Economic obsolescence

  o loss of value due to adverse **changes in surroundings**: incurable

- Curability

  o curable – cost to cure is less than resulting contribution to value

  o incurable – cost to cure exceeds contribution to value

❑ **Cost Approach**

- Types of cost appraised

  o reproduction – cost of making a precise replica

  o replacement – cost of making a functional equivalent

- Steps in the approach

  o estimate land value

  o estimate replacement cost of improvements

  o estimate total depreciation

  o subtract: (cost of improvements - depreciation) = depreciated improvements cost

  o add land back in: (land value + depreciated improvements) = value estimate of property

65

❑ **Income approach**

- Based on the principle of anticipation: the expected future income stream of a property underlies what an investor will pay for the property

- Also based on the principle of substitution: that an investor will pay no more for a subject property with a certain income stream than the investor would have to pay for another property with a similar income stream.

- Steps in the income approach

    1. estimate potential gross income

    2. estimate effective gross income (total potential income - vacancy)

    3. estimate net operating income (NOI) (effective income - expenses)

    4. select cap rate and divide it into the NOI number (NOI ÷ cap rate)

    5. For example, if a property generates $1MM gross and nets $500K NOI after expenses, and the cap rate is 10%, divide 10% into $500 K for an estimated value of $5 million.

- Gross rent multipliers (GRMs)

    o simplified, generalized income-based methods to estimate value

    o method consists of applying a multiplier to the estimated gross rent of the subject

    o multiplier is derived from market data on sale prices and gross rent

    o does not necessarily produce accurate value estimates

- GRM formula

    o GRM = price divided by *monthly* rent

    o value = GRM times *monthly* rent

❑ **Preparing a CMA**

- Scaled-down version of appraiser's sales comparison approach used to establish property listing price

- Steps

    1. identify comparables sold in last 6 months, for sale properties, and expired listings

    2. compile comparison data for each comparable: price, sale date, location, age, lot size, site aspects, living area, bedrooms, etc.

    3. complete adjustments for differences; adjustment rules:

        ♦ never adjust the subject's value or its price

        ♦ add value to the comparable if a feature is inferior to the subject

        ♦ subtract value from the comp if a feature is superior to the subject

    4. add up the net amount of total adjustments for each comparable

    5. compare and reconcile all value-adjusted comps to the subject to identify a value estimate for the subject

- CMAs and formally-completed appraisals differ in objectivity and comprehensiveness

❑ **Salesperson Role** in valuing properties

- For CMA

    o act competently and with due diligence

66

- o maintain copy of CMA and related documents
- o do not present as appraisal, or present oneself as an appraiser if not licensed as such
- For appraisal
  - o make subject property available for appraiser to inspect
  - o answer appraiser's questions
  - o provide appraiser with recent comparable sales information
- For owner
  - o explain estimates of value
  - o explain how estimates of value were determined
  - o explain impact of estimates of value to owner

UNIT TWELVE: HUMAN RIGHTS AND FAIR HOUSING

Human Rights

❑ **Federally Protected Classes**

- Race

- Color

- National origin

- Religion

- Sex, gender identity, sexual orientation

- Disability

- Familial status

❑ **NY Human Rights Law**

- Protected classes

    o race

    o creed

    o color

    o national origin

    o gender, sexual orientation, gender identity and expression

    o disability

    o familial status, children

    o age

    o military status

    o marital status

    o lawful source of income

- Laws provide anti-discrimination protection for renting, selling, leasing, and advertising housing, vacant land, commercial real estate, public housing, and membership in real estate boards

- Retaliation against complainants and witnesses of violations is prohibited

- Exemptions from anti-discrimination laws (real estate agents not exempt)

    o public housing for specific age groups if comply with requirements

    o apartment rental in two-unit building with owner occupant of one unit

    o all rooms occupied by same sex individuals

    o room rental in owner's home

    o rentals to ages 62 and older

    o rentals to at least one occupant age 55 and older

- *Exemptions based on race or color are always prohibited*

❑ **NY City Human Rights Law**
- Additional protected classes
  - o partnership status
  - o citizenship
  - o victims of domestic violence, sex offenses, stalking
  - o *military status not recognized as protected class*
- No exemption for advertised rental of owner-occupied two-family house, i.e., cannot discriminate if advertising is used to generate prospective tenants.

❑ **Americans with Disabilities Act (ADA)**
- Purpose is to prohibit discrimination against persons with disabilities, making sure disabled have same rights and opportunities as non-disabled
- Disability definition per ADA
  - o Physical or mental impairment that substantially limits one or more major life activities
- Applies to accessing public, employment, education, transportation facilities
- Applies to private employers with 15+ employees and public employees
- ADA Provisions (classified by Title)
  - o Title I: Employment
    - ◆ must have equal opportunity, enforced by U.S. Equal Employment Opportunity Commission
  - o Title II: State, local government
    - ◆ cannot discriminate in state and local services, enforced by U.S. Department of Justice
  - o Title III: Public accommodations
    - ◆ cannot discriminate in public accommodations, commercial facilities, enforced by U.S. Department of Justice
  - o Title IV: Telecommunication
    - ◆ concerns accommodations in telecommunications, public service messaging, enforced by Federal Communications Commission
  - o Title V: Miscellaneous
    - ◆ general provisions as to how ADA affects other laws, insurance providers, lawyers
- Licensees should clearly understand provisions of Title I and III
- ADA requirements
  - o landlords must modify housing and facilities to be accessible without hindrance
  - o access must be equivalent to that provided for non-disabled persons
  - o employers must make reasonable accommodations to enable disabled employees to perform essential functions of the job
  - o landlords may determine most practical accommodations

- o new construction and remodeling must meet ADA standards
  - ▪ Penalties
    - o violations can result in citations, license restrictions, fines, injunctions, remediations
    - o business owners may be liable for personal injury damages

Fair Housing

❑ **Forms of Discrimination in Residential Brokerage and Financing**

- ▪ Discriminatory misrepresentation
  - o misrepresenting property availability, price, or terms based on protected class
- ▪ Advertising
  - o restricting properties in advertising based on protected class
  - o indicating a discriminatory preference for clients and customers outside of New York's protected classes
- ▪ Social media advertising
  - o shielding and/or screening which housing ads prospects are allowed to see
  - o not monitoring whether ad language is discriminatory and/or failing to ban discriminatory comments
  - o failing to apply Fair Housing laws to personal social media accounts and advertising as well as business accounts and pages
- ▪ Unequal services
  - o altering nature or quality of services based on protected class
- ▪ Unequal amenities
  - o Limiting access to amenities and resources based on protected class or characteristics
- ▪ Steering
  - o directly or indirectly channeling customers toward or away from properties or areas
- ▪ Blockbusting
  - o inducing owners in a particular area to sell or rent to avoid impending change in ethnic or social makeup of the area that will result in lower home values
- ▪ Restricting access to market
  - o discriminatorily restricting participation in any MLS based on protected class
- ▪ Redlining
  - o financial institute refusing to provide loans within certain areas regardless of the borrower's qualifications

❑ **Federal Fair Housing Laws**

- ▪ Historical perspectives of civil rights regulation and Fair Housing laws
  - o Civil War abolished slavery, but did not end discrimination or racism
  - o since the war, black Americans mobilized and fought for equality and civil rights
  - o segregation was supported in Southern states by "Jim Crow" laws prohibiting black

people from

- using the same public facilities as white people

- living in some of the same towns

- attending the same schools

- o In 1954, American courts declared that segregation in public schools violated the equal protection clause of the 14th Amendment

- o In 1968, denial of equal housing opportunities became illegal and prohibited, with specific regard to discrimination in the sale, rental, and financing of housing based on race, religion, national origin, sex, handicap, and family status

- o Since 1968, additional laws have been developed and amended to further ensure segregation and discrimination in housing remained illegal

- Anti-discrimination

  - o federal and state laws prohibit discrimination in housing

  - o citizens entitled to live wherever they wish without discrimination

  - o state fair housing laws reflect national laws with certain differences

  - o fair housing and local zoning

    - ♦ fair housing does not preempt local zoning, but zoning cannot be discriminatory against federal or state protected classes

- Civil Rights Act of 1866

  - o no discrimination in selling or leasing housing based on race

  - o Executive Order 11063: no race discrimination involving FHA- or VA-backed loans

- Civil Rights Act of 1968

  - o Title VIII (Fair Housing Act)

  - o no housing discrimination based on race, color, religion, national origin

  - o certain exceptions permitted

  - o FHEO office administers and enforces the Act under HUD supervision

- Title VIII exemptions

  - o selling, leasing single family home without broker or discriminatory advertising, with conditions

  - o 1–4-unit rental building where owner is occupant

  - o non-commercial leasing facilities owned by private clubs

  - o facilities owned by religious organizations and leased non-commercially to members, with no membership discrimination

- Jones v. Mayer

  - o discrimination in selling/renting residential housing based on race is prohibited without exception or exemption

- HUD Equal Opportunity in Housing poster

  - o brokers must display

  - o affirms compliance with fair housing laws

71

- o failure to display can be construed as discrimination
- Fair Housing Amendments Act of 1988
  - o no discrimination based on
    - ◆ sex
    - ◆ handicap
    - ◆ families with children
  - o exemptions
    - ◆ government-designated retirement housing
    - ◆ retirement community (all residents 62+ years of age)
    - ◆ retirement community if 80% of dwellings have one person who is 55+ must have amenities for elderly residents
    - ◆ 1–4-unit dwellings and single-family houses where owners have no more than three houses
- Discrimination by the client
  - o laws apply to owner sellers as well as agents, other than exemptions
  - o illegal and prohibited for buyers or renters to
    - make discriminatory statements about communities where housing opportunities exist
    - ask pointed questions about the community where housing opportunities exist when such questions can be interpreted as discriminatory
    - refuse to be shown available housing in racially diverse communities based on the makeup of that community's citizenry
  - o requests for specific types of renters or buyers
    - licensees are prohibited from allowing sellers or landlords to limit who views and purchases or leases their property based on any protected class
  - o express concerns about neighbors' reactions to incoming protected classes moving into specific neighborhoods
    - allowing neighbors' attitudes to impact who moves into their neighborhood – potential results are blockbusting and steering violations
  - o agent equally liable if goes along with client discrimination
  - o agent should withdraw from relationship with discriminatory client
- Violations and enforcement
  - o may file HUD complaint within 1 year of violation
    - ◆ HUD investigates with federal or local enforcement authorities
    - ◆ HUD attempts to resolve complaints with merit
    - ◆ aggrieved party may file suit in state or federal court if unresolved by HUD
  - o instead of HUD complaint, party may file suit in federal or state court within 2 years of alleged violation
  - o penalties

- injection against practicing business

- damages

- equitable relief

- civil penalties for first-time or repeat offenders

❑ **Fair Financing Laws**

- Equal Credit Opportunity Act (ECOA)

  - lenders must be fair, impartial in loan qualifying

  - may not discriminate based on race, color, religion, national origin, sex, marital status, age

  - must state reasons for credit denial

- Home Mortgage Disclosure Act

  - applies to federally guaranteed or insured loans

  - prohibits redlining

  - lenders must report location of loans

Fair Housing Implications for Licensees

❑ **Broker's Responsibilities**

- Brokers liable for discriminatory behavior of salespersons and employees

- Professional standards for compliant practice

  - include fair housing logo and/or slogan in advertising

  - represent protected classes in photos and advertising

  - display HUD's Equal Housing Opportunity poster in offices

  - educate and train salespersons and employees on fair housing and anti-discrimination practices

  - establish office procedures and practices and monitor salespersons and employees for compliance

  - report Fair Housing violations

  - require salespersons to educate sellers and clients on fair housing laws and practices

  - refuse services to clients who refuse to comply with fair housing laws

  - do not provide information to clients on an area's composition based on race, religion, or ethnicity

  - practice affirmative marketing to encourage buyers to explore housing opportunities in different areas

- Testers visit brokerages to uncover discriminatory practices where services may differ from one customer to another for no apparent reason

- Unintentional discrimination and/or ignorance of the law are no excuse for violations

❑ **Salesperson's Responsibilities**

- Know and comply with Federal and State Fair Housing Laws

- Know and comply with Civil Rights Laws

- Attend training seminars, including Anti-Bias and implicit bias training

    o implicit bias essentials –

        ♦ unconscious negative association with particular groups of people which has been embedded in one's consciousness over time by history and culture

        ♦ one's mental makeup unconsciously generates stereotypes of others without knowing it

        ♦ triggers unfair / discriminatory treatment of those who are different

    o training should cover historical and social impact of biases and steps to take to recognize and address those biases

- Use the Housing and Anti-Discrimination Disclosure form (the Form)

    o as of December 2019, licensees must present Form to all prospective purchasers, tenants, sellers, and landlords upon first substantive contact by the licensee

    o Form must be posted on websites, in windows of real estate offices, and during open houses

    o applies to all property transactions, including residential, commercial, new construction, and vacant land

    o outlines protected classes and examples of discriminatory practices

    o provides consumers with information on filing complaints

    o includes signature page for prospective client to acknowledge receipt of the form

    o licensees required to maintain related records for 3 years, but encouraged to maintain indefinitely

- Reasonable Modification and Accommodation Law

    o as of May 2022, NY Human Rights Law added the requirement that landlords and real estate licensees disclose to all tenants and prospective tenants the right to request reasonable modifications and accommodations for disabilities

    o reasonable accommodation defined–

        ♦ any change, exception, or adjustment to a rule, policy, practice, or service

        ♦ structural changes within the dwelling and common use spaces

        ♦ participation in a federally-assisted program or activity

    o reasonable requests must be granted but only for a person with a disability

    o used for tenants in any housing accommodations

    o housing providers prohibited from refusing residency or placing conditions on residency to people with disabilities who require reasonable accommodations or modifications

    o Reasonable Accommodation and Reasonable Modification Disclosure Form (Form)

        ♦ licensees to provide completed Form to prospective tenants upon first substantive contact (same as agency disclosure notice)

        ♦ landlords to provide to new tenants within 30 days of tenancy or to existing tenants within 30 days of the law's effective date

- o Form covers prohibited discriminatory practices for housing provider, including
    - ♦ not permitting the disabled person to make reasonable modifications to the premises to accommodate the disabled tenant's use of the housing
    - ♦ refusing to make reasonable accommodations in the rules, policies, practices, or services to provide the disabled tenant equal opportunities to use and enjoy the dwelling
    - ♦ failing to design and construct dwellings according to NY's uniform fire prevention and building code to provide accessibility and use by disabled persons

UNIT THIRTEEN: MUNICIPAL AGENCIES

Land Use

❑ **Land Use Summary**

- Purpose of public and private control of land

    o   preservation of property values

    o   highest and best use of property

    o   balance individual property rights with public good

    o   control of growth within infrastructure capabilities

    o   regulatory and planning activities to incorporate community consensus

- Government actions impact property values which support government via taxes based on property value

- Process to achieve land use goals

    o   development of master plan by community authorities with landowners' input

        ♦   to reflect needs of local area and conform to environmental laws

        ♦   fuses state and regional laws with local objectives

    o   administration of the plan by planning commission

    o   implementation of the plan

- HOAs can impose additional standards of land use via deed restrictions

Municipal Agencies & Functions

❑ **New York City Council**

- Council makeup

    o   51 elected members, 1 from each council district; term limit of two 4-year terms

    o   38 standing committees; each chaired by Council member, includes 5 members, meets at least once a month

    o   includes several subcommittees

    o   includes caucuses to meet needs of specific communities

    o   equal partner to Mayor in governing city

- Purpose, functions of Council

    o   introduces and votes on city legislation

    o   approves city budget

    o   monitors city agencies' operation and performance

    o   reviews and decides on land use

    o   holds meetings and hearings to determine legislation regarding human services, infrastructure, and government affairs

❑ **Village Board of Trustees**

- Elected officials to manage village property and finances

- Serve 4-year term

- Number of trustees vary per village

- Mayor of village presides at board meetings

- Authority

  o adopt legislation

  o take measures for "good government" of village

  o protect safety, health, welfare of inhabitants

  o preserve and protect public works and trade

❑ **Adoption of laws and ordinances including zoning ordinance and cluster zoning approval**

- Power to enact local laws granted by State Constitution

- Scope of power and procedures for implementation are set in Municipal Home Rule Law

- Local laws same status as State legislative laws

- Home Rule powers

  o Bill of Rights for local governments

    ♦ elected legislative body

    ♦ power to adopt local laws

    ♦ power to provide cooperatively federal, state, or other government services and facilities

    ♦ eminent domain

  o limits state power related to affairs of local governments

  o empowers local governments to adopt or amend local laws

  o limits or restricts local laws to apply only to property, affairs, or government of specific village or town

- Zoning

  o municipal board appoints zoning commission to recommend district boundaries and regulations

  o board member proposes law or amendment

  o environmental impact of law determined

  o proposal referred to planning agency for review; agency to respond within 30 days or board may finalize the law

  o commission to hold public hearing with appropriate notices

  o commission to vote on proposed law and file final report with municipal clerk who is to file the law with Secretary of State within 5 days

❑ **Adoption of budget and tax rate**

- Taxing districts adopt budget for financial needs during 12-month period

- o to include estimate of expenditures and income
- o net deficit and tax rate determined
  - ◆ homesteads and non-homesteads may have different tax rates
- o deficit covered by collection of real property taxes
- o different taxing authorities sharing same services may negotiate tax shares

❑ **Planning Board**

- Members of the Planning Board are appointed either by the town board or the mayor
- Members serve terms equal to number of members on the board (7 members, 7 years, etc.) or until appointing board removes or replaces them
- Members must meet annual training requirements
- State statute or local governing board provides advisory powers for
  - o development of master plan
  - o land use regulations, studies, maps, and reports
  - o capital budgets
  - o area variance requests
- State statute or local governing board provides regulatory powers
  - o only to review subdivision plats, site plans, special use permits, sign design and only when governing board adopts resolution or ordinance providing planning board authority to do so

❑ **Zoning Board of Appeals**

- Hears appeals regarding zoning decisions and actions
- May interpret laws
- May grant use variances – using structure other than as zoned with specific conditions to be met
  - o must show unnecessary hardship
  - o land unable to produce reasonable return when used for designated purpose
  - o owner's situation is unique
  - o variance not to alter essential character of locality
  - o owner did not create hardship
- May grant area variances – using land other than as zoned with specific factors weighed
  - o whether it will create unwanted change to the area's character
  - o whether there is an alternative way to achieve the same benefit
  - o whether the area variance is substantial
  - o whether it will harm conditions of surrounding environment
  - o whether the difficulty was created by applicant
- No original jurisdiction – local zoning authority must already have made decision to be appealed
- Special circumstances for original jurisdiction – as granted by local authority and for special use permits with certain conditions to be met
- Zoning Board's decision can be appealed through state court via Article 78 administrative appeal

within 120 days of Board's decision

❑ **Architectural Review Board**

- Number of members and length of term vary per town, city, village

- Approves new construction and remodeling per municipal ordinances

- Provides regulation and guidance for maintaining quality of building exteriors and signs for either new buildings and signs or modifications to existing structures

❑ **Conservation Advisory Council (CAC)/Wetlands Commission**

- CAC assists with land use decisions with consideration of environmental issues related to development, management, and protection of natural resources

- CAC provides environmental perspective on land use proposals, master plans, stewardship of natural areas, etc.

- Clean Water Act and Tidal Wetlands Act address wetlands restoration and protection

- NYC developed a "wetlands strategy" to restore or create additional wetlands (areas with groundwater on or near surface of land)

- NY Department of Environmental Conservation – protects tidal wetlands and freshwater wetlands

- New England Interstate Water Pollution Control Commission (NEIWPCC) – New England and New York commission for preservation of water quality by monitoring and assessing regional wetlands

❑ **Historic Preservation/Landmark Commission**

- Designates and/or recommends specific areas and/or structures as historic landmarks

- Approves construction or remodeling of designated historic landmark properties; applies to exteriors only

- NY Office of Parks, Recreation, and Historic Preservation handles applications for National Register of Historic Places listings; such structures are listed on both National and State registers

❑ **Department of Building (DOB)**

- Enforces building, electrical, and zoning codes and standards along with NY labor law and multiple dwelling law

- All activities focused on public's safety, health, and welfare

- Activities include issuing building and demolition permits; performing inspections; issuing trade licenses, certificates of occupancy, and public assembly permits

- Charges permit fees based on size of structure and cost of project

  o project plans to be prepared and submitted by NY licensed engineer or architect

  o DOB legal objections provided to engineer or architect for resolution

  o once objections resolved, DOB issues permit

- Approvals and permits from additional agencies may be needed

❑ **Planning Department**

- Responsible for physical and socioeconomic planning to include

  o land use, zoning amendments and permits

  o changes in municipality maps

  o environmental reviews

- plans and policies preparation and renewals
- acquisition of publicly owned property and municipality office space
- historic and landmark district designations
  - Director of planning to provide professional advisement to other agencies and boards

❑ **Tax Assessor**
  - Responsible for tax assessments by towns, villages, cities, and some counties
  - Creates assessment roll to include the area's land and structures; open to public
  - Some areas use full value assessment; some use uniform percentage of value; NYC and Long Island use four classes of property for assessment

❑ **Receiver of Taxes/Treasurer**
  - Responsible for tax collection and accounting functions
  - No collection on tax-exempt properties

❑ **City/Town/Village Engineer**
  - Works with building, public works, and water departments to ensure proper construction and infrastructure (roads, parks, sewer and water connections, sidewalks, etc.)

❑ **County Health Department**
  - Responsible for septic system approval via plans submitted by engineer or architect
  - Mission – protect, improve, and promote health, productivity, and well being of all New Yorkers
  - Vision – New Yorkers will be the healthiest people in the world - living in communities that promote health, protected from health threats, and having access to quality, evidence-based, cost-effective health services

UNIT FOURTEEN: PROPERTY INSURANCE

Residential Property Insurance

❑ **Purpose**

- To protect asset against possible loss related to property, flood, auto, health, business, life, or pets

- May be required based on resident's location and items owned

- Homeowners and flood insurances most common types related to real estate

❑ **Provider Entities**

- Insurance companies – sell through agents, sales representatives, Internet

- Agents –

  o independent, selling for multiple companies, providing price and terms selection

  o company employed, selling only for one company

- Insurance brokers – work for client, not insurance company; search and negotiate terms and prices; assist with claims, provide risk management advice; authorized to issue or bind policy; company paid by broker, broker paid by client

❑ **Types of Coverages**

- Homeowners insurance – covers home itself, personal property or home contents, injury liability

  o lender-placed – when homeowner lets insurance lapse; higher premiums; lower coverage; premium payments added to mortgage payments; removed when owner obtains coverage

  o owner-placed – homeowner obtains his/her own policy and coverage based on

    ♦ property size and value, including potential increase or decrease in value

    ♦ contents value and age

    ♦ property location and type of structure

    ♦ rental or owner-occupied property

    ♦ mortgage lender's requirements

    ♦ policy cost and terms

- Policy types

  o monoline – one type of coverage (homeowners, liability, etc.)

  o package – two or more types of coverage

- Coverage

  o dwelling – damage to home, attached structures, major systems; typically covers fire, windstorm, hail, tornadoes, vandalism, smoke; hurricanes, earthquakes, mold must be specifically added

  o other structures – unattached structures, such as fences, sheds, pool houses

  o personal property – contents of house covered for damage, loss, theft whether or not located on the property when loss occurs

81

- o loss of use – expenses to live elsewhere when home is damaged or destroyed by covered peril

- o casualty – coverage for vandalism, theft, burglary, machinery damage

- o liability – covers suits and losses against homeowner for third-party injuries on property; covers damage to third-party property caused by policyholder

- o medical payment – covers third-party medical bills for injuries obtained on policyholder's property, unless specific cause of injury is not covered (dog bite when dogs are excluded)

- o business interruption – covers loss of business income due to inability to conduct business

- o exclusions – perils not covered under policy unless specifically added; some perils (flood) cannot be added and need separate policy

- o endorsements – adds coverage for property or perils not included in base policy

- o conditions – specifies requirement for coverage (coverage only for car parked in garage)

- o 80% rule – policies to cover at least 80% of home's replacement cost, minus deductible; no 80% coverage results in only cash value of property being paid based on depreciation and home's age

❑ **Homeowners' Policies**

- HO-1 – covers losses from basic perils; includes liability coverage for personal injury, medical payments, physical damage

- HO-2 – peril policy adds specific perils to HO-1 policy

- HO-3 – comprehensive all-risk policy covers perils unless listed as excluded

- HO-4 – renters' policy, covers personal property and liability for damage to property or injuries to third parties within the rented unit

- HO-5 – most comprehensive coverage to homeowners' policies, covering structures, personal property, and loss of use

- HO-6 – condominium and cooperatives coverage; covers personal property and interior structures such as cabinets, no coverage for structure itself; HOA carries coverage for structure

- HO-7 – extended real and personal property coverage for very expensive houses

- HO-8 – coverage for older homes where replacement costs are higher than the home's market value; covers repairs or replacements of damaged property with cheaper materials; called functional replacement

❑ **Deductibles**

- Specific amount of money policyholder pays before insurance benefits commence

- Premium amount impacted by deductible amount – the lower the deductible, the higher the premium; typically ranges from $500 to $1000

- Deductible disclosure – existence of any homeowners' insurance deductible must be disclosed to policyholder along with deductible amount and application to policy

❑ **Agent Role**

- Explain purpose and costs of property insurance to buyer

- Explain lender's interest in property insurance

- Explain escrow process for property insurance and property taxes

82

- Explain when to obtain property insurance for cash sale

❏ **Obtaining Insurance**

- New York Property Insurance Underwriting Association – meets public's basic insurance needs, including vandalism, fire, rent loss, interruption of business

- Coastal Residents Assistance – to assist with coastal and natural catastrophes such as hurricanes and other weather damages

- FEMA provides financial assistance to victims of weather-related damages

- Flood perils typically covered by the federal flood insurance program and associated flood insurance policies

❏ **Cash Value v. Replacement Cost**

- Cash value – value of item minus depreciation at time of loss

- Replacement cost – amount required to replace damaged or destroyed item at today's cost

Commercial & Umbrella Insurance

❏ **Commercial Policies**

- Protects business and employees

- Types of policies

  o Business Owner's Policy

    ♦ commercial property insurance – protects physical location and property (computers, tools, furniture, etc.)

    ♦ commercial general liability insurance – protects from claims based on bodily injury, property damage, libel and slander, advertising errors

    ♦ business income insurance – replaces lost business revenue when property damage prevents business from being conducted

  o commercial auto insurance

    ♦ covers owner and employees when driving for business

  o commercial flood insurance

    ♦ covers flood damage caused by rain, snow, hurricanes, construction; not included in standard property coverage

  o commercial umbrella insurance

    ♦ covers claims exceeding other policy limits

  o cyber insurance

    ♦ covers cyber threats and attacks

  o workers' compensation insurance

    ♦ covers employees' work-related injuries and illnesses

  o errors and omissions insurance

    ♦ covers customer suits for financial losses due to owner errors

- Commercial property
  - coverage excluded for water damage, theft, and vandalism when commercial property vacant for 60 days
  - coverage for perils reduced 15% when property vacant
  - commercial property not vacant if at least 31% total square footage occupied

❑ **Umbrella Policies**
- Provides protection beyond limits and coverages of homeowners, auto, or liability policies
- Must first obtain homeowners, auto, or liability policies before obtaining umbrella policy
- Goes into effect when limits on other policies are exhausted
- Covers claims excluded by other liability policies
- Typically covered: injuries, property damage, certain lawsuits, personal liability
- Typically not covered: policyholder's injuries, criminal or intentional act, liability assumed under a contract

UNIT FIFTEEN: LICENSEE SAFETY

Safety Precautions

❑ **Protecting Yourself**

- Meet new clients at your office and get as much personal information as possible

- Show properties before dark or turn on all lights and leave blinds open

- Know exact address; note landmarks, don't get lost; don't rely only on GPS

- Use the buddy system; do not go to properties alone.

- Make your location and client known at the office

    o tell client the office knows his/her identity

    o have the office call you at a specified time

    o establish a subtle code word to let the office know you're in trouble

- Park in well let area on the street to avoid being blocked in

- Keep your cell phone and keys with you at all times; keep handbag and valuables locked in the vehicle

- Check out the destination before entering; know all exit points

- Do not turn your back to a client or let clients follow you through doorways or up stairs

- Practice safety at open houses

    o don't be alone

    o notify at least one neighbor

    o keep an eye on groups near the end of the day

    o make sure house is empty before locking doors

- Know self-defense strategies

- Wear practical clothing

- Limit personal information you share

- Confirm your cell phone works in the area; pre-program important and emergency numbers

- Never transport cash alone

- Be aware of suspicious activity or behavior; don't advertise a property as vacant

❑ **Office Protecting Agents**

- Record each agent's vehicle information

- Record agent's outside appointment information

- Require guest registry for open houses

- No personal contact information on agents' business cards

- Keep record of agents' health conditions in case of emergency

- Do not allow agents to work alone in or out of office

- Incorporate scam and ID theft protection strategies

❑ **Protecting Clients**

- Advise clients not to show their home alone and not to allow those without an appointment to view the home

- Advise clients not to talk to other agents or buyers but to refer inquiries to you

- Remind clients that strangers will be walking through their home during showings

- Assist client in identifying items that need to be removed or secured for showings, such as valuables and medications

❑ **Protecting with Technology Applications**

- Use tracking, alarm, and distress signal software

- Provide agents with apps and devices for monitoring and safety alerts

- Use NAR's website for information, training, and other resources

UNIT SIXTEEN: TAXES AND ASSESSMENTS

Taxation

❑ **General Tax**

- Known as ad valorem taxes, levied based on value of the property

- Levied by state, cities, towns, villages, and counties, as well as school, park, lighting, drainage, water, and sanitary districts

- Non-payment results in priority lien on property enforced by court-ordered sale of property

❑ **Special Assessments**

- Levied on specific real estate that will benefit from area improvements

    o assessment based on how each land parcel will benefit from the improvement

- Municipal assessors levy assessments through approved assessing units, certified by the commissioner after completing revaluation

    o assessments made by towns, villages, cities, with assessment roll showing assessments for taxable lands and buildings in the area and open to public inspection

    o 1982 NY regulation required the State to assess property at uniform percentage of value, with NYC and Long Island dividing property into four classes for taxes

    o full value assessments continue to be challenged in court

    o NYC special assessment districts referred to as Business Improvement Districts

- Assessments differ between municipalities and between properties, with lower assessments due to

    o older construction, lower land values, or combination of both, with the opposite effect on new construction

- Undeclared improvements – made without building permit

    o permits allow taxing authority to assure compliance with local laws and building codes to protect the general public and to reassess the real estate based on the value of the improvement

❑ **Taxation**

- Reassessment – NY property being sold causes a reassessment of the property's value

    o sale year assessment is measured against target assessment (new assessment determination) from the sale

    o NYC sales require examination of

        ◆ sale year tax base

        ◆ transitional tax – difference between sale year tax and target assessment

        ◆ target assessment

    o NYC assessments not to increase more than 20% in a tax year

        ◆ higher transitional taxes to be phased in over 5-year period using two-step process:

- step 1 – determine annual transitional assessment
- step 2 – determine target assessed value

- Equalization factor – provides uniformity among districts assessing at different rates
  - NY State Board of Real Property Tax Services determines equalization rate for each municipality based on sale prices
  - factor equalizes assessments in all taxing jurisdictions within the state
  - no equalization factor used with full-value assessments
  - equalization used only with less than full value assessments
  - equalization required due to:
    - ◆ no fixed percentage for property assessments
    - ◆ varying property assessments from municipality to municipality
    - ◆ taxing boundaries for certain taxing jurisdictions, such as school districts, are not shared with cities and towns responsible for property assessments; taxes are distributed among segments of several municipalities (one to fifteen or more) with different assessment levels

❑ **Taxation Process**

- Rates
  - determined by taxing district's annual budget which includes expenditures and anticipated income
    - ◆ additional income needed to cover expenses is raised through real estate taxes
  - homesteads (dwellings with four or fewer units, owner-occupied mobile homes, condos, farms, and some vacant lands) and non-homestead (industrial and commercial) properties may utilize separate tax rates
  - different taxing districts may share taxes when also sharing expenses for the same local services, such as school districts
  - each taxing body determines tax rates separately
    - ◆ total funds needed are divided by total assessments of local real estate
    - ◆ tax rates depict the ratio of tax dollars charged in per hundred or per thousand dollars of assessed value
    - ◆ tax rates may be stated in mills, or 1 tenth of a cent, or in mills-per-dollar ratio, for example, 29 mills would equal 2.9% or $2.90 per $100 of assessed value

- Appropriation
  - authorizing expenses and providing sources of funds
  - adoption of ordinance or passage of law providing specifics of proposed taxation
  - real estate taxes are levied to raise funds to cover expenses
    - ◆ tax levy – formal action taken to impose taxes

- Tax bills
  - tax bill determined by applying tax rate to property's assessed value
    - ◆ example: $100,000 assessed value with 4% tax rate (40 mills) results in $4,000 tax bill ($100,000 x 0.040 = $4,000)

88

- example with equalization factor: $100,000 assessed value with 4% tax rate and equalization factor of 110% results in $4,400 ($110,000 x 1.10 = $110,000 x 0.04 = $4,400)
  - taxes paid late incur monthly interest charges
- Taxing jurisdictions
  - different tax districts bill at different times with varying due dates and some allowing installment payments
    - example: state, counties, and towns levy taxes from January to December and allow payments in advance while school districts levy taxes from July 1 through June 30 and payments are made in arrears
- Exemptions
  - tax exempt properties include those owned by the following when used for tax-exempt purposes:
    - city, state, and federal governments
    - schools, parks, playgrounds
    - religious organizations and corporations
    - hospitals
    - educational institutions
  - NY special exemptions and tax rate reductions include
    - veteran homeowners
    - efforts to attract industries
    - construction of low-income or multi-family housing
    - agricultural land
    - farmers claiming exemption from school taxes
    - homeowners constructing in-law apartments
    - disabled parties
    - Gold Star parents with a child lost in combat
  - elderly exemption
    - homeowners 65 and older for primary residence
    - reductions range between 10% - 50% based on income
      - income limit for 50% reduction is $3,000 to $29,000 for the state and $50,000 for NYC
      - localities may grant sliding scale exemptions less than 50% for seniors with income of $29,000 to $37,399.99
      - localities using the maximum limit provide 5% exemption
    - annual application renewal required
    - homeowners receiving an elderly exemption are also eligible for the STaR exemption (following)

- o veterans' exemption
  - ♦ must submit application with proof of honorable discharge or release from military service and letter from NY State Veterans' Services confirming character of discharge eligibility for benefits and services provided by the Restoration of Honor Act
  - ♦ may choose one of three possible exemptions only for county, city, town, village taxes
    - • alternative veterans' exemption – 15% assessed value reduction for service during war; added 10% assessed value reduction for service in combat zone; added reduction for service-related disability
    - • cold war veterans' exemption – for service from September 1945 to December 1991
    - • eligible funds exemption – for homes bought with pensions, bonuses, insurance, mustering out pay; reduces assessed value prior to taxation; also applies to school taxes
- STaR program
  - o School Tax Relief program
    - ♦ allows homeowners to apply for permanent reduction in school taxes
    - ♦ allows homeowners 65 and older to receive an age exemption and to apply annually for an enhanced reduction in school taxes
      - • eligibility based on owners' combined income; $92,000 for 2022; changes annually
    - ♦ properties eligible for STaR include houses, condos, co-ops, manufactured homes, farm houses, and mixed-use properties .

❑ **Grievance and Protesting Assessments**
- Current assessments can be disputed via the local board of assessment review
- Grievance must be submitted by Grievance Day which varies per community; March 1 is used in NYC and Nassau County
- Grievances include overassessment, disagreement of full value, unequal assessment ratios to be proven by records including incorrect property description, comparisons to neighboring properties
- Grievance steps
  - o discussion with local assessor
  - o application for hearing
  - o file grievance form with county clerk
- If requested relief not received
  - o small claims assessment review
  - o tax certiorari proceeding in NY State Supreme Court with private attorney

UNIT SEVENTEEN: CONDOMINIUMS AND COOPERATIVES

Condominiums

❑ **Definition**

- A single unit in a multiple-unit complex in which each unit's airspace and interior walls are individually owned and common elements, such as grounds, actual building structures and systems, amenities, etc., are jointly owned by all unit owners.

- Created by conversion of rental property or by new construction

- Individual units may be mortgaged, taxed, insured, sold, leased, or foreclosed with no financial impact on other units or unit owners.

❑ **Governance**

- New York Condominium Act, Article 9-B

  o regulates creation, authority, operation, and management of condominium associations

- Real Property Act

  o regulates transition of authority, governance procedures, property maintenance, etc.

- Condominium Owners Association By-laws

  o set forth the method and means for governing the condominium association, property, and finances

  o provides rules and regulations for condominium activities

  o set up covenants, conditions, restrictions for residents (CC&Rs)

  o set method for obtaining board members, officers, employees and identifying their authority, duties, and obligations

- Board of Directors

  o elected from owners to manage the condominium association; may hire professional managers

- Federal and State Fair Housing laws

  o prohibit discrimination in housing based on protected classes

- HOA laws on service and assistance animals

  o provide protection for residents with service or assistance animals

❑ **Issues; Acquisition**

- Conversions from rentals to condos in specific areas requires 51% of tenants to agree to purchase units

  o non-purchasers exempt from eviction for 3 years

  o disabled tenants and those 62 and older exempt from eviction

  o existing tenants

- may receive purchase discounts to encourage purchases
- have 90-day exclusive right to purchase
- may remain tenants and follow existing rent regulations when not purchasing under non-eviction plan

- Sponsor (condo developer/seller) creates initial offering plan to be approved by attorney general prior to units being sold
- Plan to be provided to purchasers as disclosure of property tax issues, unit square footage and floor plan, hidden fees, applicable closing date
- Plan amendments to be filed with attorney general to reflect pricing and other changes
- Sponsor appoints board of directors and manager to limit sponsor's involvement in property; sponsor retains financial liability after unit sellout but must turn over control of the board to unit owners
- Right of first refusal
  - HOA may refuse a purchaser but must then purchase the unit under the same terms

Letters of Intent

- Provided in early stages of construction in the form of a nonbinding offer to reserve a unit for purchase
- Shows buyer's willingness to purchase
- Shows lenders potential success of project to induce project funding
- Includes terms of transaction between sponsor and potential buyer

Certificate of Occupancy

- Certificate of occupancy to be obtained from Department of Buildings to confirm compliance with building codes and readiness for occupancy
- Temporary or permanent certificates to be obtained to allow purchasers to obtain financing

Title Issues

- Mortgage lenders require borrower to purchase title insurance

Closing Costs

- Deed preparation, title and tax transfers paid by sponsor-seller
- Prorated charges, deed recording, title insurance, mortgage recording taxes, and other associated items paid by purchaser
- Condominium board packages required to include verification of income, asset details, financing information

Essential Characteristics

- Common elements
  - portions of property necessary for condominium existence, operation, and maintenance (land, building structures, operating systems, recreational facilities, non-exclusive areas such as hallways, elevators, etc.)
- Owners' rights to use share common areas with other owners; may exclude non-owners from portions of common areas
- Individual units to be sold or encumbered without interference from other owners; may be foreclosed without impact on other owners

- Unit interest sale may entail limitations
- Units individually assessed and taxed

Cooperatives

❑ **Definition**

- Developer-formed association that buys housing property which becomes jointly owned and controlled by a group of individuals who hold shares, membership, and occupancy rights to the housing complex

❑ **Essential Characteristics**

- Housing complex acquired by financial nonprofit corporation with board of directors and shareholders as members

- Shareholders do not own individual units but have equal shares in the whole complex and proprietary leases

- Lease attaches to unit, not occupant; no stated or fixed rent; no term limit

- Unit value compared to total value determines individual owner's share of property expenses in lieu of rent

- Value of housing unit is reflected in number of shares purchased

- One vote per member, regardless of member's number of shares or amount of capital invested

- Profits either reinvested in the complex or returned to members

- Board of directors determine who may occupy units

- Co-op interest transferred by assigning stock certificates and lease to buyer

UNIT EIGHTEEN: COMMERCIAL AND INVESTMENT PROPERTIES

Investment Properties

❑ **Real Property Investment Characteristics**

- Conservation of capital – original investment is to grow without losing it; goal of real property investment is to purchase income

- Property ownership as tax shelter – noncash deductions for depreciation; interest; taxes, and delay or elimination of specific taxes

- Risk vs. return – more gain, more quickly equals more risk of loss; safer investments gain more slowly

- Types of risk

    o market risk

        ♦ changes in demand for invested resource may result in loss of investment value or liquidity

    o business risk

        ♦ dynamic risk – uninsurable risk based on changes in economy, income taxes, supply and demand

        ♦ static risk – insurable risk based on specific events (theft, vandalism, fire, accident liability)

    o capital risk

        ♦ chance of losing original invested cash

    o financial risk; leverage

        ♦ use of borrowed monies on the property

    o liquidity

        ♦ based on the market for the type of resource investment; is the resource exchangeable; cash is most liquid investment; illiquid investment takes longer to exchange

    o purchasing power

        ♦ changes in value of money as exchange medium could decrease value of invested resource

- Management

    o amount of attention that must be paid to the investment to result in more success, greater gain

❑ **Investment Property Types**

- Properties purchased based on investor's goals and resources

    o unimproved land – no income until there is market to develop the land

94

- commercial properties – office, retail, shopping centers, hotels/motels; income from developing and renting out space

- residential properties – greater demand than for other types of properties; multifamily properties produce rental income

- mixed-use properties – provide tax benefits and rental income

- manufacturing properties – heavy industrial, light manufacturing, loft or warehouse buildings

- fee simple ownership and leasehold – fee simple ownership preferred investment but not always possible; consequently, long-term ground leases are used

- Types of commercial lease

  - net – single tenant pays rent plus all of operating expenses and taxes; multi-tenants pay rent plus proportionate share of operating and maintenance expenses; typical for office and industrial leases

  - gross – tenant pays fixed rent with landlord paying operating expenses; lease may include rent escalation clause; also called modified gross lease; typical for residential leases

  - percentage – can be net or gross lease with no fixed rent; rent amount based on gross income generated by tenant or sales at the site; typical for retail leases

  - loft – landlord need not provide operating services; loft properties include storage and warehousing facilities

❑ Cash Flow

- Difference between actual cash flowing into investment as revenue and out of the investment for expenses, debt services, and other items; includes cash items only and not depreciation

- Deriving pre-tax cash flow

  ### Pre-tax Cash Flow

  potential rental income (full occupancy; all tenants pay rent)
  -     vacancy and collection loss
  =   effective rental income
  +   other income (laundry machines, etc.)
  =   gross operating income (GOI)

  -     operating expenses
  -     reserves (allocations made, but not spent for future outlays)
  =   net operating income (NOI)
  -     debt service (principal and interest)
  =   pre-tax cash flow

- Identifying taxable income and tax liability

  - taxable income – net operating income minus allowable deductions (depreciation, loan interest) plus amount allocated for reserves (since it was not spent)

  - tax liability – based on taxable income, not cash flow

Taxable Income

net operating income (NOI)
+   reserves
−   interest
−   depreciation
=   taxable income

Tax Liability

net operating income (NOI)
+   reserves
-       interest expense
-       cost recovery expense
=   taxable income
x   tax rate
=   tax liability

- Identifying after-tax cash flow
  - amount of income from property that actually goes into owner's pocket after income tax is paid

After-tax cash flow

pre-tax cash flow
-       tax liability
=   after tax cash flow

❑ Investment Return Analysis

- Deriving value, income, and cap rate
  - value = income ÷ rate of return
    - ♦ price of investment and amount investment should cost
  - income = rate of return x value or price
    - ♦ amount investment generates
  - cap rate = net operating income ÷ value or price
    - ♦ expected rate of return on investment
- Deriving return on investment
  - rate of return = income – operating expenses ÷ investment price
    - ♦ potential return on investment given price and performance expressed as percent
- Deriving cash-on-cash return
  - cash-on-cash return = cash flow ÷ cash invested
    - ♦ investment inclusive of financing
- Deriving return on equity
  - equity = market value – current debt principal
  - return on equity = net operating income ÷ equity
    - ♦ return on total stake in investment including cash invested, accumulated

96

depreciation, equity build-up, appreciation expressed by current market value

- ♦ ROE derived by cash flow = cash flow ÷ equity

❏ **Rentable vs Usable Area**

- ▪ Rentable area

  - ○ square footage of floor or unit of space used to calculate annual rent based on full floor tenancy, often includes non-income producing common areas; formula varies based on method of measurement used in commercial marketplace (Real Estate Board of NY or Building Owners and Managers Association) chosen by property owner

- ▪ Usable area

  - ○ methods to determine usable area vary; typically determined by subtracting space used by office furniture, personnel, equipment from rentable area; does not include common areas

- ▪ Loss (load) factor

  - ○ difference between interior usable area and rentable area

  - ○ expressed as percentage = (rentable area – usable area) ÷ rentable area

  - ○ expressed as square footage = rentable area – usable area

- ▪ Add-on factor

  - ○ difference between usable and rentable square footage when added to the usable square footage; considered reciprocal of loss factor

  - ○ expressed as percentage = square footage loss factor ÷ usable area

Commercial Properties

❏ **Key Commercial Property Terms**

- ▪ **Use clause** – defines what business the tenant may conduct within the leased property to guarantee lawful use and compliance with the property's certificate of occupancy

- ▪ **Attornment** – defines who is to be paid rent and who is to pay the rent; can be defined in letter of attornment instead of lease clause, typically when leased property is sold to another party honoring the lease

- ▪ **Lease escalation** – periodic increases in a lease's rent; protects owner against inflationary rises in operation costs by passing the increased costs on to the tenant

- ▪ **Proportionate share** – as result of lease escalation, defines tenant's share of operation cost increases; uses tenant's space percentage of gross rentable area of the entire building to determine how much of the increased costs the tenant will pay; calculation methods vary resulting in varying amounts to be paid by tenant

  - ○ proportionate share = tenant rentable area ÷ building gross rentable area

- ▪ **Base year** – used in commercial leases to pass increased operations costs to tenant; defines when the tenant's liability for property taxes and increased operational costs begins

  - ○ typically year of occupancy for property with operating history

  - ○ operating bases estimated by developers of new construction

  - ○ proportionate share of occupancy applied to difference between base year and current year's costs

- **Operating stop and tax stop** – defines landlord responsibility to cover increases in annual operating expenses as dollar per square foot; excess costs over the "stop" become tenant's responsibility
    - some leases protect tenants by using stops as limits on annual rent increases
- **Porters wage escalation** – an index of wage escalations that is tied directly to the rents paid on leased property. Movements of this index trigger like movements in the tenant's rent obligation.
    - amount of rent increases are denominated in rent per square foot; specific amounts determined through negotiations at lease commencement

UNIT NINETEEN: INCOME TAX ISSUES IN REAL ESTATE TRANSACTIONS

Income Tax Issues

❑ **Tax Reform Act of 2018**

1. Added alternative minimum tax exemptions

2. Created seven income tax brackets

3. Limits mortgage interest deduction amount

4. Limits real estate tax deduction

5. Reduced top corporate tax rate

- Homeowner deductions

    o **property taxes** – maximum $10,000 deduction from total tax bill during year tax is paid

    o **mortgage interest** – limited deduction based on home acquisition financing, loan refinancing, home equity loans

    o **second homes** – limited property tax and interest deductions

- Points and closing costs

    o **points** – interest prepaid to lender; conditional deduction in payment year; applies to acquisition financing only

    o **closing costs** – not deductible in acquisition year for owner-occupied properties; amounts are added to property's depreciable basis and deducted from rental income over the depreciation period allowed

- Capital gains and recapture

    o **short-term gains (loss)** –value gain or loss of property owned for 1 year or less; gain taxed at ordinary income rates

    o **long-term gains (loss)** – net increase or decrease in value of property owned for 2 or more income tax years; taxed at ordinary income tax rate

    o **deriving income property gains** – calculated based on property's adjusted basis

        ♦ ending basis – beginning basis = gain

        ♦ beginning basis = initial price minus deductible acquisition costs

        ♦ adjusted basis – purchase price plus capital improvements minus depreciation

        ♦ ending basis = adjusted basis minus deductible selling costs

        ♦ IRS-based financial interest to determine annual depreciation and gain/loss on sale of property

    o **recapture** – time-of-sale recovery of depreciation claimed in previous tax years; recapture tax rate = 25%; cannot depreciate primary residences for tax purposes

- Active vs passive income

    o **active** – employment income (salaries, commissions, gratuities, etc.)

- o **passive** – income without owner's day-to-day involvement (rent, investments, etc.); limited deductions for passive capital losses

- o **portfolio** – income from dividends from ownership stock, interest from any source, royalties on intellectual property

❑ **Calculating Capital Gain**

- Straight-line depreciation – method for calculating annual depreciation allowance

  - o recovery periods

    - ◆ 27 ½ year – residential income property wherein 80% of income is from improvement.

    - ◆ 39 year – commercial income property such as office buildings, retail centers, industrial parks, professional buildings

  - o depreciable basis – total purchase cost (to include realtor commission, legal fees, appraisals, etc.) minus land value; used to calculate annual allowable deductions

❑ **Like-kind Exchanges (1031 Exchanges)**

- No $250,000/$500,000 capital gains tax exclusion for investment property sale

- Investment properties use IRS code 1031 as tax shelter for tax-deferred exchanges of like-kind property (property for property, not property for money); allows capital gains taxes to be deferred but not forgiven

- Qualified property for exchanges must be "like-kind property" only

- Qualifying properties

  - o investment real properties only; commercial, industrial, income residential, vacant property held for investment, hotels, motels, leaseholds for 30+ years

- Non-qualifying properties

  - o property primarily for sale, property held by developer or dealer, securities, stocks and bonds, interests in partnership, properties outside U.S., personal residences

- 45-day rule

  - o replacement property to be designated within 45 days of sale of first property; identification rules to be followed

- 180-day rule

  - o delayed exchange closing on replacement property within 180 days of sale of first property

- Failure to meet time limits results in entire gain being taxable

- Reverse exchange

  - o replacement property obtained prior to sale of first property; must be completed within 180 days

- Exchanging parties must use facilitator/intermediary

❑ **Low-income Housing Tax Incentives**

- Created by the Tax Reform Act of 1986,

- Tax credit for developers and investors for the acquisition, rehabilitation, or new construction of rental housing targeted to lower-income households

- Paid by federal government; administered by state

100

- Housing eligibility criteria
  - include a specific minimum percentage of affordable units
  - remain affordable for a minimum of 30 years.
- Tax credits
  - 4% credit for new construction that involves other government assistance such as subsidies or buying an existing project.
  - 9% credit for new construction (or significant rehabilitation) with no other government assistance.
  - credits applied for 10 years and cover most tax expenses for the property

UNIT TWENTY: MORTGAGE BROKERAGE

Mortgage Brokerage

❑ **Mortgage Broker Defined**

- Person or entity registered according to the NY State Banking Department to solicit, process, place, or negotiate residential or commercial mortgage loans for others for a fee (paid by either the borrower or the lender) or to offer to do the same

❑ **Mortgage Broker Licensing Requirements**

- Have 2 or more years of experience in credit analysis

- Have education and/or experience in underwriting

- Obtain business registration with NY State Banking Department

- Obtain workers compensation insurance

- Pass criminal and state background check

- Provide business formation documents, such as financial statements, credit reports, business plan, agent and employee information, etc.

- Complete pre-licensing education requirements; pass state and national exam

- Submit application and licensing fee

- Obtain a NY mortgage broker surety bond to guarantee legal compliance

- Renew license annually

❑ **Mortgage Broker Responsibilities**

- Work with potential borrower to determine financial and borrowing needs and qualifications

- Assist borrower with loan preapproval

- Handle loan application paperwork

- Seek and obtain an appropriate lender

- Negotiate with multiple lenders to find best loan option and interest rate for borrower

- Assure borrower understands loan and payment terms

- Obtain loan commitment letter from lender

- Comply with all federal and state finance and lending laws

- Avoid undisclosed dual agency relationships when the mortgage broker is also a real estate licensee

❑ **Mortgage Broker versus Mortgage Banker**

- Broker acts as middleman between lenders and real estate purchasers

    o   finds lenders and loans for the borrower;

    o   handles loan approval and application;

    o   charges a fee for services

- Banker originates the loan
  - issues mortgage loan commitments;
  - advances funds for the loan, and
  - may service the loan; but
  - most bankers sell the loan to the secondary market (investors)

❑ **Role of Mortgage Broker in a Real Estate Transaction**
- To connect borrowers with the best loan terms based on their financial situation and interest rate needs
- To collect information from the borrower regarding income, assets, employment, credit
- To obtain a mortgage commitment from a lender to confirm the borrower's ability to purchase the property
- To analyze the borrower's financial potential and creditworthiness to establish preapproval and prequalification for the loan
  - preapproval includes having all necessary documents on file with no substantial credit or income issues
  - prequalification includes the broker having established that the borrower will most likely meet the loan requirements of a specific lender
  - both preapproval and prequalification are based on the borrower's honesty
- To take care of and submit all preapplication loan documents
- To prepare and present the fee agreement to the borrower
- To present the borrower to all potential lenders
- To complete and submit all loan applications
- To help the borrower gather the documents required by the lender
  - 2 or more years of the borrower's tax returns
  - financial statement of the borrower's net worth, assets, and liabilities
  - reconstructed operating statement that includes income, expenses, and supporting leases for any rental properties
- To obtain and explain to the borrower the terms of any lending offers and rebates paid to the mortgage broker
- To explain to the borrower the difference between types of loans and payment options
  - fixed rate
  - variable rate
  - amortized
  - interest only
  - short term
  - long term
  - rate lock for the length of the loan
- To bring the loan process and transaction to a close

UNIT TWENTY-ONE: PROPERTY MANAGEMENT

Property Management

❑ **Property Management**

- Property management is the business of overseeing daily operations and financial aspects of property owned by others

- Property managers and staff oversee specific properties on behalf of the owners, assuring the property condition and financial performance meet set standards

❑ **The Management Agreement**

- Components

  o parties' names; property description; contract term; owner's purpose; owner's responsibilities; manager's authority and responsibilities; budget; allocation of costs; reporting; compensation; HUD Equal Opportunity statement

- Rights, duties, and liabilities

  o landlord – receive rent; receive premises in specified condition; enter and inspect; examine books; contract; hire vendors; set rents; pay management fee; comply with applicable laws

  o manager – based on authority granted in contract, may hire and fire; enter into contracts; perform management tasks without interference; maintain financial records; make reports; budget; collect rent; find tenants; maintain property; meet owner goals; hold liability for trust funds; comply with applicable laws

❑ **Property Management Functions and Skills Required**

- Types of managers

  o individual – managing properties for multiple owners

  o building manager – employed to manage a single property

  o resident – employed to live and manage on site

  o may specialize in a property type

  o fiduciary of the principal

  o specific functions determined by management agreement

- Reporting

  o monthly, quarterly, annually

  o annual operating budget, cash flow reports, profit and loss statements, budget comparison statements

- Budgeting

  o operating budget – based on expected expenses and revenues; determines rental rates, capital expenditures, reserves, salaries and wages; projects income based on past performance and current market

  o income

104

- ◆ potential gross income – rents plus revenues

- ◆ effective gross income – potential gross income minus uncollected rents, vacancies, and evictions

- ◆ net operating income – effective gross income minus operating expenses

- ◆ cash flow – net operating income minus debt service and reserves

- ○ expenses

  - ◆ fixed expenses remain constant, e.g., operating expenses, regular maintenance costs, administration

  - ◆ variable expenses change from month to month or occur sporadically, e.g., repairs, capital expenditures

- ○ capital expenditures – outlays for major renovations and construction; cash reserves set aside for variable expenses

- ○ cash reserve – a fund set aside from operating revenues for variable expenses; amount based on variable expenses from previous year

- ○ operating statements itemizing income and expenses presented to owner on scheduled basis for evaluation of manager's performance in regard to budget

- ▪ Renting

  - ○ keep property rented and occupied

  - ○ develop periodic marketing plans

  - ○ select compatible tenants and collect scheduled rents

  - ○ maintain tenant relations

  - ○ comply with fair housing laws, Americans with Disabilities Act, and ECOA

- ▪ Property maintenance

  - ○ balance costs of services, owner financial objectives, and tenant needs

  - ○ routine, preventive, or corrective; staffed in-house or contracted out

- ▪ Construction

  - ○ tenant alterations, renovations, expansion, environmental remediation

  - ○ legal concerns – Americans with Disabilities Act requires same level of access to facilities for disabled and nondisabled, reasonable accommodations, necessary modifications, barrier removal

❑ **Leasing Considerations**

- ▪ Landlord rights

  - ○ enter premises, receive payment, retake on termination, pursue remedies

- ▪ Landlord responsibilities

  - ○ provide habitable conditions; maintain heating, cooling, electrical, plumbing; keep clean and in repair

- ▪ General tenant's rights

  - ○ quiet enjoyment

  - ○ habitable conditions

- o right to sue for default
- New York City and Buffalo's Multiple Dwelling Law requirements
  - o automatic self-closing and self-locking doors
    - ♦ additional tenant-installed locks allowed
  - o two-way voice buzzers
  - o heat provided by landlord from October 1 to May 31
  - o mirrors in self-serviced elevators in buildings with eight or more units
  - o chain guards and peepholes on apartment entrance doors in buildings with eight or more units
- Other requirements
  - o window guards for children under 11 years
  - o guards on public hall windows
  - o smoke and carbon monoxide detectors
  - o secure mailboxes in buildings with three or more units
- Tenant responsibilities
  - o pay rent, obey rules, give proper notice, return property in prescribed condition, use only for intended purpose
- Rent regulations
  - o NY rent regulation administered by Office of Rent Administration of the New York State Division of Housing and Community Renewal (DHCR)
    - o rent control – based on location; applies to buildings with three or more units; properties built before February 1947; applies to tenant occupying unit since July 1, 1971; control only lasts until unit is vacated
    - o rent stabilization – based on location; limited annual rent increases; tenants renew for 1 or 2 years
      - in NYC, applies to buildings with six or more units built between February 1, 1947 and January 1, 1974; also applies to buildings with three or more units built or renovated since 1974 with special tax benefits
      - outside NYC, applies to communities under Emergency Tenant Protection Act; community limits size of building covered; applies only to properties with six or more units
  - o Rent Act of 2015 – effective June 15, 2015 through June 15, 2019; changed method for calculating rents on vacancy leases;
    - o if unit's rent is controlled at $2,700 and tenant's income exceeds $200,000 for 2 consecutive years, landlord may request to remove the unit's rent stabilized status
    - o if a vacant unit's legal DHCR registered rent is at least $2,700, landlord may request to remove the unit's rent control
- Eviction
  - o actual – requires NY State court order to remove tenant

- constructive – tenant vacates on account of landlord failure to maintain premises
- Termination of lease
  - expiration
  - performance
  - agreement
  - abandonment
  - breach
  - notice
  - destruction of premises
  - condemnation
  - foreclosure
  - death of either party (tenancy at will)
  - death of landlord (life estate)

UNIT TWENTY-TWO: REAL ESTATE MATH

Basic Math

Fractions

Adding and subtracting same denominator:

    Formula: *a / c + b / c = (a + b) ÷ c*

    Example: 1/2 + 1/2 = (1 + 1) / 2 = 2/2 = 1

Adding and subtracting different denominators:

    Formula: *a / c + b / d = (ad + bc) / cd*

    Example: 1/2 + 1/3 = (3 +2) / 6 = 5/6

Multiplying:

    Formula: *(a / c) x (b / d) = ab / cd*

    Example: (2/5) x (4/6) = 8/30 = 4/15

Decimals and Percents

Converting decimals to percentages

    Formula: *Decimal number x 100 = Percentage number*

    Example: .022 x 100 = 2.2%

Converting percentages to decimals

    Formula: *Percent number ÷ 100 = Decimal number*

    Example: 2.2 ÷ 100 = .022

Multiplying percents

    Formula: *1. Percent number ÷ 100 = Decimal number*

                     2. Beginning number x Decimal number = Product

    Example: 75% of 256 (75% x 256) = ?

                     1.   75 ÷ 100 = .75

                     2.   256 x .75= 192

Dividing by percents

Formula: 1. *Percent number ÷ 100 = Decimal number*

                 2. *Beginning number ÷ Decimal = Dividend*

Example: 240 ÷ 75% = ?

                 1. 75% ÷ 100 = .75

                 2. 240 ÷ .75 = 320

Decimals, Fractions, and Percentages

Converting fractions to percents

Formula: (1)   a / b or a ÷ b = a divided by b = decimal number

                 (2)   decimal number x 100 = percent number

Example: (1)   2 / 5 = 2 divided by 5 = 0.4

                 (2)   .4 x 100 = 40%

Converting a percent to fraction and reducing it

Formula: (1)   X% = X ÷ 100 or X / 100

                 (2)   X ÷ a   where a is the largest number that divides evenly
                         100 ÷ a   into both numerator and denominator

Example: (1)   40% = 40 ÷ 100, or 40 / 100

                 (2)   40 ÷ 20 =   2
                         100 ÷ 20 =   5

Converting fractions to decimals and percentages

Formula: *Decimal x 100 = Percent number*

Example: .75 x 100 = 75%

Equations

Additions and Subtractions

Formula: *if* $a = b + c$

                 then $b = a - c$ *(subtracting c from both sides)*

                 and $c = a - b$ *(subtracting b from both sides)*

Example: 10 $= 6 + 4$

                 6         $= 10 - 4$

$$4 \quad = 10 - 6$$

Multiplications and Divisions

Formula: *if* $a = b \times c$

            then $b = a / c$ *(dividing both sides by c)*

            and $c = a / b$ *(dividing both sides by b)*

Example: $10 = 2 \times 5$

            $2 = 10 \div 5$

            $5 = 10 \div 2$

Linear and Perimeter Measurement
Linear measure of rectangles

Formula: *Side A = Area ÷ Side B*

Example: A rectangular house has one side 40' side long and area of 1,200 SF. What is the length of the other side?

         Side A = (1,200' ÷ 40') = 30'

Perimeter measurement

Formula: *Perimeter = Sum of all sides of an object*

Example: A five-sided lot has the following dimensions:

         Side A = 50' Side B = 60'
         Side C= 70' Side D = 100'
         Side E = 30'

         What is the perimeter of the lot?

         P = 50' + 60' + 70' + 100' + 30' = 310'

Area Measurement

Square and rectangle

Formula: *Area = Width x Depth (Horizontal) or Width x Height (Vertical)*

            Width= Depth (Height) ÷ Area

            Depth (Height)= Width ÷ Area

Example: A house is 40' deep and 30' wide. What is its area?

         Area = 40' x 30' = 1,200 SF

Triangle

Formula: *Area = (Height x Base) ÷ 2*

                Note: Base is also sometimes referred to as "width"

Example: An A-frame house has a front facade measuring 30' across and 20' in height. What is the area of the facade?

                Area = (30' x 20') ÷ 2 = 300 Square feet (SF)

Square foot-to-acre conversion

Formula: *Acres = Area SF ÷ 43,560 SF*

Example: How many acres is 196,020 SF?

                196,020 SF ÷ 43,560 SF = 4.5 acres

Acre-to-square foot conversion

Formula: *SF = Number of acres x 43,560 SF*

Example: How many square feet is .75 acres?

                .75 acres x 43,560 SF = 32,670 SF

Linear and Area Conversion Chart

Linear measures

(cm = centimeter; m = meter; km = kilometer)

1 inch	=	1/12 foot	=	1/36 yard		
1 foot	=	12 inches	=	1/3 yard		
1 yard	=	36 inches	=	3 feet		
1 rod	=	16.5 feet	=	1/320 mile		
1 mile	=	5280 feet	=	1760 yards	=	320 rods
1 centimeter	=	1/100 m				
1 meter	=	100 cm	=	1/1000 km		
1 kilometer	=	1,000 m				

Area measures

1 square inch	=	1/144 sq. foot				
1 square foot	=	1/9 sq. yard	=	144 sq. inches		
1 square yard	=	9 sq. feet	=	1,296 sq. inches		
1 acre	=	1/640 sq. mi	=	43,560 SF	=	208.71 ft x 208.71 ft
1 square mile	=	640 acres	=	1 section	=	1/36 township
1 section	=	1 mi x 1 mi	=	640 acres	=	1/36 township
1 township	=	6 mi x 6 mi	=	36 sq. mi	=	36 sections

Metric conversions

(cm = centimeter; m = meter; km = kilometer)

1 inch	=	2.54 cm				
1 foot	=	30.48 cm	=	.3048 m		
1 yard	=	91.44 cm	=	.9144 m		
1 mile	=	1609.3 m	=	1.60 km		
1 centimeter	=	.3937 inch				
1 meter	=	39.37 inches	=	3.28 feet	=	1.094 yards
1 kilometer	=	3,281.5 feet	=	.621 mile		

Fractions of sections, acres, and linear dimensions

Fraction		# Acres
1 section	=	640 acres
1/2 section	=	320 acres
1/4 section	=	160 acres
1/8 section	=	80 acres
1/16 section	=	40 acres
1/32 section	=	20 acres
1/64 section	=	10 acres

Calculating Area from the Legal Description

Formula: (1) *First multiply all the denominators of the fractions in the legal description together.*

(2) *Then divide 640 by the resulting product.*

Examples: How many acres are in the Northern 1/2 of the Southwestern 1/4 of Section 6?

640 / (2 x 4) = 640 / 8 = 80 acres

How many acres are in the Western 1/2 of the Northwestern 1/4 of the Northeastern 1/4 of Section 8?

640 / (2 x 4 x 4) = 640 / 32 = 20 acres

Volume Measurement

Formula: *Volume = Width x Height x Depth   (assume objects with 90 degree angles)*

Base = (Height x Depth) ÷ Volume

Height = (Base x Depth) ÷ Volume

Depth = (Base x Height) ÷ Volume

Example: What is the volume of a 40' x 30' x 20' house?

40' x 30' x 20' = 24,000 cubic feet

Leases

Percentage Lease Rent Calculation

Formula: *Monthly percentage rent = Sales x percent of sales charged*

Example: A store generates $50,000 per month. The lease calls for 1.5% percentage rent. Monthly rent amount?

($50,000 x .015) = $750 / month

Contracts for the Sale of Real Estate

Percentage of Listing Price Calculation

Formula: *Percentage of listing price = Offer ÷ Listing price*

Example: A property listed for $150,000 receives an offer for $120,000. The offer's percentage of listing price is:

$120,000 ÷ $150,000 = 80%

Earnest Money Deposit Calculation

Formula: *Deposit = Offering price x required or market-accepted percentage*

Example: A seller requires a 2% deposit on a property listed for $320,000. The required deposit (assuming a full price offer) is:

$320,000 x 2% = $6,400

Appraisal & Value

Adjusting Comparables

Rules:
1. Never adjust the subject!

2. If the comparable is superior to the subject, subtract value from the comparable.

3. If the comparable is inferior to the subject, add value to the comparable.

Example: The subject has a $10,000 pool and no porch. A comparable that sold for $250,000 has a porch ($5,000), an extra bathroom ($6,000), and no pool.

Adjustments to comp: $250,000 (+10,000 - 5,000 - 6,000) = $249,000 indicated value of subject

113

Gross Rent Multiplier

Formulas: *Sales price = Monthly rental income x GRM*

Monthly rental income = Sales price / Gross Rent Multiplier

Note: Gross rent multiplier is often abbreviated as GRM.

Examples:
1. What is the value of a fourplex with monthly rent of $2,800 and a GRM of 112?

   $2,800 rent x 112 GRM = $313,600

2. What is the GRM of a fourplex with monthly rent of $2,800 and a value of $313,600?

   313,600 price ÷ $2,800 rent = 112 GRM

Gross Income Multiplier

Formulas *Gross Income Multiplier = Sales price ÷ Annual income*

Sales price = Annual income x Gross Income Multiplier

Annual income = Sales price ÷ Gross Income Multiplier

Note: Gross income multiplier is often abbreviated as GIM.

Examples:
1. What is the value of a commercial property with an annual income of $33,600 and a GIM of 9.3?

   $33,600 income x 9.3 GIM = $312,480

2. What is the GIM of a commercial property with annual income of $33,600 and a value of $312,480?

   $313,600 price ÷ $33,600 = 9.3 GIM

Cost Approach Formula

Formula: *Value = Land value + (Improvements + Capital additions - Depreciation)*

Example: Land value = $50,000; home replacement cost = $150,000; new garage added @ $30,000; total depreciation = $10,000

Value = $50,000 + (150,000 + 30,000 - 10,000) = $220,000

Depreciation

Formulas: *Annual depreciation = Beginning depreciable basis ÷ Depreciation term*

Depreciable basis = (Initial property value + Any capital improvements - Land value)

Note: The depreciation term is in number of years.

Example: Property value = $500,000; land value = $110,000; depreciation term = 39 years

Step 1: ($500,000 - $110,000) = $390,000 depreciable basis

Step 2: ($390,000 ÷ 39 years) = $10,000 annual depreciation

Income Capitalization Formula

Formulas: *Value = Annual Net Operating Income ÷ Capitalization rate*

Capitalization rate = Annual Net Operating Income ÷ Value

Annual Net Operating Income = Value x Capitalization rate

Examples:
1. A property generates $490,000 net income and sells at a 7% cap rate. What is its value?

$490,000 ÷ 7% = $7,000,000 value

2. A property has a net income of $490,000 and sells for $7,000,000. What is its cap rate?

$490,000 ÷ 7,000,000 = .07, or 7%

3. A property's value is $7,000,000 and the cap rate is 7%. What is the property's net operating income?

$7,000,000 x .07 = $490,000

Net Operating Income (NOI, Net Income)

Formula: *NOI = Potential rent - Vacancy loss + Other income - Operating expenses*

Note: NOI does not include debt payments!

Example: A building has 10 office suites generating annual potential rent of $10,000 each. Vacancy = 10% and annual expenses are $35,000. Vending machines yield $5,000. What is the NOI?

$100,000 rent - 10,000 vacancy + 5,000 other income - 35,000 expenses = $60,000 NOI

Finance

Points

Definition: 1 point = 1% of the loan amount or .01 x loan amount

Formulas: *Points = Fee paid ÷ Loan amount*

                        Fee paid = Loan amount x Points

                        Loan amount = Fee paid ÷ Points

Examples:

1. A borrower pays $500 for a $10,000 loan. How many points are paid?

   $500 ÷ 10,000 = .05 = 5 points

2. A borrower pays 5 points on a $10,000 loan. What is the fee paid?

   $10,000 x .05 = $500

3. A borrower pays $500 as 5 points on a loan. What is the loan amount?

   $500 ÷ .05 = $10,000

Rules of
Thumb: 1 point charged raises lender's yield by .125%

              8 points charged raises lender's yield by 1%

Example: A lender wants to yield 7% on a 6.5% loan. How many points must he or she charge?

              (7% - 6.5%) = .5%

              .5% ÷ .125% = 4 points

Interest Rate, Principal and Payment

Caveat!
          Interest rates in mortgage financing apply to the annual interest payment and exclude principal payment. Remember to convert annual payments to monthly or vice versa as the question requires, and to exclude principal payments from your calculations!

Formulas: *Payment = Principal x Rate*

              Principal = Payment ÷ Rate

              Rate = Payment ÷ Principal

Examples:

1. A borrower has a $100,000 loan @ 6% interest. What are the annual and monthly payments?

   Annual payment = $100,000 x .06 = $6,000
   Monthly payment = $6,000 ÷ 12 = $500

2. A borrower has a $500 monthly payment on a 6% loan. What is the loan principal?

   Principal = ($500 x 12) ÷ 6% = ($6,000 ÷ .06) = $100,000

3. A borrower has a $500 monthly payment on a $100,000 loan. What is the loan rate?

   Rate = ($500 x 12) ÷ $100,000 = ($6,000 ÷ 100,000) = .06 = 6%

Total Interest, Interest Rate, and Loan Term

Formulas: *Interest-only loan:*   *Total interest = Loan amount x Rate x Term in years*

             Amortized loan: *Total interest = (Monthly PI payment x 12 x term) - Loan amount*

Examples: 1. A borrower obtains a 10-year interest only loan of $50,000 @ 6%. How much interest will he or she pay?

                ($50,000 x .06 x 10) = $30,000

             2. A borrower obtains a 10-year amortized loan of $50,000 @ 6% with monthly payments of $555.10. How much interest will he or she pay?

                ($555.10 x 12 x 10) - $50,000 = $16,612

Amortization Calculation

Formulas: *Month 1:*   *Principal paid = Monthly payment - (Loan amount x Rate ÷ 12)*

             Month 2:   *New loan amount = (Previous month principal - Principal paid)*

                          Principal paid = Monthly payment - (New loan amount x Rate ÷ 12)

Example: A borrower obtains a 30-year $100,000 amortized loan @ 7% with a $665.31 monthly payment. What is the principal paid in the second month?

             Month 1:   Principal paid = $665.31 - ($100,000 x 7% ÷ 12) = $665.31 - (583.33 interest paid) = $81.98

             Month 2:   New loan amount = $100,000 previous month beginning loan amount - $81.98 principal paid = $99,918.02

                        Principal paid = $665.31 - ($99,918.02 x 7% ÷ 12) = $665.31 - (582.86 interest paid) = $82.45

Loan Constants

Formulas: *Monthly payment = (Loan amount x Loan constant) / 1000*

             Loan amount = (Monthly payment ÷ Loan constant) x 1000

             Loan constant = (Monthly payment ÷ Loan amount) x 1000

117

Examples:

1. A borrower obtains a loan for $100,000 with a 6.3207 constant. What is the monthly payment?

   Monthly payment = ($100,000 ÷ 1,000) x 6.3207 = $632.07

2. A borrower has a monthly payment of $632.07 on a loan with a monthly constant of 6.3207. What is the loan amount?

   Loan amount = ($632.07 ÷ 6.3207) x 1000 = $100,000

3. A borrower obtains a loan for $100,000 with a monthly payment of $632.07. What is the loan constant?

   Loan constant = ($632.07 ÷ $100,000) x 1,000 = 6.3207

Loan - to - Value Ratio (LTV)

Formulas:

LTV ratio = Loan ÷ Price (Value)

Loan = LTV ratio x Price (Value)

Price (Value) = Loan ÷ LTV ratio

Examples:

1. A borrower can get a $265,600 loan on a $332,000 home. What is her LTV ratio?

   LTV Ratio = $265,600 ÷ 332,000 = 80%

2. A borrower can get an 80% loan on a $332,000 home. What is the loan amount?

   Loan = $332,000 x .80 = $265,600

3. A borrower obtained an 80% loan for $265,600. What was the price of the home?

   Price (value) = $265,600 ÷ .80 = $332,000

Financial Qualification

Income ratio qualification

Formula: *Monthly Principal & Interest (PI) payment = Income ratio x Monthly gross income*

Example: A lender uses a 28% income ratio for the PI payment. A borrower grosses $30,000 per year. What monthly PI payment can the borrower afford?

Monthly PI payment = ($30,000 ÷ 12) x .28 = $700

How much can the borrower borrow if the loan constant is 6.3207? (See also- loan constants)

Loan amount = ($700 ÷ 6.3207) x 1,000 = $110,747.22

Debt ratio qualification

Formulas: *Debt ratio = (Housing expense + Other debt payments) ÷ Monthly gross income*

118

Housing expense = (Monthly gross income x Debt ratio) - Other debt payments

Example: A lender uses a 36% debt ratio. A borrower earns $30,000 / year and has monthly non-housing debt payments of $500. What housing payment can she afford?

Housing expense = ($30,000 ÷ 12 x .36) - 500 = ($900 - 500) = $400

Investment

Appreciation Calculations

Simple appreciation

Formulas: *Total appreciation = Current value - Original price*

Total appreciation rate = Total appreciation ÷ Original price

Average annual appreciation rate = Total appreciation rate ÷ number of years

One year appreciation rate = (Annual appreciation amount) ÷ (Value at beginning of year)

Examples:
1. A home purchased for $200,000 five years ago is now worth $300,000. What are the total appreciation amount, total appreciation rate, and average appreciation rate?

   Total appreciation = ($300,000 - 200,000), or $100,000

   Total appreciation rate = ($100,000 ÷ 200,000), or 50%

   Average annual appreciation rate = 50% ÷ 5 years = 10%

2. A home costing $250,000 is worth $268,000 one year later. What is the one-year appreciation rate?

   One-year appreciation rate = ($18,000 ÷ 250,000) = 7.2%

Compounded appreciation

Formula: *Appreciated value = Beginning value x (1+ annual rate) x (1+ annual rate) ...... for the number of years in question*

Example: A $100,000 property is expected to appreciate 5% each year for the next 3 years. What will be its appreciated value at the end of this period?

Appreciated value = $100,000 x 1.05 x 1.05 x 1.05 = $115,762.50

Rate of Return, Investment Value, Income

Formulas: Where Income = net operating income (NOI); Rate = rate of return, cap rate, or percent yield; and Value = value, price or investment amount:

Rate = Income ÷ Value

119

Value = Income ÷ Rate

Income = Value x Rate

Examples:

1. An office building has $200,000 net income and sold for $3,200,000. What was the rate of return?

   Rate = ($200,000 NOI ÷ 3,200,000 price) = 6.25%

2. An office building has $200,000 net income and a cap rate of 6.25%. What is its value?

   Value = ($200,000 ÷ 6.25%) = $3,200,000

3. An office building sells for $3,200,000 at a cap rate of 6.25%. What is its NOI?

   Income = $3,200,000 x 6.25% = $200,000

Basis, Adjusted Basis, and Capital Gain

Formulas:

Capital gain = Amount realized - Adjusted basis, where

Amount realized = Sale price - Selling costs

Adjusted basis = Beginning basis + Capital improvements - Total depreciation

Total depreciation = (Beginning depreciable basis ÷ Depreciation term in years) x Years depreciated

Depreciable basis = Initial property value + Capital improvements - Land value

Example:

Tip: work example backwards from last formula to first formula.

An apartment building was purchased for $500,000, with the land value estimated to be $100,000. The owner added a $100,000 parking lot. The property was depreciated on a 40-year schedule (for present purposes!). Three years later the property sold for $700,000, and selling costs were $50,000. What was the capital gain?

1. depreciable basis = $500,000 purchase price + 100,000 parking lot - 100,000 land = $500,000

2. total depreciation = ($500,000 ÷ 40 years) x 3 years = $37,500

3. adjusted basis = $500,000 purchase price + 100,000 parking lot - 37,500 total depreciation = $562,500

4. amount realized = $700,000 sale price - 50,000 selling costs = $650,000

5. capital gain = $650,000 amount realized - 562,500 adjusted basis = $87,500

Depreciation

Formulas: *Annual depreciation = (Beginning depreciable basis) ÷ (Depreciation term in number of years)*

Depreciable basis = (Initial property value + Capital improvements - Land value)

Example: Property value = $500,000; land value = $110,000; depreciation term = 39 years

1. ($500,000 - 110,000) = $390,000 depreciable basis

2. ($390,000 ÷ 39 years) = $10,000 annual depreciation

Equity

Formula: *Equity = Current market value - Current loan balance(s)*

Example: A home that was purchased for $150,000 with a $100,000 loan is now worth $300,000. The current loan balance is $80,000. What is the homeowner's equity?

Equity = $300,000 value - $80,000 debt = $220,000

Net Income

Formula: *NOI = Potential rent - Vacancy loss + Other income - Operating expenses*

Note: NOI does not include debt payments!

Example: A building has 10 office suites generating annual potential rent of $10,000 each. Vacancy = 10% and annual expenses are $35,000. Vending machines yield $5,000. What is the NOI?

$100,000 rent - 10,000 vacancy + 5,000 other income - 35,000 expenses = $60,000 NOI

Cash Flow

Formula: *Cash flow = (Net Operating Income - Debt service) where debt service is PI payment*

Example: A building generates $100,000 NOI after expenses and has a debt payment of $40,000. What is its cash flow?

Cash flow = $100,000 - 40,000 = $60,000

Investment Property Income Tax Liability

Formula: *Tax liability = (NOI + Reserves - Interest expense - Depreciation) x Tax bracket*

Example: An office building has NOI of $200,000, an annual reserve expense of $20,000, interest expense of $130,000 and annual depreciation of $50,000. Assuming a 28% tax bracket, what is its income tax liability?

Tax liability = ($200,000 + 20,000 - 130,000 - 50,000) x 28% = $11,200

Return on Investment

Formula: $ROI = NOI \div Price$

Example: An investment property generates a cash flow of $100,000 and appraises for $1,500,000. What is the owner's return on investment?

ROI = $100,000 ÷ 1,500,000 = 6.67%

Return on Equity

Formula: $ROE = Cash\ flow \div Equity$

Example: An investment property generates a cash flow of $100,000. The owner has $500,000 equity in the property. What is the owner's return on equity?

ROE= $100,000 ÷ 500,000 = 20%

Real Estate Taxation

Converting Mill Rates

Definition: 1 mill = $.001; a mill rate of 1 mill per $1,000 = .1%; a 1% tax rate = 10 mills

Formula: $Tax = (Taxable\ value \div 1000)\ x\ Mill\ rate$

Example: A tax rate on a house with a $200,000 taxable value is 7 mills per thousand dollars of assessed valuation. What is the tax?

Tax = ($200,000 ÷ 1,000) x 7 mills = $1,400

Tax Base

Formula: $Tax\ base = Assessed\ valuations - Exemptions$

Example: A town has a total assessed valuation of $20,000,000 and exemptions of $4,000,000. What is the tax base?

$20,000,000 - 4,000,000 = $16,000,000

Tax Rate, Base, and Requirement

Formulas: $Tax\ rate = Tax\ requirement \div Tax\ base$

$Tax\ base = Tax\ requirement \div Tax\ rate$

$Tax\ requirement = Tax\ base\ x\ Rate$

Example: A town has a tax base of $160,000,000 and a budget of $8,000,000. What is the tax rate?

Tax rate = ($8,000,000 ÷ 160,000,000) = .05, or 5%, or 50 mills

Special Assessments

Formula: *Special assessment = Total special assessment cost x Homeowner's share*

Example: A homeowner owns 100' of an 800' seawall that must be repaired. The total assessment will be $80,000. What is the homeowner's assessment?

1.   Homeowner's share = 100' ÷ 800' = .125, or 12.5%

2.   Special assessment = $80,000 x 12.5% = $10,000

Commissions

Commission Splits

Formulas: *Total commission = Sale price x Commission rate*

Co-brokerage split = Total commission x Co-brokerage percent

Agent split = Co-brokerage split x Agent percent

Broker split = Co-brokerage split - Agent split

Example: A $300,000 property sells at a 7% commission with a 50-50 co-brokerage split and a 60% agent split with her broker. What are total, co-brokerage, agent's, and broker's commissions?

Total commission = $300,000 x .07 = $21,000

Co-brokerage splits = $300,000 x .07 x .50 = $10,500

Agent split = $10,500 x .60 = $6,300

Agent's broker's split = $10.500 - 6,300 = $4,200

Seller's Net

Formula: *Seller's net = Sale Price - (sale price x commission) - Other closing costs - Loan balance*

Example: A home sells for $260,000 and has a loan balance of $200,000 at closing. The commission is 7% and other closing costs are $2,000. What is the seller's net?

Seller's net = ($260,000 - (260,000 x .07) - 2,000 - 200,000) = $39,800

Price to Net an Amount

Formula: *Sale Price = (Desired net + Closing costs + Loan payoff)) (1 - Commission rate)*

123

Example: A homeseller wants to net $50,000. The commission is 7%, the loan payoff is $150,000, and closing costs are $4,000. What must the price be?

Sale price = ($50,000 + 4,000 + 150,000) ÷ .93 = $219,355

Closing Costs, Prorations

30-Day 12-Month Method

Formulas: *Monthly amount = Annual amount / 12*

Daily amount = Monthly amount / 30

Proration = (Monthly amount multiplied by the # months) + (Daily amount multiplied by the # days)

Example: An annual tax bill is $1,800. Closing is on April 10. What is the seller's share of the taxes?

1.   Monthly amount = ($1,800 ÷ 12) = $150; no. of months = 3

2.   Daily amount = ($150 ÷ 30) = $5.00; no. of days = 10

3.   Proration = ($150 x 3) + ($5 x 10) = ($450 + 50) = $500 seller's share

365-Day Method

Formula: *Daily amount = (Annual amount ÷ 365) or (Monthly amount ÷ Length of month)*

Proration = Daily amount multiplied by the # days

Example: An annual tax bill is $1,800. Closing is on April 10. What is the seller's share of the taxes?

1.   Daily amount = ($1,800 ÷ 365) = $4.93

2.   Jan 1 thru April 10 = (31 + 28 + 31 + 10) days, or 100 days

3.   Proration = $4.93 x 100 days = $493 seller's share

Income Received in Advance (Rent)

Logic: *Credit buyer and debit seller for buyer's share*

Example: Seller receives $1,000 rent. The month is ¾ over.

1.   Buyer's share is ($1,000 x 25%) = $250

2.   Credit buyer / debit seller $250.

Expenses paid in Arrears (Tax)

Logic: *Credit buyer and debit seller for seller's share*

Example: Buyer will pay $1,000 taxes. The year is ¾ over.

1.   Buyer's share is ($1,000 x 25%) = $250

2.   Credit buyer / debit seller $750.

Insurance Coverage

Recovery with Co-Insurance Clauses

Formula: Recovery = (Damage claim) x (Percent replacement cost covered ÷ Minimum coverage requirement)

Example: An owner insures a home for $100,000. Replacement cost is $150,000. A co-insurance clause requires coverage of 80% of replacement cost to avoid penalty. Fire destroys the house. What can the owner recover from the insurer?

Claim recovery = $150,000 x (67% cost covered ÷ 80% required) = $125,625

Section II: Practice Tests

UNIT ONE TEST: LICENSE LAW AND REGULATIONS

1.1   What is one purpose of licensing real estate practitioners?

   a.   To fund state projects
   b.   To maintain professional standards
   c.   To create a database of real estate agents statewide
   d.   To provide agents with proof of educational coursework completion

1.2   New York offers the following license types:

   a.   Broker, assistant broker
   b.   Broker, salesperson, assistant
   c.   Assistant broker, salesperson
   d.   Broker, associate broker, salesperson

1.3   Which of the following is not a salesperson's responsibility?

   a.   Perform all business in affiliated broker's name
   b.   Fair and honest dealings with public
   c.   Supervision, guidance, training
   d.   Accountability for escrow funds belonging to others

1.4   To become licensed as a salesperson, one must be at least _____ years old.

   a.   18
   b.   20
   c.   21
   d.   25

1.5   Applicants for a real estate salesperson license must complete _____ hours of salesperson education coursework.

   a.   22 ½
   b.   45
   c.   77
   d.   120

1.6   Antoine was convicted of shoplifting more than $5000 worth of electronics from a nearby electronics store. Now he would like to become a real estate salesperson. What must he do to become an eligible applicant for licensure?

   a.   He must have his criminal record expunged.
   b.   He must appeal his conviction.
   c.   He must have the Secretary of State determine whether his conviction bars or does not bar his licensure.
   d.   There is nothing he can do; he is a convicted criminal.

1.7   Applicants for a real estate broker license must complete a 152-hour broker education course. How many of those hours are actually a broker course?

a. 22 ½
b. 75
c. 40
d. 100

1.8   To be eligible for a real estate broker's license, an applicant must have

a. 5 years of salesperson experience.
b. 2 years of salesperson experience.
c. 1 year of salesperson experience and 1 year of experience in the general real estate field.
d. 4 years of experience in the general real estate field.

1.9   Which of the following acts does not require a New York real estate license?

a. Collecting rent from tenants of a residential unit
b. Negotiating residential loans that are secured by a mortgage
c. Negotiating the sale of real property
d. Negotiating the rent of residential property

1.10   Which of the following individuals needs a New York real estate license?

a. An executor acting under a court order
b. An attorney acting as a broker
c. A resident manager employed by a single property owner to manage rental property
d. A public officer performing official duties

1.11   When an applicant qualifies for licensure, a license and pocket card are issued. Who must maintain possession of the actual license?

a. The licensee
b. The licensee's sponsoring broker
c. The Department of State
d. The Secretary of State

1.12   Which of the following acts is not the current sponsoring broker's responsibility when terminating association with a salesperson?

a. File a change of association notice with the Department of State
b. Return the license to the terminated salesperson
c. File a termination notice with the Department of State
d. Collect all transaction related documents from the terminated salesperson

1.13   Under what condition does an applicant seeking a nonresident license in New York not need to take additional education courses or examinations?

a. Mutual recognition
b. Reciprocity agreement
c. Both mutual recognition and reciprocity
d. Neither mutual recognition nor reciprocity

1.14 Which of the following is not required for a nonresident license in New York?

    a.   Meet NY licensing requirements
    b.   Meet NY exam requirements
    c.   Maintain a place of business in NY and in home state
    d.   File an irrevocable consent form

1.15 When a salesperson holds licenses under multiple brokers, it's called

    a.   illegal licensure.
    b.   unsponsored practice.
    c.   split licensure.
    d.   dual licensure.

1.16 New York real estate licenses must be renewed every

    a.   year.
    b.   2 years.
    c.   3 years.
    d.   4 years.

1.17 Continuing education completed in a classroom setting requires _____ attendance.

    a.   50%
    b.   75%
    c.   83%
    d.   90%

1.18 Licensees are required to complete _____ hours of continuing education every licensure period.

    a.   14
    b.   18 ½
    c.   22 ½
    d.   45

1.19 Continuing education coursework must include 3 hours of

    a.   business math.
    b.   fair housing.
    c.   advertising.
    d.   marketing.

1.20 Failure to renew a real estate license within 2 years of the expiration date results in

    a.   the license being revoked.
    b.   the license being suspended for 1 year.
    c.   the licensee retaking the state licensure exam.
    d.   the licensee being charged a late renewal fee.

1.21 Branch offices must hold separate licenses and be approved by the

    a.   broker owner.
    b.   Department of State.
    c.   Secretary of State.
    d.   real estate board.

1.22 What type of license must an associate broker hold to operate a branch office under the broker owner's supervision?

  a. Broker license
  b. Manager license
  c. Associate broker license
  d. Associate brokers are not permitted to operate branch offices regardless of license type.

1.23 Which of the following statements is false?

  a. Licensees' individual websites must include a link to the brokerage website.
  b. All email ads must include the brokerage name and identify the advertiser as a real estate broker.
  c. Ads must not confuse the public.
  d. For sale signs must include the name of the listing brokerage.

1.24 Which of the following statements is true?

  a. Nicknames are not allowed to be included in advertisements.
  b. Ads that include team names must always include the team members' names.
  c. Ads that include team names must also include the word "team" in the name.
  d. Only licensed team members' names are to be included in the ad,

1.25 When advertising another broker's exclusive listing,

  a. the listing broker's consent is required.
  b. the other broker's name may or may not be included.
  c. the advertising broker must be included as the listing broker.
  d. the advertising broker's name must be included conspicuously in the ad.

1.26 Which of the following is a common license law violation?

  a. Salesperson Gary is licensed under multiple sponsoring brokers.
  b. Broker Dan hired unlicensed Sue to relocate tenants.
  c. Salesperson Cory refused to accept a kickback payment.
  d. Broker Melanie presented an offer to seller Joan after another offer had already been accepted.

1.27 A broker's unlicensed assistant is violating license law if he/she

  a. places for sale signs on a client's property.
  b. computes commission checks.
  c. is paid on a per-transaction basis.
  d. accepts a salary instead of hourly pay.

1.28 Who is required to complete a property condition disclosure statement?

  a. Seller's broker
  b. Seller
  c. Buyer's agent
  d. No one is required to complete the statement.

1.29 Which of the following statements is false?

  a. Both the seller and the buyer must sign a property condition disclosure statement.
  b. The seller's agent is required to inform the seller of the obligation to disclose the property's condition.
  c. When a property condition disclosure statement is provided to the buyer, there is no need for a property inspection.
  d. The property condition statement should be attached to the purchase contract.

1.30   Which of the following property transfers must comply with the property condition disclosure requirements?

    a.   A transfer to the property owner's brother
    b.   A transfer to a trust beneficiary
    c.   A transfer to the owner's unrelated roommate
    d.   A transfer to a mortgage lender to avoid foreclosure

UNIT TWO TEST: LAW OF AGENCY AND DISCLOSURE

2.1   The principal in a real estate transaction is the

    a. broker.
    b. client.
    c. customer.
    d. prospect.

2.2   _____ is the type of agency wherein the client uses a power of attorney to empower the agent to perform all of the actions legally delegated to an agency representative.

    a. Universal agency
    b. General agency
    c. Special agency
    d. Limited agency

2.3   In which type of agency may the agent have the authority to enter into contracts on behalf of the principal?

    a. Universal agency
    b. Special agency
    c. Limited agency
    d. General agency

2.4   Real estate brokerage is typically based on which type of agency?

    a. Universal
    b. General
    c. Special
    d. All of the above

2.5   When the parties to a transaction behave as though there is an agency agreement even though one has not been discussed, _____ is created.

    a. an implied agency
    b. an oral agreement
    c. a written agreement
    d. fiduciary agency

2.6   An agent who represents both the buyer and seller in the same transaction is a

    a. broker's agent.
    b. designated sales agent.
    c. dual agent.
    d. seller's agent.

2.7   Which of the following statements is true?

    a. A seller's agent has the duty to balance the seller's interests with those of the buyer.
    b. A broker's agent works for the listing agent's firm.
    c. A dual agent has a fiduciary duty of undivided loyalty to both clients.
    d. A designated agent works as a single agent within the broker's dual agency.

2.8   Which of the following duties does an agent not owe to a customer?

   a.   Honesty
   b.   Confidentiality
   c.   Reasonable skill
   d.   Proper disclosure

2.9   Which duty does an agent still owe to a client after the agency agreement has expired?

   a.   Loyalty
   b.   Full disclosure
   c.   Accounting
   d.   Confidentiality

2.10   Which of the following duties does a principal owe to the agent?

   a.   Compensation
   b.   Honesty
   c.   Obedience
   d.   Loyalty

2.11   Which of the following statements is true?

   a.   Agents can be held liable for breaching fiduciary duties to a client.
   b.   A breach of duty does not negate the client paying any compensation owed to the agent.
   c.   Clients are prohibited from filing lawsuits against agents who breach their fiduciary duties.
   d.   An agent's breach of duty is judged only after the listing agreement has expired.

2.12   If an agent fails to disclose facts he is unaware of but should have known, he is guilty of

   a.   intentional misrepresentation.
   b.   negligent misrepresentation.
   c.   misrepresentation of expertise.
   d.   misrepresentation resulting in fraud.

2.13   The Clayton Act prohibits

   a.   restrictions on interstate commerce.
   b.   the use of tie-in agreements.
   c.   practices that create monopolies.
   d.   practicing group boycotting.

2.14   Brokers John and Sue got together and decided to split a particular area in their town. The agreement was that John would do business in one section while Sue does business in the other section and neither would do business in the other's section. John and Sue are illegally practicing

   a.   market allocation.
   b.   group boycotting.
   c.   price fixing.
   d.   tie-in agreements.

2.15   A tie-in agreement occurs when

   a.   two or more competitors join together and agree to boycott a third brokerage competitor.
   b.   two or more competitors conspire to set like commissions regardless of market conditions or competition.
   c.   competing firms agree to divide a market area and restrict their competitive activities to their own area.
   d.   the sale of one product or service is contingent upon the sale of another, less desirable product or service.

2.16 An individual who violates antitrust laws can be penalized by

    a. up to 5 years in prison.
    b. fines up to $350,000.
    c. either a fine or prison time but not both.
    d. all of the above.

2.17 A business entity who violates antitrust laws can be penalized by

    a. fines up to $25,000.
    b. fines up to $1,000,000.
    c. separate DOJ fines.
    d. up to 5 years in prison.

2.18 When an agent represents one party in a transaction, the agent is

    a. engaged in cooperative sales.
    b. a subagent.
    c. a single agent.
    d. dual agent.

2.19 Which of the following allows a listing broker to split the commission with another broker who provides the buyer with no seller's liability for the agent's actions?

    a. Subagency
    b. Cooperative sales
    c. Brokerage without subagency
    d. Single agency

2.20 An agent of the broker who is the agent of the client is a

    a. dual agent.
    b. single agent.
    c. brokerage without subagency.
    d. subagent.

2.21 Dual agency

    a. can be oral or written.
    b. can only be created intentionally.
    c. is illegal in New York.
    d. results in a conflict of interest.

2.22 An agent in a dual agency relationship does not owe the clients the duty of

    a. full disclosure.
    b. obedience.
    c. accounting.
    d. diligence.

2.23 Requirements of a dual agency do not include

    a. written consent by all parties.
    b. agent's undivided loyalty.
    c. agency disclosure to all parties.
    d. keeping each party's pricing strategy confidential.

2.24 Barry is the listing broker for Sarah's property. As such, Barry is a single agent. However, one of Barry's salespersons has found a buyer for the property and has agreed to represent the buyer in the transaction.

    a. Barry's salesperson must not represent the buyer as it will be a conflict of interest.
    b. Barry's representation changes from a single agency to a dual agency, requiring both parties' consent.
    c. Barry must terminate this salesperson.
    d. Barry will now collect commission from both the seller and the buyer.

2.25 Listing broker Barry has ended up in a dual agency relationship. Consequently, he has decided to allow another salesperson to represent the buyer and is appointing another salesperson to represent the seller. While Barry will remain the dual agent, the two salespersons are considered

    a. designated single agents.
    b. subagents.
    c. cooperative sales agents.
    d. agents at a brokerage without subagency.

2.26 _____ listings are illegal in New York.

    a. Open
    b. Exclusive right-to-sell
    c. Exclusive agency
    d. Net

2.27 Which of the following is the most commonly used type of listing?

    a. Exclusive right-to-sell
    b. Exclusive agency
    c. Open listing
    d. Net listing

2.28 In which listing is the broker paid a commission regardless of who actually procures the buyer prior to the listing expiration?

    a. Exclusive right-to-sell
    b. Exclusive agency
    c. Open listing
    d. Net listing

2.29 Which listing allows the seller to contract with multiple brokers?

    a. Exclusive right-to-sell
    b. Exclusive agency
    c. Open listing
    d. MLS

2.30 When using a multiple listing service, who receives compensation when the property sells?

    a. Only the listing broker
    b. Only the broker who procured the buyer
    c. The listing broker and the cooperating broker who procured the buyer
    d. No commission is paid when an MLS is used.

2.31 Which of the following is not required for a listing agreement?

    a. Automatic extension clause
    b. Confirmation the seller owns the property
    c. Property description
    d. Property's zoning classification

2.32 Which of the following statements is false?

    a. New York agency disclosures must be in writing.
    b. Agency disclosures must be presented to prospective clients after a listing agreement is signed.
    c. Agency disclosure forms are required for the sale of residential property with four or fewer units.
    d. Clients may sign an advanced consent to dual agency.

2.33 An agency disclosure is not required for

    a. the sale of a condominium.
    b. a transaction involving a cooperative.
    c. residential property with five units.
    d. the sale of a condominium in a building with twenty units.

2.34 When may a broker accept compensation from more than one party in a transaction?

    a. When both parties agree to pay commission to the broker
    b. When the property being sold includes five or more units
    c. When all parties to the transaction consent
    d. When the broker charges fees in addition to the commission

2.35 Brokers must maintain signed agency disclosure forms for

    a. 1 year.
    b. 2 years.
    c. 3 years.
    d. 5 years.

2.36 Property condition disclosure statements are to be completed by the

    a. seller.
    b. seller's agent.
    c. buyer's agent.
    d. property inspector.

2.37 New York City requires landlords to inspect rental units for lead hazards _____ when children under 6 years are involved.

    a. each time a new lease is signed
    b. each year
    c. at the termination of the lease
    d. each time a tenant complains

2.38 New York's truth-in-heating law requires sellers to provide buyers with heating and cooling bills for the previous _____ for one to two-family properties when the buyer submits a written request.

    a. 6 months
    b. 1 year
    c. 2 years
    d. month

2.39 Lead disclosures must be made

    a. when the property is listed and again before closing or lease signing.
    b. each year when the tenant's lease is renewed.
    c. when the buyer or tenant first inspects the property.
    d. lead disclosures are not required.

2.40 Landlords are to provide prospective tenants with rental unit's bedbug infestation history for the previous

    a. 6 months.
    b. month.
    c. year.
    d. There is no requirement for bedbug disclosure.

UNIT THREE TEST: ESTATES AND INTERESTS

3.1   Which of the following would be defined as real estate as opposed to real property?

a. Wells, driveways, and signs on a parcel of land.
b. Mobile homes temporarily parked on a parcel of land.
c. Timber that has been cut and is lying on a parcel of land.
d. Business equipment an owner or tenant has placed on a parcel of land.

3.2   The "bundle of rights" refers to a set of rights

a. enjoyed by the owner of a property.
b. that is synonymous with the Bill of Rights.
c. guaranteed to citizens by the Statute of Rights.
d. specified in a deed or land contract.

3.3   Which of the following best describes the legal concept of personal property?

a. Any item which is acquired in a fee simple sale transaction.
b. Any item of property that is not definable as real property.
c. Any movable property owned by an individual, partnership, or corporation.
d. Any item that is not a natural item affixed to the earth.

3.4   A homeowner is very upset over a drone that a neighbor flies over his house. He takes his case to court to end this possible violation of rights. Does he have a case, and on what basis?

a. No. The neighbor is not physically on his property.
b. No. The drone is in the air, so he cannot exercise any surface rights.
c. Yes. The owner has the right to stop encroachments.
d. Yes. The drones infringe on his air rights.

3.5   Littoral rights apply to which of the following?

a. Boatable ponds entirely contained within the boundaries of an owner's property.
b. Streams and rivers.
c. Navigable lakes, seas, and oceans.
d. Navigable streams and rivers.

3.6   A retired couple has just bought a retirement home with a pier on a large lake. In this case the retirees' water rights extend to

a. the high water mark of the body of water at the shoreline.
b. the low water mark of the body of water at the shoreline.
c. the center of the lake.
d. the end of the pier.

3.7   Riparian rights concern which of the following bodies of water?

a. Lakes.
b. Seas and oceans.
c. Streams and rivers.
d. Navigable lakes.

3.8 Which of the following best describes a "fixture?"

a. Any item of personal property positioned within the boundaries of a parcel of real estate.
b. An item of personal property that has been converted to real property.
c. An item of real property temporarily placed on land for the purpose of conducting a business.
d. An item of personal property that has been left in one location for a period of six months.

3.9 An item may be considered personal property as opposed to real property provided that

a. the owner intended to remove it after a period of time.
b. it can be removed without altering the appearance of the structure.
c. it is unnecessary to the physical integrity of the structure.
d. the owner installed it at some time after acquiring the real property.

3.10 Two people own a house, each having an undivided equal interest. Which of the following best describes what each party owns?

a. Fifty percent of the physical house and the land it rests on.
b One hundred percent of the home and the land.
c. Fifty percent of the estate consisting of the indivisible whole of the real property.
d. Each owns one hundred percent of the estate represented by the real property and fifty percent of the physical house and the land it rests on.

3.11 A real property interest that includes the right to possess is considered

a. an estate in land.
b. a leasehold estate.
c. a fee simple estate.
d. the bundle of rights.

3.12 If the duration of an owner's rights in an estate is not determinable, the owner has

a. a tenancy at sufferance.
b. a leased fee simple estate.
c. a freehold estate.
d. a leasehold estate.

3.13 The distinguishing feature of a leasehold estate is

a. ownership of an interest by a tenant.
b. temporary ownership of the full bundle of rights in a property.
c. unlimited ownership of one right in the bundle of rights in a property.
d. that the estate is limited by a lease term.

3.14 A landowner conveys a parcel of property with the provision that the land cannot be developed for retail purposes. The new owner immediately begins to develop a retail shopping outlet, the grantor finds out and takes the property back. What kind of estate did this landowner convey?

a. Fee simple absolute.
b. Life estate with reversion.
c. Life estate with condition subsequent.
d. Fee simple defeasible.

3.15 Ned grants his sister Alice an estate for as long as she lives. Her descendants, however, cannot inherit the estate. What kind of estate is it?

a. An estate pur autre vie.
b. An estate for years.
c. An ordinary life estate.
d. A legal life estate.

3.16 Louis owned a boat and a house before marrying Barbara. While she was single, Barbara owned a new car. The two got married and bought a second home. As an engagement present, Barbara's father bought Louis a motorcycle. Under the law of community property, what property can Louis sell without his wife's consent or signature?

a. The boat and house.
b. The boat, house, and motorcycle.
c. The second home and the motorcycle.
d. The boat and motorcycle.

3.17 An estate from period-to-period will continue as long as

a. the tenant makes, and landlord accepts, regular rent payments.
b. the term specified in the lease.
c. the period is less than a year.
d. the landlord has not sold the property.

3.18 A tenant continues to occupy an apartment after lease expiration without the consent of the landlord. This type of estate is called

a. an estate at sufferance.
b. a holdover estate.
c. a canceled leasehold.
d. a hostile leasehold.

3.19 A tenant without a lease has been sending the landlord monthly rent checks, and the landlord continues to accept the payments. What kind of leasehold estate exists?

a. Estate for years.
b. Estate from period to period.
c. Estate at will.
d. Estate at sufferance.

3.20 A fee or life estate is held by an individual. This form of estate is referred to as a(an)

a. tenancy in severalty.
b. tenancy by the entireties.
c. absolute fee simple.
d. legal fee simple.

3.21 Six people have identical rights in a property and enjoy an indivisible interest. However, any of the owners may sell or transfer his/her interest without consent of the others. This form of ownership is a

a. joint tenancy.
b. homestead ownership.
c. tenancy in common.
d. estate in severalty.

3.22   The "four unities" required to create a joint tenancy include which of the following conditions?

    a. Parties must acquire respective interests at the same time.
    b. Parties must be residents of the same state at the time of acquiring the interest.
    c. Parties must be family members.
    d. Parties must have joint financial responsibility.

3.23   Unlike tenants in common, joint tenants

    a. own distinct portions of the physical property.
    b. cannot will their interest to a party outside the tenancy.
    c. may own unequal shares of the property.
    d. cannot encumber their interest to outside parties.

3.24   Which of the following life estates is created by operation of law rather than by the owner?

    a. Conventional life estate.
    b. Ordinary life estate.
    c. Legal life estate.
    d. Community property life estate.

3.25   Under what conditions can two individuals own a property as tenants by the entireties?

    a. If they so elect at the time of acquiring title.
    b. If they are blood relatives.
    c. If they are married.
    d. If they incorporate.

UNIT FOUR TEST: LIENS AND EASEMENTS

4.1   Which of the following is true of easements in general?

    a. They involve the property that contains the easement and a non-owning party.
    b. They apply to a whole property, not to any specific portion of the property.
    c. They only involve the legal owner of the property.
    d. They may require a specific use, but cannot prohibit one.

4.2   Mr. King wants to offer 100 acres of his property for sale. Since the property is landlocked, he will have to put in a driveway to the road that will run across his remaining property. What kind of easement will he have to grant?

    a. An easement in gross.
    b. A commercial easement.
    c. A personal easement.
    d. An easement appurtenant.

4.3   If property Alpha has a court-ordered easement across property Beta in order for Alpha to have access to a public road, the easement is a(n)

    a. easement by prescription.
    b. personal easement.
    c. easement by necessity.
    d. easement in gross.

4.4   An encroachment is

    a. an easement that has not been recorded on the title of the burdened property.
    b. an unauthorized physical intrusion of one property into another.
    c. a right granted by a property owner to the owner of an adjoining property to build a structure that protrudes across the property boundary.
    d. a structure that does not comply with a zoning ordinance.

4.5   A court might grant an easement by prescription if

    a. a town needs to dig a trench across an owner's property to install a sewer line to a neighboring property, and the owner refuses permission.
    b. a property owner sells the front half of a lot and wants to continue using the driveway to access the rear of the lot.
    c. a trespasser has been using an owner's property for a certain period with the owner's knowledge but without permission.
    d. a property owner wants to prevent the owner of an adjoining property from building an improvement that blocks her view.

4.6   The purpose of a deed restriction is to enable an owner to specify

    a. the form of ownership in which a property may be held.
    b. how long a property must be owned before it can be legally transferred.
    c. what groups of people are legally excluded from future ownership of a property.
    d. how a property may be used and what improvements may be built on it.

4.7   Melinda purchases a house and finances it. The lender in turn places a lien on Melinda's title. The lien in this mortgage transaction is

a. evidence of debt incurred by a property owner.
b. a promissory note granted by a property owner as security for a debt.
c. the creditor's claim against the property as collateral security for the loan.
d. the document required to clear clouded title.

4.8   How is a lien terminated?

a. Payment of the debt that is the subject of the lien and recording of the satisfaction.
b. Transfer of the property that has the lien.
c. Recording of another lien that is superior.
d. Death of the lienor or lienee.

4.9   A real estate tax lien, a federal income tax lien, a judgment lien, and a mortgage lien are recorded against a property. Which lien will be paid first when the property is sold?

a. Real estate tax lien.
b. Federal income tax lien.
c. Judgment lien.
d. Mortgage lien.

4.10   A lienholder can change the lien priority of a junior lien by agreeing to

a. change the date of recording.
b. lower the amount of the claim.
c. cancel the lien.
d. subordinate the lien.

4.11   A property owner gives Deanna permission to cross his property as a shortcut to her kindergarten school bus. One day the property owner dies. What right was Deanna granted originally, and will it survive the owner's death?

a. A personal easement in gross, which continues after the owner's death.
b. An easement by prescription, which continues after the owner's death.
c. A license, which continues after the owner's death.
d. A license, which terminates upon the owner's death.

4.12   A property owner who is selling her land wants to control how it is used in the future. She might accomplish her aim by means of

a. an injunction.
b. a deed restriction.
c. an easement.
d. a land trust.

4.13   What distinguishes a lien from other types of encumbrances?

a. It involves a monetary claim against the value of a property.
b. It lowers the value of a property.
c. It is created voluntarily by the property owner.
d. It attaches to the property rather than to the owner of the property.

4.14 A judge rules in favor of the creditor in a court proceeding and places a judgment lien against all the debtor's assets, including his real property. This is an example of a(n)

    a. voluntary junior lien.
    b. involuntary superior lien.
    c. involuntary specific lien.
    d. involuntary general lien.

4.15 Which of the following describes an encumbrance?

    a. A third party's right to encroach upon a property without the permission of the property owner.
    b. A third party's right to claim the sale proceeds of a property that has been mortgaged as collateral for a loan.
    c. A third party's interest in a real property that limits the interests of the freehold property owner.
    d. Another's right to acquire a freehold interest in a property against the property owner's wishes.

4.16 Violations of a deed condition can result in

    a. an injunction to force compliance.
    b. an injunction for payment of compensatory damages.
    c. ownership reverting to the previous owner.
    d. a forced sale of the deeded property.

4.17 Deed restrictions take precedence over zoning ordinances if

    a. the restrictions are created prior to the zoning ordinance.
    b. the deed restriction is more restrictive than the zoning ordinance.
    c. the restrictions are created after the zoning ordinance.
    d. the deed restriction is less restrictive than the zoning ordinance.

4.18 Which of the following liens is a junior lien?

    a. Mortgage lien
    b. Real estate tax lien
    c. State inheritance tax lien
    d. Federal estate tax lien

4.19 An easement is an encumbrance that affects a property's

    a. transfer.
    b. use.
    c. ownership.
    d. title.

4.20 Which of the following statements is true?

    a. An encroachment increases the value of the affected property.
    b. An encroachment must be recorded on the property's title.
    c. An owner may sue to have an encroachment removed from his/her property.
    d. When remedied, an encroachment automatically becomes a prescriptive easement.

UNIT FIVE TEST: DEEDS AND CONVEYANCES

5.1   Which of the following defines actual notice?

    a. It is notice published in a newspaper.
    b. It is knowledge one could have or should have obtained.
    c. It is notice explicitly stated in a legal document.
    d. It is knowledge received or imparted through direct experience.

5.2   Which of the following defines constructive notice?

    a. It is notice published in a newspaper.
    b. It is knowledge one could have or should have obtained.
    c. It is notice explicitly stated in a legal document.
    d. It is knowledge received or imparted through direct experience.

5.3   Ownership of real estate can be transferred voluntarily or involuntarily. The three ways title can be transferred voluntarily are by

    a. grant, deed, and will.
    b. escheat, deed, and covenant.
    c. title certificate, will, and deed.
    d. sale contract, deed, and warrant of seizin.

5.4   What is the function of recording a deed?

    a. It makes the deed valid.
    b. It causes title to pass.
    c. It gives constructive notice of ownership.
    d. It removes all prior recorded encumbrances.

5.5   The only clause that is actually required in a deed is the

    a. habendum clause.
    b. granting clause.
    c. reserving clause.
    d. tenendum clause.

5.6   The type of deed that offers the grantee the fullest protection against claims to the title is the

    a. general warranty deed.
    b. special warranty deed.
    c. quitclaim deed.
    d. bargain and defend deed.

5.7   Which of the following best describes the documentary stamp tax?

    a. A transfer tax based on the price of the property being conveyed.
    b. A tax a title company must pay in order to examine title records in the recorder's office.
    c. A tax collected by attorneys and paid to the state when transfer documents are prepared.
    d. A tax on stamps used to certify the authenticity of a conveyance.

5.8   The court proceeding that generally settles a decedent's estate is called

a. testate.
b. probate.
c. escheat.
d. distribution.

5.9   If an owner of real property dies intestate and has no legal heirs, what will happen to the property?

a. It will escheat to the state or county.
b. It will transfer to the decedent's executor.
c. It will be divided equally among adjoining property owners.
d. It will become a public easement.

5.10   A municipality wants to build a sewage treatment facility which will require the acquisition of several parcels of privately owned land. What legal power enables the municipality to buy the necessary properties, even against the owners' wishes?

a. Estoppel.
b. Escheat.
c. Alienation.
d. Eminent domain.

5.11   An adverse possessor must be able to successfully demonstrate that he or she has been

a. openly possessing and claiming the property without the owner's consent.
b. occupying the property without an occupancy permit.
c. using the property intermittently and without permission over a period of years.
d. building a permanent structure on the property.

5.12   A person wishes to convey any and all interests in a property to another without assurance of the property's marketability. This party would most likely use which of the following types of deed?

a. A sheriff's deed.
b. A special warranty deed.
c. A partition deed.
d. A quitclaim deed.

5.13   A drifter secretly lives in an abandoned shack on a large ranch property. After twenty years, the person makes a claim of ownership to the shack and the land immediately surrounding it that he had cleared. This claim will likely be

a. upheld through adverse possession.
b. upheld because of the length of possession.
c. declined through the doctrine of prior appropriation.
d. declined because possession was secretive.

5.14   What is a deed of conveyance?

a.   A document that proves a property is owned by the listed person
b.   A legal instrument used to transfer a real estate title voluntarily to another party
c.   A legal instrument used when a real estate title is being transferred involuntarily to another party
d.   A document used when a government is taking ownership of a property through eminent domain

5.15 Which of the following is not required for a title to pass to the new owner?

    a. The grantee must sign the deed.
    b. The grantor must be competent.
    c. The grantee must receive and accept the deed.
    d. The grantor must intend to deliver the deed beyond the act of physical delivery.

5.16 Which of the following is not a means of a voluntary title transfer?

    a. Deed
    b. Will
    c. Escheat
    d. Public grant

5.17 When transferring a title, what is the purpose of a notice?

    a. To inform the clerk that the title is ready to be recorded
    b. To allow the clerk to notify the grantee that the title has been recorded
    c. To provide evidence of the land's ownership to the public
    d. To notify the grantor that the grantee has received and accepted the title

5.18 The legal document used by a land owner to transfer ownership of the land to another party is a(n)

    a. deed of conveyance.
    b. constructive notice.
    c. actual notice.
    d. equitable title.

5.19 Which of the following is a covenant clause found in a deed?

    a. Haben clause
    b. Warrant of seisin clause
    c. Reddum clause
    d. Tendum clause

5.20 A tax deed is what type of deed?

    a. Bargain and sale
    b. General warranty
    c. Special warranty
    d. Special purpose

UNIT SIX TEST: TITLE CLOSING AND COSTS

6.1   The buyer and seller verifying the terms of the sales contract have been met is a step in the

   a.   sale contract creation process.
   b.   title closing process.
   c.   title recording procedures.
   d.   TRID required procedures.

6.2   RESPA applies to

   a.   commercial property.
   b.   industrial property.
   c.   residential property.
   d.   all property.

6.3   RESPA requires lenders to provide borrowers an estimate of loan settlement costs within _____ of the loan application.

   a.   24 hours
   b.   10 days
   c.   5 business days
   d.   3 days

6.4   During what process are the transaction funds actually disbursed?

   a.   settlement process.
   b.   title closing process.
   c.   title recording procedures.
   d.   TRID required procedures.

6.5   Which of the following is typically a seller's non-prorated expense?

   a.   Title insurance
   b.   Document stamp tax
   c.   Mortgage recording fees
   d.   Impound reserves

6.6   Which of the following would potentially be classified as a prorated item for closing?

   a.   Attorney fees
   b.   Mortgage fees
   c.   Utilities bill
   d.   Title insurance

6.7   Which proration method determines the proration by multiplying the daily amount by the number of days?

   a.   30-day 12 month
   b.   31-day
   c.   365-day
   d.   365-day 12 month

6.8 If John sells his house to Barbara with a closing date of April 1, what would John's prorated responsibility be for $2,700 paid in advance for property hazard insurance? Use the 30-day 12-month proration method and assume the day of closing is part of John's share.

    a. $674.75
    b. $225
    c. $2,700
    d. $682.50

6.9 Which of the following replaces the Good Faith Estimate and the HUD-1 forms?

    a. Real Estate Settlement Procedures Act
    b. Truth-In-Lending Act
    c. Truth-in-Lending Integrated Disclosures Rule
    d. None of the above

6.10 Under TRID/TILA, the closing disclosure must be provided to the borrower

    a. 3 business days after the loan application.
    b. 3 business days before loan consummation.
    c. 3 days before real estate transaction closing.
    d. 3 days after closing.

6.11 The Truth-in-Lending Integrated Disclosures Rule is applicable to

    a. home equity loans.
    b. reverse mortgages.
    c. loans on mobile homes.
    d. construction loans.

6.12 In what document are the parties responsible for which closing costs first identified?

    a. Good faith estimate
    b. Sales contract
    c. Closing disclosure form
    d. Loan estimate form

6.13 The closing statement is typically completed during the

    a. loan application process.
    b. title recording procedures.
    c. title insurance procedures.
    d. settlement process.

6.14 Are kickbacks permitted during the title closing procedures among firms involved in the transaction?

    a. Yes, as long as they are disclosed
    b. No, mortgage lenders prohibit them.
    c. No, RESPA prohibits them.
    d. Yes, they should be included in the closing statement.

6.15 Sue is purchasing Charlie's house with a closing date of January 30. If the brokerage fee is $2,400, what prorated amount will Sue be responsible to pay based on the 365-day method of proration?

    a. $197.40
    b. $2,202.60
    c. $2,400 as Sue is responsible for the non-prorated brokerage fee
    d. $0.00 as Charlie is responsible for the non-prorated brokerage fee

6.16   Which of the following is not considered evidence of title?

    a.   A title insurance policy
    b.   An attorney's opinion of the title abstract
    c.   A notary stamp on the title
    d.   A title certificate

6.17   A cloud on the title is

    a.   the successive property owners from the original grant to the present.
    b.   unrecorded claims.
    c.   a lawsuit to settle claims.
    d.   a written chronology of recorded owners, transfers, encumbrances.

6.18   A written chronology of recorded owners, transfers, encumbrances is called a(n)

    a.   suit to quiet title.
    b.   cloud on the title.
    c.   abstract of marketable title.
    d.   abstract of title.

6.19   A lawsuit to settle claims against the title is called

    a.   a suit to quiet title.
    b.   a title record.
    c.   a title plant.
    d.   an abstract of title.

6.20   Under TRID/TILA, a good faith estimate is where

    a.   no written loan estimate is provided.
    b.   the borrower trusts the lender to provide the cost estimate based only on the lender's experience.
    c.   loan estimate costs are based on the best information available.
    d.   closing disclosure costs must exactly equal estimate costs.

UNIT SEVEN TEST: CONTRACTS, CONTRACT OF SALE AND LEASE

7.1   Which of the following describes a gross lease?

a. The tenant pays a base rent plus some or all of the operating expenses.
b. The tenant pays a fixed rent, and the landlord pays all operating expenses.
c. The tenant pays a base rent plus an amount based on income generated in the leased space.
d. The tenant pays a rent that increases at specified times over the lease term.

7.2   If an apartment contains a refrigerator that is not included in the lease,

a. the lessee is required to buy it from the landlord.
b. the landlord is required to remove it.
c. the lease is invalidated because of an incomplete property description.
d. the landlord does not have to maintain it.

7.3   A basic responsibility of a landlord is to

a. provide leased space at market rental rates.
b. deliver a habitable property.
c. keep the rental space freshly painted.
d. refrain from entering the leased space at any time during the lease term.

7.4   How does a constructive eviction occur?

a. A landlord obtains a court order to force the tenant to vacate the leased premises.
b. A court officer forcibly removes the tenant from the premises.
c. A tenant declares a landlord in default and vacates the leased premises.
d. A landlord declares a tenant in default and takes possession of the leased premises.

7.5   A store owner enters into a lease that charges rent per square foot, a common area fee, and a portion of the store owner's gross income from the property. This kind of lease is a

a.   triple charge, or triple net lease.
b.   proprietor's lease.
c.   percentage lease.
d.   retailer's gross lease.

7.6   An owner leases a property to a business in exchange for rent. The tenant is required to pay all operating expenses as well. This is an example of a

a.   proprietary lease.
b.   percentage lease.
c.   gross lease.
d.   net lease.

7.7   A lease automatically terminates under which of the following circumstances?

a.   The tenant fails to pay rent.
b.   The leased property is foreclosed.
c.   The tenant goes out of business.
d.   The landlord cancels the lease.

7.8   Which of the following types of leasehold estate lacks a specific term?

   a. Estate for years.
   b. Estate from period-to-period.
   c. Estate at will.
   d. Estate by the entireties.

7.9   When a tenant rents an apartment, he or she is usually responsible for

   a. compliance with the rules and regulations of the building.
   b. payment for any alterations to the leased space.
   c. recording the lease in title records.
   d. occupying the premises throughout the lease term.

7.10   While a one-year lease is in effect, the tenant dies of a sudden illness. In this situation,

   a. the lease automatically terminates.
   b. the tenant's estate has the option of canceling the contract.
   c. the landlord can record a lien against the leased fee interest.
   d. the tenant's estate is still obligated under the lease.

7.11   Three students rent a house together, and all three sign a one-year lease. Six months later, two students move out. Which of the following is true of the remaining rent obligation?

   a. The remaining tenant is responsible for the full rent obligation.
   b. The remaining tenant is responsible for one third of the rent obligation.
   c. The lease is cancelled due to abandonment. Therefore, the rent obligation is extinguished.
   d. The departing tenants have no further rent obligation.

7.12   A tenant transfers a portion of the leasehold interest to another party. The instrument that accomplishes this transfer is a(n)

   a. deed.
   b. novation.
   c. sublease.
   d. reconveyance

7.13   Vijay enters into a lease for his new store. The provisions of the lease require Vijay to pay the operating expenses of the premises such as janitorial and repair expenses. This is an example of a

   a. gross lease.
   b. percentage lease.
   c. land lease.
   d. net lease.

7.14   A tenant obtains a lease where the landlord agrees to pay all operating expenses in exchange for an additional $5.00 rent per square foot. Another term for this lease is a(n)

   a. gross lease.
   b. proprietary lease.
   c. exchange lease.
   d. full-service net lease.

7.15 Which of the following circumstances is the most likely scenario for a ground lease?

    a. A developer wants to acquire a necessary parcel that separates two parcels she already owns.
    b. An owner-developer wants to retain ownership of the land portion of the improved real property.
    c. A fast food company wants to place a restaurant in an existing building without buying either land or improvement.
    d. A farmer wants to sell his property to a mining company.

7.16 If a lease does not state a specific ending date, when does it terminate?

    a. Immediately, since it is an invalid lease.
    b. After one year.
    c. When either party gives proper notice.
    d. Whenever the property is sold.

7.17 Which of the following is an executory contract?

    a. An expired lease.
    b. A sale contract before closing.
    c. A recorded sale contract.
    d. An option to buy after it is exercised.

7.18 A bilateral contract is one in which

    a. both parties promise to do something in exchange for the other party's performance.
    b. both parties receive equal consideration.
    c. two parties agree to perform a service together.
    d. both parties promise to do something if the other party performs first.

7.19 A breach of contract is

    a. a termination of the contract by the mutual consent of the parties.
    b. financial damage suffered by a party because another party has nullified a contract provision.
    c. a lawsuit to force a party to discharge the contract.
    d. the failure of a party to perform according to the terms of the contract.

7.20 What is rescission?

    a. The act of withdrawing an offer before it has been accepted.
    b. The act of declaring that a contract is no longer in effect for a given party.
    c. The act of declaring a contract unenforceable.
    d. The act of modifying the terms of an offer.

7.21 To be valid, a contract must

    a. reflect a mutual understanding or agreement.
    b. use precise wording in a document.
    c. not be executable.
    d. be created only by an attorney.

7.22 Two parties enter into a contract. The agreement fulfills all the requirements for a valid contract, with no disqualifying circumstances. Given this situation, it is still possible that the contract may be

    a. void.
    b. illegal.
    c. unenforceable.
    d. voidable.

7.23 The purpose of the statute of frauds is to

   a. invalidate certain oral contracts.
   b. require certain conveyance-related contracts to be in writing.
   c. nullify oral leases and listing agreements.
   d. eliminate fraud in real estate contracts.

7.24 An unintentional agreement that is deemed to exist based on terms that were expressed by one party's actions is called a(n)

   a. express agreement.
   b. implied agreement.
   c. bilateral agreement.
   d. executed agreement.

7.25 Which of the following contracts is exempt from requirements under the Statute of Frauds?

   a. A 2-year real estate listing agreement
   b. A sales contract
   c. A 6-month lease
   d. None of the above; all contracts must comply with the Statute's requirements.

7.26 Which of the following may legally prepare a contract?

   a. A real estate broker
   b. An escrow officer
   c. An attorney
   d. An mortgage loan officer

7.27 Which of the following is an example of an executed contract?

   a. A sales contract after transaction closing
   b. An offer to purchase real property
   c. An unsigned 1-year lease
   d. A builder's contract to begin remodeling an owner's home

7.28 When does an offer expire?

   a. On a date and time indicated by the offeree
   b. On a date and time indicated by the offeror
   c. On the date of the transaction closing
   d. On the date the offeree signs the offer

7.29 An option to buy is

   a. a unilateral contract requiring the seller to perform.
   b. a unilateral contract requiring the buyer to perform.
   c. a bilateral contract requiring both the buyer and the seller to perform.
   d. not a valid contract.

7.30 In accordance with the statute of frauds,

   a. leases in excess of one year must be recorded to be enforceable.
   b. oral leases are not enforceable.
   c. a five-year lease must be in writing to be enforceable.
   d. an unwritten lease is fraudulent.

UNIT EIGHT TEST: REAL ESTATE FINANCE

8.1   What are the key instruments used in a mortgage transaction?

   a.   Loan and lien
   b.   Promissory note and mortgage
   c.   Borrower's application and lender's quote
   d.   Note and PMI

8.2   The difference between a property's market value and the balance of the mortgage loan on the property is called

   a.   interest.
   b.   loan-to-value.
   c.   equity.
   d.   hypothecation.

8.3   What is a PITI mortgage clause?

   a.   A clause that requires the borrower to carry private mortgage insurance
   b.   A clause providing the annual loan balance
   c.   A clause requiring the borrower to take and maintain occupancy as the principal residence
   d.   A clause covering the escrow payment for principal, interest, taxes, and insurance

8.4   What is the purpose of PMI?

   a.   It protects the lender against monetary loss if the borrower defaults.
   b.   It protects the borrower against foreclosure in the event the borrower is unable to make loan payments.
   c.   It protects the borrower against monetary loss if the property is damaged by a covered hazard.
   d.   It provides the lender an additional avenue to obtain a profit on the loan.

8.5   What is a loan-to-value ratio?

   a.   The percentage of a lender's portfolio that is composed of mortgage loans.
   b.   The ratio of borrowed principal plus total interest to the appraised value of the collateral property.
   c.   The ratio of a lender's return on a mortgage loan to the value of the collateral property.
   d.   The ratio of the loan amount and the value of the property expressed as a percent

8.6   For a loan that is not backed by the Federal Housing Administration or Veterans Administration, and for which the borrower is making a down payment of less than 20%, the lender is likely to require the borrower to obtain

   a.   a subrogation agreement.
   b.   private mortgage insurance.
   c.   a letter of credit.
   d.   a co-signer on the note.

8.7   The difference between what a borrower has to pay to purchase a property and the amount a lender will lend on the property is the

   a.   mortgage insurance coverage amount.
   b.   lender's profit margin.
   c.   buyer's down payment.
   d.   origination fee.

8.8   The Equal Credit Opportunity Act prohibits a lender from

a. refusing a loan because the borrower does not match the lender's target market.
b. including income from self-employment in the borrower's qualifying income.
c. requiring both spouses to sign the loan application form.
d. refusing a loan because a borrower has a defective credit report.

8.9   A loan applicant has an annual gross income of $72,000. How much will a lender allow the applicant to pay for monthly housing expense to qualify for a loan if the lender uses an income ratio of 28%?

a. $2,160.
b. $1,680.
c. $1,068.
d. $840.

8.10   AMC Bank discovers, in considering buyer Bob's application for a mortgage loan, that Bob has borrowed the down payment from an uncle and has to repay that loan. Bob should expect that AMC Bank will

a. refuse the application.
b. adjust the applicant's debt ratio calculation and lower the loan amount.
c. increase the loan amount to enable the borrower to pay off the loan to the relative.
d. require the borrower to make payments to an escrow account for repayment of the relative's loan.

8.11   The Federal Reserve's Regulation Z applies to which loans?

a. All loans.
b. All loans secured by real estate.
c. All loans secured by a residence.
d. All loans over $25,000.

8.12   If a particular loan falls under Regulation Z's right of rescission provision,

a. the lender has the right to change the terms of the loan within a certain period.
b. the lender has the right to accelerate repayment of the loan because of a change in the borrower's credit status.
c. the borrower has the right to pay off the loan ahead of schedule with no penalty.
d. the borrower has a limited right to cancel the transaction within a certain period.

8.13   Under the Equal Credit Opportunity Act, a lender, or a real estate agent who assists a seller in qualifying a potential buyer, may not

a. tell a rejected loan applicant the reasons for the rejection.
b. ask the buyer/borrower about his/her religion or national origin.
c. ask the buyer/borrower to explain unconventional sources of income.
d. use a credit report that has not been provided to the borrower.

8.14   A conventional mortgage loan is one that is

a. backed by the Federal National Mortgage Association.
b. insured under Section 203(b) of the Federal Housing Administration loan program.
c. guaranteed by the Government National Mortgage Association.
d. not FHA-insured or VA-guaranteed.

8.15 Which of the following correctly describes the flow of money and documents in a mortgage loan transaction?

   a. The borrower gives the lender a note and a mortgage in exchange for loan funds.
   b. The lender gives the borrower a mortgage and receives a note in exchange for loan funds.
   c. The borrower receives a note in exchange for a mortgage from the lender.
   d. The lender gives the borrower a note, loan funds and a mortgage.

8.16 In a deed of trust transaction, which of the following occurs?

   a. The beneficiary conveys title to a trustee in exchange for loan funds.
   b. The trustee conveys title to a beneficiary in exchange for loan funds.
   c. The trustor conveys title to a trustee in exchange for loan funds from the beneficiary.
   d. The trustee conveys title to a trustor in exchange for loan funds from the beneficiary.

8.17 When the terms of the mortgage loan are satisfied, the mortgagee

   a. may retain any overage in the escrow account.
   b. may inspect the property before returning legal title.
   c. may be entitled to charge the borrower a small fee to close the loan.
   d. may be required to execute a release of mortgage document.

8.18 The Equal Credit Opportunity Act (ECOA) requires lenders to

   a. extend equal credit to all prospective borrowers.
   b. consider the income of a spouse in evaluating a family's creditworthiness.
   c. discount the income of a person involved in child-rearing or child-bearing.
   d. specialize lending activity by geographical area for improved customer service.

8.19 Lenders use an income ratio in qualifying to

   a. insure a borrower has the earning power to make the loan payments.
   b. compare a borrower's earnings to the borrower's short-term debt.
   c. identify the highest possible interest rate that the borrower can afford.
   d. quantify the borrower's assets to the fullest extent.

8.20 At the closing of a mortgage loan

   a. the borrower pays off the note and receives clear title.
   b. the lender issues a firm loan commitment.
   c. the parties complete all loan origination documents and the loan is funded.
   d. the borrower's loan application is complete and the file closed.

8.21 Which laws or regulations require mortgage lenders to disclose financing costs and annual percentage rate to a borrower before funding a loan?

   a. The Equal Credit Opportunity Act.
   b. Truth-in-Lending laws and Regulation Z.
   c. The Real Estate Settlement and Procedures Act.
   d. Federal Fair Housing Laws.

8.22 Which laws or regulations prevent mortgage lenders from discriminating in extending credit to potential borrowers?

   a. The Equal Credit Opportunity Act.
   b. Truth-in-Lending laws.
   c. The Real Estate Settlement and Procedures Act.
   d. Federal Fair Housing Laws.

8.23 Which laws or regulations require mortgage lenders to provide an estimate of closing costs to a borrower and forbid them to pay kickbacks for referrals?

a. The Equal Credit Opportunity Act.
b. Truth-in-Lending laws.
c. the Real Estate Settlement and Procedures Act.
d. Federal Fair Housing Laws.

8.24 The major organizations operating in the secondary mortgage market are

a. Fannie Mae, Freddie Mac, and Ginnie Mae.
b. Fannie Mae, GMAC, and MGIC.
c. Freddie Mac, FHA, and VA.
d. Fannie Mae, Freddie Mac, and the Federal Reserve.

8.25 How does the secondary mortgage market aid borrowers seeking a mortgage loan?

a. It cycles funds back to primary lenders so they can make more loans.
b. It issues second mortgages and sells them in the home equity market.
c. It lends funds to banks so they can make more loans.
d. It pays off defaulted loans made by primary mortgage lenders.

8.26 What is the role of Fannie Mae in the secondary mortgage market?

a. It guarantees FHA-backed and VA-backed loans.
b. It insures FHA-backed and VA-backed loans.
c. It purchases FHA-backed and VA-backed loans.
d. It originates FHA-backed and VA-backed loans.

8.27 The requirement to repay a mortgage loan before the scheduled due date is called

a. escalation.
b. acceleration.
c. loan termination.
d. alienation.

8.28 A defeasance clause may require

a. the promissory note to be filed with the county clerk.
b. the lender to execute a satisfaction of mortgage document.
c. the lender to place a lien on the mortgaged property.
d. the lender to void the loan.

8.29 Under which type of mortgage is a down payment not required?

a. Conventional
b. FHA
c. VA
d. None of the above

8.30 Under which of the following does a lender sell a mortgage to a third-party investor?

a. Assumption of mortgage
b. Alienation clause
c. Subject to mortgage
d. Assignment of mortgage

UNIT NINE TEST: LAND USE REGULATIONS

9.1 Which of the following is true regarding master planning and zoning?

   a. The aggregate of zoning ordinances is the master plan.
   b. A master plan eliminates the need for zoning ordinances.
   c. Master planning is a county-level function; zoning is limited to the city level.
   d. Zoning ordinances are a primary means of keeping land use in harmony with the master plan.

9.2 The basic intent of zoning ordinances is to

   a. establish the basis for public ownership of land for the common good.
   b. establish subdivision rules and regulations.
   c. specify usage for every parcel within the zoning authority's jurisdiction.
   d. restrict development in unincorporated areas.

9.3 Why do zoning authorities create different types of zones?

   a. To ensure that a variety of building structures are available in the community.
   b. To separate land uses so that they do not interfere with each other.
   c. To preserve high density land uses.
   d. To discourage industrial and commercial users from relocating.

9.4 The key consideration in granting a zoning exception known as a special exception is which of the following?

   a. Hardship
   b. Change of zones
   c. The public interest
   d. The use was legal prior to the new zone creation

9.5 The intensity of land usage generally refers to what?

   a. The number of residential building lots per acre.
   b. The number of people per square mile.
   c. The number of building permits issued per year within a zoning jurisdiction.
   d. The area of a commercial or industrial facility in relation to the size of the site.

9.6 How does Planned Unit Development zoning vary from ordinary zoning?

   a. It applies only to office parks.
   b. It incorporates a number of different zones within a single property boundary.
   c. It requires that multiple tracts of land be developed according to a single design.
   d. It requires developers to obtain a separate building permit for every structure.

9.7 Which of the following situations is most likely to represent an illegal nonconforming use?

   a. A homeowner in a residential zone converts her residence to a private school.
   b. A homeowner builds a toolshed in a neighborhood where there are no toolsheds.
   c. A storeowner remodels a storefront in accordance with regulations, and then the zoning is changed to residential.
   d. A new zoning ordinance outlaws two-story additions after a homeowner completes an addition.

9.8   What is the difference between a variance and a nonconforming use?

    a. A variance, once granted, is unconditional and permanent.
    b. A variance is granted by the zoning board if the owner has a justifiable reason.
    c. A nonconforming use is allowed if the owner requests it in advance of building.
    d. A nonconforming use violates current zoning, but a variance does not.

9.9   A document certifying that a structure complies with building codes and is ready for use is referred to as a(n)

    a. inspection report.
    b. satisfaction bond.
    c. certificate of occupancy.
    d. user permit.

9.10   Which of the following is true of an eminent domain proceeding?

    a. It cancels the property owner's mortgage loan balance.
    b. It leaves the property owner with equitable title in place of legal title.
    c. It conveys legal title to the acquiring entity.
    d. It clouds the chain of title by canceling the original grant.

9.11   Public land use planning strives to balance which of the following potentially conflicting interests?

    a. Individual property rights and the public's interest.
    b. Public policy makers and community business leaders.
    c. Tenant occupancy specifications and construction contractors.
    d. Individual property owners and municipal planning agencies.

9.12   Zoning, building codes, and environmental restrictions are forms of local land use control known as

    a. master planning.
    b. preemption.
    c. police power.
    d. concurrency.

9.13   If a municipality exerts its power of eminent domain against a certain property owner, what happens?

    a. The owner must pay higher property taxes or give up the property.
    b. The owner must cede an easement without receiving any compensation.
    c. The municipality annexes the property.
    d. The owner must sell the property in exchange for market-value compensation.

9.14   To be valid, a local zoning ordinance must

    a. reasonably promote community health, safety and welfare.
    b. comply with federal zoning laws.
    c. apply only to unique properties.
    d. be published periodically in the local newspaper.

9.15   Why do communities require building permits?

    a. To promote development.
    b. To establish the basis for an inspection.
    c. To promote certificates of occupancy.
    d. To ensure that improvements comply with codes.

9.16 What is the purpose of residential zoning?

    a. To increase home values in a neighborhood.
    b. To regulate the density of dwellings in the residential zone.
    c. To prevent families from residing in commercial and industrial sites.
    d. To maximize intensity of usage.

9.17 A non-profit organization wants to erect an urgent care facility in a residential zone. Given other favorable circumstances, the local authorities may grant permission by allowing

    a. a special exception.
    b. an illegal nonconforming use.
    c. an easement.
    d. a license.

9.18 A property that conformed with zoning ordinances when it was developed but does not conform to new ordinances is said to be

    a. an illegal special exception.
    b. a variance.
    c. a legal nonconforming use.
    d. unmarketable.

9.19 A policy that holds developers responsible for the impact their projects have on the local infrastructure is called

    a. zone density.
    b. impact report.
    c. concurrency.
    d. set backs.

9.20 Standards are established for every aspect of a construction project by

    a. zoning.
    b. building codes.
    c. environmental restrictions.
    d. land use controls.

9.21 Which of the following requires environmental impact surveys?

    a. Clean Air Amendment
    b. National Environmental Policy Act
    c. Water Quality Improvement Act
    d. Residential Lead-based Paint Hazard Reduction Act

9.22 Which of the private land use controls can result in the grantor repossessing the property when a use violation occurs?

    a. Deed restrictions
    b. Declaration restriction
    c. Deed condition
    d. All of the above

9.23 Asbestos can adversely impact

    a. air quality.
    b. soil quality.
    c. water quality.
    d. All of the above

9.24 In relation to eminent domain, which of the following statements is false?

    a. At the resolution hearing, owners are permitted to voice their opinion about losing the property.
    b. The entity seeking the property must show it is necessary for the project.
    c. The property title is ultimately transferred in exchange for the property's market value.
    d. The ultimate title transfer extinguishes all existing encumbrances.

9.25 In a coding appeal, when a property owner petitions the zoning board for a zoning change, it's called a(n)

    a. special exception.
    b. nonconforming use.
    c. variance.
    d. amendment.

9.26 When a zoning change results in the use of existing properties being in violation of the new ordinance, that is called a(n)

    a. special exception.
    b. legal nonconforming use.
    c. variance.
    d. illegal nonconforming use.

9.27 Which of the following is not considered a type of zone?

    a. Residential
    b. Retail
    c. Industrial
    d. Agricultural

9.28 For a zoning ordinance to be valid, it must

    a. promote community health, safety, and welfare.
    b. be approved by the general public in the associated area.
    c. address all zone types equally.
    d. not allow exceptions.

9.29 Long term growth and usage strategies are included in

    a. zoning ordinances.
    b. plan development.
    c. the master plan.
    d. enabling acts.

9.30 A government's legal authority to create, regulate, tax, and condemn real property in the interest of the public's health, safety, and welfare is called

    a. a zoning ordinance.
    b. police power.
    c. eminent domain.
    d. land use control.

UNIT TEN TEST: CONSTRUCTION AND ENVIRONMENTAL ISSUES

10.1 A written narrative of the materials needed for a construction project along with the techniques to be used is called the

    a. specifications.
    b. blueprints.
    c. building permit.
    d. certificate of occupancy.

10.2 A certificate of occupancy indicates

    a. how many residents are currently living in the building.
    b. the maximum number of residents that can safely occupy the building.
    c. the building is in compliance with building codes and is ready for occupancy.
    d. the modifications to be performed prior to the building becoming occupied.

10.3 Which of the following documents is implied and not required to be in writing?

    a. Construction specifications
    b. New York new home warranty
    c. Certificate of occupancy
    d. Contract for home improvement work

10.4 The National Electric Code is renewed

    a. annually.
    b. every 2 years.
    c. every 3 years.
    d. as needed.

10.5 The New York Merchant Implied Warranty provides a _____ warranty for material defects.

    a. 1-year
    b. 3-year
    c. 5-year
    d. 6-year

10.6 Amanda's Law requires

    a. carbon monoxide alarms in specific dwellings.
    b. smoke detectors in all New York dwellings.
    c. sprinklers in buildings with specific square footage and occupancy.
    d. written contracts for home improvement work in dwellings with occupants under the age of 12.

10.7 A building envelope consists of

    a. wooden privacy fencing around the perimeter of the property.
    b. the external walls of a home's basement.
    c. the building's roof, walls, doors, windows, and foundation.
    d. the land on which the building sits.

10.8　Which of the following is not a component of construction?

　　a.　Doors
　　b.　Carpeting
　　c.　Downspouts
　　d.　Termite shield

10.9　As a component of construction, a conduit

　　a.　is metal piping used to carry flexible wiring.
　　b.　interrupts a circuit when an overload occurs on the line.
　　c.　is the main control box for an electrical system.
　　d.　the measure of overall capability of the household supply.

10.10　Which of the following is not a window part?

　　a.　Jamb
　　b.　Louver
　　c.　Mullion
　　d.　Sash

10.11　A cross gable is a type of

　　a.　plumbing.
　　b.　insulation.
　　c.　roof.
　　d.　foundation.

10.12　Stucco is a type of

　　a.　roof.
　　b.　foundation.
　　c.　insulation.
　　d.　exterior covering.

10.13　When is asbestos harmful?

　　a.　When used as insulation
　　b.　When left undisturbed
　　c.　When disturbed and dust is released
　　d.　Never

10.14　John owns a rental house in New York City that was built in 1960. Does John need to perform any lead dust testing? If so, when?

　　a.　No, houses built in 1960 did not contain any lead.
　　b.　Yes, every time John leases to any new tenant, he must have lead dust testing performed.
　　c.　No, John does not lease to anyone with children.
　　d.　Yes, John must lead dust test annually.

10.15　How does radon enter homes?

　　a.　Within the insulation
　　b.　Through ground water
　　c.　Through certain types of wood used for the home's foundation
　　d.　Through foundation cracks and floor drains

10.16 Possible lead-based paint hazard must be disclosed

    a. on structures built before 1978.
    b. on all New York City rental properties.
    c. only on single-family homes.
    d. when any New York home is being sold.

10.17 Water damage in a home could result in

    a. termites.
    b. mold.
    c. septic tank damage.
    d. neurological problems for the home's occupants.

10.18 The manufacture of Polychlorinated Biphenyls has been banned since

    a. 1978.
    b. 1979.
    c. 1976.
    d. 1973.

10.19 CERCLA established the Superfund for

    a. remediating mold in multi-unit dwellings, such as apartment buildings.
    b. testing and removing lead-based paint from rental units with occupants under age 7.
    c. cleaning up uncontrolled hazardous waste dumps and spills.
    d. inspecting and removing leaking underground storage tanks.

10.20 CERCLA's Phase III audit of property being sold

    a. identifies prior users and the presence of hazardous materials.
    b. performs the chemical analysis to find hazardous substances on the property.
    c. remediates, cleans up, and performs follow-up monitoring of the site.
    d. prosecutes and imposes penalties of those liable for the contamination.

10.21 Under CERCLA, who may potentially be held liable for contamination and the resulting cleanup?

    a. Tenant
    b. Real estate licensee
    c. Previous land owner
    d. All of the above

10.22 When did the original Superfund expire?

    a. 1979
    b. 1985
    c. 1986
    d. 1988

10.23 The Superfund Amendments and Reauthorization Act removed contamination liability from

    a. tenants.
    b. innocent landowners.
    c. previous landowners.
    d. real estate licensees.

10.24 The Superfund Amendments and Reauthorization Act of 1986

    a. cancelled the original Superfund.
    b. provided more lenient standards for contamination cleanup.
    c. provided higher funding than CERCLA's original Superfund.
    d. none of the above.

10.25 To prevent termite issues, when constructing new homes, contractors should

    a. not use wood for foundations and structures.
    b. use only concrete blocks for foundations.
    c. allow only treated wood to touch the ground.
    d. treat the ground prior to building the home's foundation.

10.26 The Toxic Substances Control Act of 1976 provides the EPA with authority to

    a. require reporting, testing, and restrictions on Polychlorinated Biphenyls.
    b. assist homeowners in mold remediation when present in multi-family dwellings.
    c. remove underground storage tanks when present on same site as family dwellings.
    d. ban the use of insulation that contains urea formaldehyde.

10.27 The Brownfields legislation regulates

    a. asbestos remediation.
    b. industrial site cleanup.
    c. underground storage tank inspections.
    d. polychlorinated biphenyls.

10.28 Which of the following laws regulates solid waste disposal?

    a. Resource Conservation and Recovery Act
    b. National Environmental Policy Act
    c. The EPA PCB ban
    d. Brownfields legislation

10.29 The EPA was created under which legislation?

    a. Resource Conservation and Recovery Act
    b. Solid Waste Disposal Act
    c. Comprehensive Environmental Response, Compensation and Liability Act
    d. National Environmental Policy Act

10.30 When was the manufacture of asbestos banned in the U.S.?

    a. 1978
    b. 1979
    c. 1985
    d. 1989

10.31 What is urea formaldehyde used in?

    a. Paint
    b. Pressed wood products
    c. Wall paper
    d. HVAC systems

10.32 What is the environmental impact of chlorofluorocarbons use?

    a. Respiratory issues in humans
    b. Contamination of wetlands
    c. Depletion of earth's ozone layer
    d. Contamination of ground water

10.33 Which construction electrical component contains wire splices or cable connections?

    a. Junction box
    b. Fuse
    c. Circuit breaker
    d. Service entrance panel

10.34 An awning window is one that

    a. is hinged on the bottom.
    b. swings out at the bottom.
    c. has horizontal glass slats.
    d. is arched.

10.35 New York site preparation requirements do not include

    a. landscaping considerations.
    b. grading the land.
    c. providing drainage.
    d. blueprint preparation.

UNIT ELEVEN TEST: VALUATION PROCESS AND PRICING PROPERTIES

11.1 If the price of an item is increasing, one can usually assume that

    a. demand for the item is decreasing in relation to supply of the item.
    b. demand for the item is increasing in relation to supply of the item.
    c. supply of the item is increasing.
    d. demand for the item and supply of the item are increasing.

11.2 When the market for an item has achieved market equilibrium, which of the following statements is true?

    a. New suppliers will enter the market and drive the price down.
    b. Demand will slowly taper off, driving the price down.
    c. Unmet demand for the item is directed toward demand for some other item.
    d. Supply and demand are equal, and price and value are equal.

11.3 As an economic product, real estate is distinguished by

    a. its homogeneity.
    b. its variety.
    c. the uniqueness of every parcel.
    d. its ability to appreciate in value.

11.4 The city of Stevensville has declared a moratorium on new construction. If demand is increasing, what will be the likely effect on real estate prices in the area?

    a. Prices level off.
    b. Prices continue to follow the trend that preceded the moratorium.
    c. Prices fall.
    d. Prices rise.

11.5 If Okapi, Inc., a company that markets its sports clothing worldwide, moves into Stevensville and hires 100 employees, it is reasonable to expect that the town will experience

    a. an immediate rise in the demand for industrial real estate, but no other changes in the real estate market.
    b. an increase in demand for all types of real estate.
    c. a housing boom, but no other changes in the real estate market.
    d. an immediate increase in the prices for industrial and office real estate, but no impact on the residential market.

11.6 A town is rapidly growing, but all the buildable vacant lots in the most desirable area have already been occupied. In this case, it is likely that the price of existing homes in that area

    a. will stabilize, since the population must stabilize.
    b. will increase.
    c. will decline, since no further building can take place.
    d. will not show any predictable movement.

11.7 If there is a significant undersupply of homes in a market, construction will tend to increase. This is an example of

    a. supply outstripping demand.
    b. demand outstripping value.
    c. consumer optimism.
    d. the market tending toward equilibrium.

11.8 If commercial real estate rental prices are falling in a market, it is likely that

    a. demand has outstripped supply of space.
    b. the market is in equilibrium.
    c. the market is over-supplied.
    d. employment is increasing.

11.9 A construction boom in a market is an indication that prices

    a. have been increasing.
    b. have been declining.
    c. have been in equilibrium.
    d. have exceeded supply.

11.10 Bill Parsons paid $150,000 for a house to operate as a rental property, figuring that he could rent it out at a rate of $900 a month. In paying a price based on the property's ability to generate a desired future income, Parsons was motivated by the economic principle known as

    a. substitution.
    b. anticipation.
    c. supply and demand.
    d. utility.

11.11 Which of the following situations illustrates the principle of contribution?

    a. A homebuyer makes a down payment of 20% instead of the 10% the lender requires.
    b. A homeowner adds a third bathroom to a house and thereby increases the appraised value by $10,000.
    c. The appraised value of a house goes up by $20,000 over a two-year period because of the prices recently paid for other houses in the neighborhood.
    d. Because of a decline in mortgage interest rates, a homeowner in a certain market is able to list her house at a higher price.

11.12 When a property owner combines two adjacent properties to create a single property with a higher value than the sum of the values of the two separate properties, the applicable principle of value is called

    a. assemblage.
    b. accretion.
    c. progression.
    d. subdivision.

11.13 What is the difference between market value and market price, if any?

    a. There is no difference.
    b. Market value is a broker's estimate; market price is a precise number derived by a licensed appraiser.
    c. Market value is an average price derived from comparable sales; market price is a price based on the cost of creating the property.
    d. Market value is an estimate; market price is the price at which a property sold.

11.14 The first step in the appraisal process, regardless of the appraisal method, is to

    a. identify the highest and best use of the property to be appraised.
    b. collect and analyze property data.
    c. estimate the value of the land as if it were vacant.
    d. define the appraisal problem and the purpose of the appraisal.

11.15 In the final step of an appraisal, the appraiser reconciles the value estimates derived by the various appraisal approaches by

    a. disregarding the high and low extreme results.
    b. averaging the results of all three approaches.
    c. weighing the applicability of the approaches and considering the quality of data supporting each approach.
    d. choosing the result that is closest to the average for properties in the immediate neighborhood.

11.16 Which of the following statements properly describes the central concept of the sales comparison approach?

    a. Find the median price of recently sold comparable properties and add or subtract dollar amounts in the subject property to account for competitive differences.
    b. Make dollar adjustments to the sale prices of comparable properties to account for competitive differences with the subject.
    c. Find at least three comparable properties that are currently for sale and make dollar adjustments to the listing prices to account for competitive differences with the subject.
    d. Apply an appreciation factor to the price at which the subject property most recently sold and make dollar adjustments to account for competitive differences with comparable properties currently for sale.

11.17 One of the strengths of the sales comparison approach is that it

    a. takes into account the subject property's investment value.
    b. reveals the profit margin of the builder or developer of the subject property.
    c. discovers the underlying value of the subject property apart from the influence of competing properties.
    d. takes into account the competitive value of specific amenities of the subject property.

11.18 In making dollar adjustments in the sales comparison approach, the appraiser

    a. adds value to a comparable that is inferior to the subject property.
    b. adds value to the subject property if it is inferior to a comparable.
    c. subtracts value from a comparable that is inferior to the subject property.
    d. subtracts value from the subject property if it is inferior to a comparable.

11.19 The best comparable property for use in the sales comparison approach is the one that

    a. requires the most and largest adjustments.
    b. requires the fewest and smallest adjustments.
    c. sold most recently at the highest price.
    d. is located closest to the subject property.

11.20 A house is being appraised using the sales comparison approach. The house has three bedrooms, two bathrooms, and a patio. The appraiser selects a comparable house that has three bedrooms, 3 bathrooms, and no patio. The comparable house just sold for $200,000. A bath is valued at $7,000, and a patio at $2,000. Assuming all else is equal, what is the adjusted value of the comparable?

    a. $202,000.
    b. $207,000.
    c. $195,000.
    d. $205,000.

11.21 Which of the following statements properly describes the central methodology of the cost approach to appraisal?

a. Apply a depreciation factor to the reported actual cost of acquiring and improving the subject property.
b. Estimate the cost of building the improvements on the subject property.
c. Estimate the land value and add to this the actual cost of the improvements adjusted for competitive differences with similar properties.
d. Add the estimated land value and cost of improvements and subtract the accrued depreciation of the improvements.

11.22 One of the strengths of the cost approach is that it

a. takes into account the amount of money required to develop a similar property.
b. is very accurate for a property with new improvements that represent the highest and best use.
c. results in an actual price in dollars instead of an estimated value.
d. reveals the owner's return on money invested in the cost of development.

11.23 The principle underlying depreciation from physical deterioration is that

a. eventually, a property loses all of its value.
b. a property loses a portion of its value each year because of economic obsolescence.
c. a property loses the same increment of value each year over the economic life of the property.
d. the value lost to depreciation is incurable.

11.24 A property is being appraised by the cost approach. The appraiser estimates that the land is worth $30,000 and the replacement cost of the improvements is $95,000. Total depreciation from all causes is $10,000. What is the indicated value of the property?

a. $135,000.
b. $130,000.
c. $125,000.
d. $115,000.

11.25 Which of the following statements properly describes how to apply the income capitalization approach to appraisal?

a. Apply a rate of return to the price paid for an income property.
b. Divide the income a property generates by a rate of return.
c. Estimate the amount of income a property must generate to return the capital amount invested in it.
d. Estimate the rate of return a property owner receives from income generated by the property.

11.26 A strength of the income capitalization approach is that it

a. uses a rate of return that is required for all potential purchasers in a market.
b. yields an accurate projection of investment income.
c. uses a method that is also used by investors to determine how much they should pay for an investment property.
d. can be used with any type of property in any market.

11.27 A property is being appraised using the income capitalization approach. Annually, it has an estimated gross income of $60,000, vacancy and credit losses of $3,000, and operating expenses of $20,000. Using a capitalization rate of ten percent, what is the indicated value (to the nearest $1,000)?

a. $370,000.
b. $400,000.
c. $570,000.
d. $600,000.

11.28 An apartment building that sold for $450,000 had monthly gross rent receipts of $3,000. What is its monthly gross rent multiplier?

a. 12.5
b. .01.
c. .08.
d. 150.

11.29 As a component of real estate value, the principle of substitution states that

a. if two similar properties are for sale, a buyer will purchase the cheaper of the two.
b. if one of two adjacent homes is more valuable, the price of the other home will tend to rise.
c. if too many properties are built in a market, the prices will tend to go down.
d. people will readily move to another home if it is of equal value.

11.30 Highest and best use of a property is that use which

a. is physically and financially feasible, legal, and the most productive.
b. is legal, feasible, and deemed the most appropriate by zoning authorities.
c. entails the largest building that zoning ordinances will allow developers to erect.
d. conforms to other properties in the area.

11.31 Lynne just bought a house. She paid $187,500, for it, even though it had been listed at $195,000. An adjoining property owner, Ken, had tried to buy the property for $185,000, but had been refused. He now offers Lynne $190,000 for the house. Lynne is interested, so she hires an appraiser. The appraiser returns an estimate of value of $200,000. Which of these numbers can be called the market value?

a. $187,500.
b. $190,000.
c. $195,000.
d. $200,000.

11.32 A notable weakness of the sales comparison approach to value is that

a. there may be no recent sale price data in the market.
b. the approach is not based on the principle of substitution.
c. the approach is only accurate with unique, special purpose properties.
d. sale prices cannot be compared, since all real estate is different.

11.33 In the sales comparison approach, an adjustment is warranted if

a. the buyer obtains conventional financing for the property.
b. the seller offers below-market seller financing.
c. a comparable is located in another, albeit similar neighborhood.
d. one property has a hip roof and the other has a gabled roof.

11.34 To complete the sales comparison approach, the appraiser

a. averages the comparable values.
b. weights the comparables.
c. identifies the subject's value as that of the middle value of the comparables.
d. identifies the subject's value as that of the nearest comparable.

11.35 One weakness of the cost approach for appraising market value is that

    a. builders may not pay market value for materials or labor.
    b. market value is not always the same as what the property cost.
    c. comparables used may not have similar quality of construction.
    d. new properties have inestimable costs and rates of depreciation.

11.36 A home is located in a neighborhood where homeowners on the block have failed to maintain their properties. This is an example of

    a. curable external obsolescence.
    b. incurable economic obsolescence.
    c. functional obsolescence.
    d. physical deterioration.

11.37 In appraisal, loss of value in a property from any cause is referred to as

    a. deterioration.
    b. obsolescence.
    c. depreciation.
    d. deflation.

11.38 In the cost approach, after estimating the value of the land and the cost of the improvements, the appraiser

    a. estimates depreciation, subtracts depreciation from cost, and adds back the land value.
    b. subtracts deterioration from cost, estimates land depreciation, and totals the two values.
    c. estimates depreciation of land and improvements and subtracts the total from original cost.
    d. estimates obsolescence and subtracts from the cost of land and improvements.

11.39 What is the difference between a CMA and an appraisal?

    a. Details and preparation time
    b. Objectivity and comprehensiveness
    c. Professionalism and cost
    d. Approach and use of comparables

11.40 CMAs do not use which of the following information?

    a. Location of comparables
    b. Scaled-down version of an appraiser's sales comparison approach
    c. Sale prices for homes sold in the previous year
    d. Properties still for sale

UNIT TWELVE TEST: HUMAN RIGHTS AND FAIR HOUSING

12.1   The fair housing law that first protected people against discrimination in housing based on race was the

   a. Civil Rights Act of 1866.
   b. Civil Rights Act of 1968.
   c. Executive Order 11063 of 1962.
   d. Title VIII amendment to the Fair Housing Act.

12.2   The classes protected against discrimination by the Fair Housing Act of 1968 are

   a. race only.
   b. religion and gender only.
   c. race, color, religion, and national origin.
   d. age and gender only.

12.3   An agent is committing an act of discriminatory advertising by doing which of the following?

   a. Telling prospective buyers about the positive and negative aspects of a certain neighborhood.
   b. Telling a prospective seller that now would be a good time to put a property on the market.
   c. Advertising a property as available to individuals of a particular race.
   d. Telling a prospective buyer that the agent is too busy to show the buyer properties personally on a given day.

12.4   Which of the following is an example of blockbusting?

   a. An agent shows a minority home buyer property located in a neighborhood where there are no other minority home owners.
   b. An agent persuades a minority home buyer to avoid looking in a neighborhood where there are no minority home owners.
   c. An agent persuades a family to put their house on the market because minority families are beginning to move into the neighborhood.
   d. An agent persuades a minority home buyer to buy a property located in an area where most of the home owners are minorities.

12.5   The practice of redlining is specifically prohibited by

   a. The Home Mortgage Disclosure Act.
   b. The Real Estate Settlement Procedures Act.
   c. The Civil Rights Act of 1866.
   d. The Americans with Disabilities Act.

12.6   Title VIII of the Civil Rights Act of 1968 applies to the sale of

   a. all single-family residences.
   b. all privately owned single-family residences.
   c. privately owned single-family residences listed with a broker.
   d. privately owned single-family residences for sale by owner.

12.7 A broker signs a listing agreement to sell a home for $200,000. An immigrant couple are interested in the house and ask the agent the price. The agent states the price as $210,000. According to the fair housing laws, such an action is

   a. illegal, because the agent changed the terms of the sale to discourage this particular couple.
   b. illegal, because the agent violated the listing agreement.
   c. legal, because the quoted price increase did not exceed 10% of the listing price.
   d. legal, because the increased price does not necessarily exclude the couple.

12.8 Which of the following actions is allowed under federal fair housing laws?

   a. A broker, following the instructions of the seller, advertises the property as for sale to Christian families only.
   b. A home seller, acting without a broker, places a "for sale-- mature, single men only" sign in front of the house.
   c. The owner of four rental houses advertises one of the properties for rent to married couples, no children, no pets.
   d. The owner of a duplex who resides in one of the units refuses to rent the other unit to a non-Christian.

12.9 Cecily Longstreet believes a real estate agent has kept her from seeing a certain property for rent because she is a woman. What actions should she take if she wants legal satisfaction for her complaint?

   a. File charges of illegal discrimination with the police department that has jurisdiction over the local area.
   b. File a complaint with HUD and/or file suit against the offending parties in a state or federal court within the prescribed time period.
   c. Wait two years and then file a civil suit in federal court.
   d. Sue HUD for damages under the Civil rights Act of 1866.

12.10 George Scott hires Shannon Lang to sell his house, with the condition that he will not be the first one in the neighborhood to sell to members of a certain ethnic group. What should Shannon do about this condition?

   a. Inform Scott that the condition is illegal and that she cannot comply with it.
   b. Note the condition on the listing agreement and have Scott initial it.
   c. Pretend that she did not hear the condition and proceed to market the property to all groups.
   d. Tell Scott that she will try to discourage members of that group from looking at the property, but that she cannot control cooperating brokers.

12.11 Under federal fair housing laws, the owner of a ten-unit apartment building may legally

   a. advertise that the property is not available to anyone requiring wheelchair access.
   b. refuse to rent to aliens.
   c. require families without children to pay the same security deposit that families with children must pay.
   d. require tenants to move out when they become 62 years old.

12.12 Sam Gough wants to rent out his home, but wants to exclude families with children because of his belief that they cause damage. Under what conditions would federal fair housing laws allow Gough to rent on these terms?

   a. The owner has a consistent no-children policy in all his rental properties.
   b. The owner can prove that costs to repair damage caused by previous tenants with children exceeded the tenants' security deposit.
   c. It is a single-family house that is part of a federally-designated planned unit development.
   d. It is a single-family house, and the owner owns only one other rental home in addition to his own residence.

12.13 Which of the following laws or rulings extended discrimination to include gender, handicapped status, and family status?

    a. Executive Order 11063.
    b. the Civil Rights Act of 1968.
    c. the Fair Housing Amendments Act of 1988.
    d. Jones v Mayer.

12.14 The Wallaces, a bi-racial family, would like to buy a home in a certain price range. Agent Ambrose shows the family all available properties in a neighborhood of families with similar racial makeups. Ambrose does not mention a number of homes in the family's price range in other neighborhoods. This agent could be liable for

    a. blockbusting.
    b. providing unequal services.
    c. steering.
    d. nothing; his services were legal and acceptable.

12.15 An agent does not like a particular minority buyer, and is very short with the person, refusing to engage in lengthy conversation or show him any properties. A second minority party visits the office the next day. The agent is very forthcoming, and shows the person five prospective properties. This agent could be liable for

    a. providing unequal services.
    b. steering.
    c. misrepresentation.
    d. nothing; both parties were minorities, and therefore, no discrimination occurred.

12.16 Following the client's recommendation, an agent conceals the availability of a property from an employed but pregnant and unmarried woman. This agent could be liable for

    a. discriminatory misrepresentation by omission.
    b. steering.
    c. violating fiduciary duty.
    d. nothing: an agent may show or not show any property at his or her discretion.

12.17 A principal instructs an agent to inform minority buyers that the property for lease was just leased an hour ago and is no longer available. The agent refuses to comply. In this case,

    a. the agent should exercise caution until the listing expires, then decline to renew it.
    b. the principal has proposed an illegal act, which should not be obeyed.
    c. the agent is liable for breaching the listing terms.
    d. the agent may sue the principal for discrimination and misrepresentation.

12.18 An agent receives a full-price offer from a minority party. The agent presents the offer to the seller and discloses the buyer's minority status. The seller at that point instructs the agent to inform the buyer that the property has just gone under contract. The agent duly complies, telling the offeror that the home has just been temporarily removed from the market and is unavailable – but may be available soon if the contract falls through. Which party or parties, if any, have violated fair housing laws?

    a. The agent only.
    b. The owner only.
    c. The agent and the owner.
    d. Neither agent nor owner.

12.19 The sections of the Americans with Disabilities Act that most concern real estate agents are those that deal with

    a.   telecommunications and insurance.
    b.   public accommodations and employees.
    c.   state and local government.
    d.   agency and public service.

12.20 Blockbusting is a form of discrimination that

    a.   induces owners in a particular area to sell to avoid an impending change in the ethnic makeup of the neighborhood.
    b.   alters the nature or quality of services based on any protected class.
    c.   misrepresents property availability, price, or terms based on any protected class.
    d.   channeling customers toward or away from properties or particular areas.

12.21 The law or ruling that prohibited discrimination based on race without exemptions or exceptions is

    a.   the Fair Housing Amendments Act of 1988.
    b.   Civil Rights Act of 1968.
    c.   Jones v. Mayer.
    d.   Title VIII.

12.22 The Home Mortgage Disclosure Act applies to

    a.   public housing.
    b.   condominium sales.
    c.   federally guaranteed or insured loans.
    d.   leases with options.

12.23 Which law adds victims of domestic violence as a protected class in housing?

    a.   Americans with Disabilities Act
    b.   NYC Human Rights Law
    c.   NY Human Rights Law
    d.   All Federal Fair Housing Laws

12.24 Exemptions to the New York Human Rights Law do not apply to

    a.   homeowners.
    b.   real estate agents.
    c.   renters 62 years and older.
    d.   landlords.

12.25 Which of the following protected classes is only recognized by the NY Human Rights Law?

    a.   Military status
    b.   Citizenship
    c.   Sexual orientation
    d.   Victims of stalking

12.26 The New York Human Rights Law provides anti-discrimination protection for all of the following except

    a.   housing advertisements.
    b.   commercial real estate.
    c.   real estate board membership.
    d.   agricultural real estate.

12.27 Which of the following is not an exemption under the NY Human Rights Law?

    a. Apartment rentals in five-unit buildings with the owner occupying one unit
    b. Public housing for a specific age group
    c. Room rental in an owner's home
    d. Buildings where all rooms are occupied by same sex individuals

12.28 Which of the following is not an exemption to the NY City Human Rights Law?

    a. Room rentals in an owner's home
    b. Advertisements for rental of an owner-occupied two-family house
    c. Public housing for a specific age group
    d. Rentals to ages 62 and older

12.29 Sarah applied for a rental in an apartment in Albany, NY. The landlord's background check on Sarah revealed that she is a survivor of domestic violence. Not wanting to deal with potential problems, the landlord refused to allow Sarah to rent the apartment, telling her he did not want to risk having incidents occur on his property. Sarah filed a complaint with HUD for discrimination, but HUD declined to process the complaint. Why?

    a. The landlord was within his rights to refuse a rental to anyone for any reason.
    b. The landlord did not specifically say the domestic violence was the reason for the refusal.
    c. Being a victim of domestic violence is not a protected class in Albany.
    d. Sarah had no witnesses to the discrimination.

12.30 Title III Public Accommodations of the Americans with Disabilities Act is enforced by the

    a. Federal Communications Commission.
    b. U.S. Equal Employment Opportunity Commission.
    c. Federal Trade Commission.
    d. U.S. Department of Justice.

12.31 Which of the following would not be required by the Americans with Disabilities Act or Fair Housing laws as a reasonable accommodation?

    a. Installation of a wheelchair ramp at the entrance of an apartment building
    b. Installation of an elevator inside a two-story apartment building
    c. Widening of building doorways to allow wheelchair access
    d. Permitting a disabled person to have a service dog in an area where pets are not allowed

12.32 While registering to use a multiple listing service, Broker Terrance came across a question asking for his race. Once he answered the question, he found himself locked out of the program. This is an example of illegally

    a. restricting access to market.
    b. blockbusting.
    c. redlining.
    d. steering.

12.33 Federal law allows landlords to refuse to rent to families with children when the building's occupancy is restricted to residents who are at least

    a. 57 years old.
    b. 60 years old.
    c. 62 years old.
    d. 70 years old.

12.34 A financial institution that refuses to provide residential mortgage loans simply because of where the property is located is guilty of

a. blockbusting.
b. restricting access to market.
c. steering.
d. redlining.

12.35 For which protected class are there no exceptions from housing discrimination?

a. Religion
b. Age
c. Race
d. Gender

12.36 Which of the following discriminatory acts were allowed by the Jim Crow laws in the southern states?

a. Slavery
b. Black people banned from shopping in same grocery stores as white people
c. Banning black people from attending the same churches as white people
d. Banning black people from attending the same public schools as white people

12.37 When did segregation in public schools become illegal?

a. 1866
b. 1954
c. 1968
d. 1988

12.38 Licensees must provide the Reasonable Accommodation and Reasonable Modification Disclosure Form to prospective tenants

a. within 30 days of residency.
b. upon first substantive contact.
c. within 30 days of the law's effective date.
d. Licensees are not required to provide the form to prospective tenants.

12.39 If a prospective tenant is disabled and has a service dog, but the housing rules state no dogs allowed, which of the following statements is true?

a. The prospective tenant should find another housing opportunity where dogs are allowed.
b. The landlord can deny or accept the service dog for residency.
c. The landlord must modify the rules to accommodate the disabled tenant's need for the service dog.
d. The landlord must change the no dogs rule for all tenants so as to allow the service dog's residency.

UNIT THIRTEEN TEST: MUNICIPAL AGENCIES

13.1   Which of the following statements is true regarding the purpose of public and private control of land?

    a.   The purpose is to decrease property values.
    b.   The purpose is to assure the highest and best use of property.
    c.   The purpose is to assure the preference of individual property rights over the public good.
    d.   The purpose is to allow continued growth regardless of infrastructure capabilities.

13.2   New York City Council members may serve

    a.   two 4-year terms.
    b.   one 3-year term.
    c.   two 1-year terms.
    d.   unlimited 3-year terms.

13.3   The New York agency that serves as an equal partner to the mayor in governing the city is the

    a.   Village Board of Trustees.
    b.   Planning Board.
    c.   Zoning Board.
    d.   New York City Council.

13.4   Village Board of Trustee board meetings are presided over by

    a.   alternating members of the Board.
    b.   president of the Board.
    c.   village mayor.
    d.   the trustee with the most seniority.

13.5   Which of the following establishes the scope of power for implementing laws and ordinances?

    a.   Municipal Home Rule Law
    b.   Local Bill of Rights
    c.   Village Constitution
    d.   Local legislative laws

13.6   When a zoning board member submits a new law proposal to the planning agency, the agency must respond within _____ or the board may go ahead and finalize the law.

    a.   10 business days
    b.   6 months
    c.   30 days
    d.   60 days

13.7   When the zoning commission votes on a proposed law and files the final report with the municipal clerk, the clerk must file the law with the _____ within 5 days.

    a.   Secretary of State
    b.   Mayor
    c.   Governor
    d.   local municipal board

13.8 Taxing districts adopt a budget for meeting their financial needs every

    a. 30 days.
    b. 6 months.
    c. 12 months.
    d. 2 years.

13.9 Deficits in municipal budgets are met by

    a. increasing property values.
    b. collecting real property taxes.
    c. imposing fees on properties sales.
    d. decreasing property taxes.

13.10 If a town board appoints six members to the Planning Board, what is the length of the term those members will serve?

    a. 4 years
    b. 2 years
    c. 6 years
    d. 7 years

13.11 The Planning Board is provided regulatory powers for

    a. subdivision plat review.
    b. master plan development.
    c. land use regulation.
    d. capital budgets.

13.12 Use variances are granted based on whether

    a. the owner's situation is unique.
    b. the variance will harm conditions of in the surrounding environment.
    c. there is an alternative way to achieve the same benefit.
    d. the variance is substantial.

13.13 An area variance is necessary when

    a. using a structure in a way other than as it is zoned.
    b. using a master plan for a municipality other than as it is zoned.
    c. using specific land in a way other than as it is zoned.
    d. dividing a subdivision plat other than as it is zoned.

13.14 Other than providing regulations for maintaining building exteriors, the Architectural Review Board also provides regulations and guidance for

    a. building interiors.
    b. building signs.
    c. building landscaping.
    d. building use.

13.15 Which agency assists with land use decisions while considering environmental issues related to development, management, and protection of natural resources?

    a. Planning Board
    b. NY Zoning Board
    c. NY Department of Natural Resources
    d. Conservation Advisory Council

13.16 The two types of wetlands protected by the NY Department of Environmental Conservation are

    a.   salt water and fresh water.
    b.   ocean and river.
    c.   tidal and freshwater.
    d.   groundwater and surface water.

13.17 Applications for placing a structure on the National Register of Historic Places listings are handled by

    a.   NY Department of Building.
    b.   Historic Preservation and Landmark Commission.
    c.   NY Office of Parks, Recreation, and Historic Preservation.
    d.   National Historic Registry.

13.18 The agency responsible for issuing demolition permits and certificates of occupancy is the

    a.   Department of Building.
    b.   Planning Department.
    c.   Architectural Review Board.
    d.   Planning Board.

13.19 Which type of tax assessment is used in New York City and Long Island?

    a.   Four classes of property
    b.   Full value assessment
    c.   Uniform percentage of value
    d.   None of the above

13.20 Which New York agency is responsible for septic system approval?

    a.   Village/city engineer
    b.   County Health Department
    c.   Department of Building
    d.   Planning Department

UNIT FOURTEEN TEST: PROPERTY INSURANCE

14.1   What will likely happen if a homeowner lets his or her homeowners' insurance coverage lapse?

   a. The mortgage lender will place coverage on the home.
   b. The mortgage lender will foreclose on the home.
   c. The home will not be protected if there is a flood.
   d. The homeowner will not be allowed to purchase a new policy.

14.2   Depending on a home's location, a mortgage lender may require the borrower to carry

   a. liability insurance.
   b. health insurance.
   c. personal property insurance.
   d. flood insurance.

14.3   Which homeowners' policy covers condominiums?

   a. HO-3
   b. HO-4
   c. HO-5
   d. HO-6

14.4   Which homeowners' policy covers older homes with replacement costs higher than the home's market value?

   a. HO-4
   b. HO-5
   c. HO-8
   d. HO-6

14.5   Which homeowners' policy is also known as renters' insurance?

   a. HO-1
   b. HO-3
   c. HO-4
   d. HO-5

14.6   Which of the following is a true statement about the "80% rule" for homeowner's policies?

   a. 80% of replacement value is the maximum an insurance company will pay.
   b. If insured for less than 80% of replacement cost, a home's coverage will include a deduction for depreciation.
   c. If insured for 80% of replacement cost, a home is covered for the full cost of replacement.
   d. Insurance companies will not insure residences for less than 80% of their replacement cost.

14.7   Which of the following is not covered in the standard HO-1 policy?

   a. Damage caused by terrorism
   b. Damage caused by aircraft
   c. Damage caused by cars
   d. Damage caused by earthquakes

14.8   Insurance companies may remove coverage for certain perils when a commercial property has been vacant for

    a.   one year.
    b.   120 days.
    c.   90 days.
    d.   60 days.

14.9   Insurance policies can either be package or _____ policies

    a.   personal property
    b.   monoline
    c.   all coverage
    d.   dwelling

14.10   The most common types of insurance related to real estate are

    a.   flood and homeowners.
    b.   homeowners and auto.
    c.   liability and casualty.
    d.   dwelling and loss of use.

14.11   Which of the following would not be covered under a dwelling policy?

    a.   An attached garage
    b.   A fence
    c.   An air conditioning system
    d.   A home

14.12   Which of the following would be covered under a casualty policy?

    a.   Fire
    b.   Windstorm
    c.   Theft
    d.   Smoke

14.13   An endorsement

    a.   specifies requirements for coverage under the policy.
    b.   adds coverage for property or perils that are not included in the base policy.
    c.   lists the perils not covered under the policy.
    d.   specifies structure contents that are covered under the base policy.

14.14   HO-2 policies are known as

    a.   exclusion policies because they exclude specific perils from base policies.
    b.   comprehensive all-risk policies because they cover all perils.
    c.   peril policies because they add specific perils to HO-1 policies.
    d.   comprehensive coverage policies that cover structures, personal property, and loss of use.

14.15   What is the prerequisite of obtaining an umbrella policy?

    a.   A $500 - $1000 deductible must be escrowed for use in a claim.
    b.   The homeowner must add the umbrella coverage to his base policy as an endorsement.
    c.   The agent must explain the lender's interest in the insurance to the home buyer.
    d.   The home buyer must first obtain a homeowners', auto, or liability policy.

UNIT FIFTEEN TEST: LICENSEE SAFETY

15.1   Which of the following statements is false?

    a.   Female agents should lock their purses in their vehicles during showings.
    b.   Agents should have visitors enter doorways ahead of the agent.
    c.   Agents should not let the person they are meeting know the office has been given the person's name and location of the meeting place.
    d.   Agents should rely strictly on their GPS in unfamiliar areas.

15.2   The purpose of having a secret word or phrase when contacting the office is to

    a.   let the broker know if the potential buyer has submitted an offer.
    b.   let the office know the potential buyer did not arrive for the property showing.
    c.   let the office know the agent is in trouble.
    d.   let the office know the open house is over and the agent is leaving.

15.3   Why should the broker keep a record of agents' health conditions?

    a.   To judge the agent's performance
    b.   To determine the agent's work load
    c.   To be aware of situations that may result in a medical emergency
    d.   To select appropriate health benefits

15.4   Which of the following items should clients remove or secure for an open house?

    a.   Family photos
    b.   Large televisions
    c.   Toys
    d.   Expensive jewelry

15.5   Which of the following would be a safety concern during an open house?

    a.   The agent locking his/her cell phone in the vehicle
    b.   A neighbor's interest in the event
    c.   Finding the house completely empty prior to the agent leaving
    d.   The agent parking on the street instead of in the driveway

15.6   Which of the following statements is true?

    a.   Agents should meet new clients at the client's house for the first time to assess the property.
    b.   Agents should bring a second person along for a house showing.
    c.   Agents should lead clients through the house being shown, even into attics or basements.
    d.   Agents should park in the driveway during an open house to leave street parking open to the visitors.

15.7   Brokers should not

    a.   record each agent's vehicle information.
    b.   print an agent's personal address on business cards.
    c.   keep a schedule of an agent's outside appointments.
    d.   require an agent to have a guest registry at all open houses.

15.8 An agent should

    a. advise the client to talk to other agents and buyers during an open house.
    b. not scare clients by reminding them that strangers will be walking through the house during a showing.
    c. encourage clients to show the home to buyers that may not have an appointment to view the home.
    d. advise the client to refer all inquiries about the home to the agent.

15.9 Marie is an agent who is meeting her new client, Joe, for the second time. She has agreed to meet Joe at the house he wants to sell. Once there, Marie locked her purse in her car, let her broker know the address and client's name, and then turned off her cell phone so she would not be disturbed while viewing the house. What did Marie do that could jeopardize her safety?

    a. Although she let her broker know where she was, she met the client away from her office.
    b. Two things: she locked her purse in the car instead of keeping it with her at all times and turned off her cell phone.
    c. Two things: she met the client alone and then turned off her cell phone.
    d. She didn't do anything that would jeopardize her safety.

15.10 As a broker, Jose has identified procedures for protecting his affiliated agents' safety. The procedures include keeping a record of the agents' vehicles, health conditions, and their outside appointments. Jose also requires his agents to use a guest registry at open houses, to never work alone in or out of the office, to include their personal contact information on business cards, and to utilize scam and ID theft protection strategies. However, Jose made a mistake by including one of these items in his safety procedures.

    a. The agents' personal contact information should not be included on business cards.
    b. Requiring a guest registry at open houses imposes on the guests' personal information.
    c. Keeping a record of the agents' health conditions is a violation of HIPAA laws.
    d. Not allowing the agents to work alone increases the work load for all agents.

15.11 Which of the following is not a recommended strategy for agents to protect their safety?

    a. Wear practical clothing.
    b. Carry a gun.
    c. Do not turn your back on a client.
    d. Establish a code word with the office.

15.12 Broker Sherri keeps a record of her agents' health conditions. Why should she do that?

    a. To determine if an agent is physically fit for the job
    b. To determine if an agent's health conditions are impacting the cost of health insurance for the brokerage
    c. To provide critical information to first responders in case of an emergency
    d. She should not be keeping a record of agents' health conditions.

15.13 Agent Alex gave the following advice to his home seller client. Which statement is valid in protecting the client's safety?

    a. Talk to other agents to provide them with information on the client's home and sale details.
    b. Do not turn away a potential buyer even if one shows up without an appointment.
    c. Instead of providing potential buyers information about the home, refer all inquiries Alex.
    d. Do not allow strangers to walk through the home during open houses.

15.14 Jerry had his client remove the following items from the home prior to an open house. Which removal was unnecessary?

    a. A large screen television from the family room
    b. Opioids from the bathroom medicine cabinet
    c. Heirloom jewelry from the master bedroom
    d. A gun collection from an unlocked cabinet in the home office

15.15 If it is necessary to show a property after dark, what should the agent do to protect his/her safety?

    a. Let the broker know he/she is showing the property alone.
    b. Park in the property's driveway to be closer to the house.
    c. Carry any cash on the agent's person instead of leaving it in the car where it could be stolen.
    d. Open all of the blinds in the house.

UNIT SIXTEEN TEST: TAXES AND ASSESSMENTS

16.1 Taxes based on the value of the property are

    a. special assessment taxes.
    b. undeclared improvement taxes.
    c. ad valorem taxes.
    d. reassessment taxes.

16.2 A priority lien resulting from non-payment of taxes is enforced by

    a. court-ordered sale of the property.
    b. fines up to 10% of the property's assessed value.
    c. imposition of an equalization factor.
    d. imposition of a special assessment on the property.

16.3 Special assessments are levied on

    a. all properties in the township.
    b. all properties in the specific school district.
    c. only properties that will benefit from the specific improvements.
    d. homeowners who fail to pay their ad valorem taxes.

16.4 Which of the following does not result in lower assessments?

    a. Older construction
    b. New construction
    c. Lower land value
    d. Combination of older construction and lower land value

16.5 Undeclared improvements are those

    a. not reported to the county.
    b. not taxed.
    c. made with no building permit.
    d. made by individual homeowners.

16.6 An examination of which of the following is not required with a New York City property sale.

    a. Sale year tax base
    b. Transitional tax
    c. Special assessment tax
    d. Target assessment

16.7 Which of the following is an allowable assessment increase in New York City in a tax year?

    a. 15%
    b. 25%
    c. 28%
    d. 30%

16.8 _____ provides uniformity among districts that assess at different rates.

    a. Transitional tax
    b. Equalization factor
    c. Reassessment
    d. An annual budget

16.9 An equalization factor is not used with

    a. full-value assessments.
    b. transactional taxes.
    c. homestead assessments.
    d. varying property assessments.

16.10 When a taxing district's budget shows expenditures higher than anticipated income, how are the additional funds raised to cover the expenditures?

    a. Through school taxes
    b. By increasing property assessments
    c. Through real estate taxes
    d. By using an equalization factor

16.11 Which of the following does not qualify as a homestead?

    a. Condominiums
    b. Farms
    c. Owner-occupied mobile homes
    d. Apartment buildings with more than four units

16.12 A tax rate of 35 mills equals _____ per $100 of assessed value.

    a. 35%
    b. $0.35
    c. 3.5%
    d. $35

16.13 Authorizing expenses and providing sources of funds to cover those expenses is called

    a. equalization.
    b. appropriation.
    c. reassessment.
    d. assessing.

16.14 Taxing districts issue tax bills each year

    a. in January with a March due date.
    b. In June with a July due date.
    c. at the end of December with a January due date.
    d. at different times with varying due dates.

16.15 Which of the following properties may be eligible for a tax exemption?

    a. Private clubs and organizations
    b. Privately owned commercial properties
    c. Hospitals
    d. Zoos

16.16 Construction of low-income housing qualifies for

   a. New York special exemptions and reductions.
   b. General tax exemption.
   c. Federal tax exemption
   d. Special assessment tax exemption

16.17 The income limit for an elderly party's 50% tax reduction in New York City is

   a. $3,000.
   b. $50,000.
   c. $29,000.
   d. $37,399.

16.18 The alternative veterans tax exemption provides a _____ assessed property value reduction for the veteran's service during war.

   a. 10%
   b. 15%
   c. 20%
   d. 25%

16.19 Properties eligible for tax relief under the STaR program do not include

   a. farm houses.
   b. condominiums.
   c. cooperatives.
   d. commercial properties.

16.20 Assessment grievance day in New York City

   a. is March 1.
   b. is January 30.
   c. June 1.
   d. varies year to year.

UNIT SEVENTEEN TEST: CONDOMINIUMS AND COOPERATIVES

17.1 Which of the following statements is false?

    a. Condominiums can be created by converting rental property into condos.
    b. Condominiums are only created by converting rental properties into condos.
    c. Condominiums may be foreclosed without impacting other unit owners.
    d. Condominium owners jointly own common elements within the condo community.

17.2 Which of the following sets up covenants, conditions, and restrictions for condominium residents?

    a. New York Condominium Act
    b. Real Property Act
    c. Condominium Owners Association By-laws
    d. State Fair Housing laws

17.3 To convert rental units to condominiums in specific areas of the state, _____ of the tenants must agree to purchase the units.

    a. 25%
    b. 51%
    c. 76%
    d. 100%

17.4 When a rental property is converted to condominiums, those tenants who choose not to purchase a unit are exempt from eviction for

    a. 3 years.
    b. 2 years.
    c. 1 year.
    d. 90 days.

17.5 When condominiums are being sold, the initial offering plan is created by the

    a. real estate agent handling the sales.
    b. attorney general.
    c. board of directors.
    d. condo sponsor.

17.6 Letters of intent

    a. are legally binding offers to purchase a condominium unit.
    b. guarantee a project's success so as to induce funding for the project.
    c. are provided only when condominium construction is completed.
    d. include the terms of the transaction between the sponsor and a potential buyer.

17.7 Who pays for condominium deed preparations when selling condo units?

    a. Buyer
    b. Title agent
    c. Sponsor-seller
    d. Real estate agent

17.8 Condominium board packages are required to include

   a. asset details.
   b. title insurance.
   c. deed recording confirmation.
   d. copy of binding offer for purchase of unit.

17.9 Which of the following is not a condominium common area?

   a. Elevators
   b. Operating systems
   c. Appliances
   d. Recreational facilities

17.10 A condominium certificate of occupancy is obtained from

   a. the board of directors.
   b. the Department of Buildings.
   c. the developer.
   d. the sponsor.

17.11 Which document is provided to condo purchasers to disclose the property tax issues, the unit square footage and floor plan, any hidden fees, and the applicable closing date?

   a. Letter of Intent
   b. Certificate of Occupancy
   c. Condominium Owners Association By-laws
   d. Initial Offering Plan

17.12 Who appoints the initial manager for a condominium association?

   a. Board of Directors
   b. Sponsor
   c. Unit owners
   d. None of the above

17.13 Who actually owns individual cooperative units?

   a. The developer maintains ownership.
   b. Shareholders jointly own the units.
   c. Individual shareholders own their own units.
   d. Developer, founding corporation, and shareholders own the units.

17.14 Mr. Flemming purchased 6 shares in the Broad County Co-op. Ms. Johnson purchased 3 shares. When issues require shareholder votes, how many votes are each of these shareholders allowed?

   a. Mr. Flemming – 6 votes; Ms. Johnson – 3 votes
   b. Mr. Flemming – 2 votes; Ms. Johnson – 1 vote
   c. Mr. Flemming – 1 vote; Ms. Johnson – 1 vote
   d. Mr. Flemming – 0 votes; Ms. Johnson – 0 votes

17.15 What provides cooperative shareholders the right to occupy units within the co-op?

   a. A proprietary lease
   b. The number of shares owned
   c. The board of directors
   d. The ownership deed to the unit

UNIT EIGHTEEN TEST: COMMERCIAL AND INVESTMENT PROPERTY ANALYSIS

18.1   The goal of real property investment is

   a.   to establish a tax shelter.
   b.   to acquire a cash flow.
   c.   to earn noncash tax deductions for depreciation.
   d.   to gain as much as possible as quickly as possible to avoid risk of loss.

18.2   Which of the following is a type of business risk?

   a.   capital risk
   b.   liquidity
   c.   static risk
   d.   leverage

18.3   Which of the following best describes liquidity?

   a.   The degree to which an asset is convertible to cash in a market transaction
   b.   The intensity of management required to safeguard an investment
   c.   The readily an asset can be exchanged for a like-kind asset
   d.   The net profit, or positive cash flow, of a given asset

18.4   Which type of investment property has a greater demand than for than other types of property?

   a.   Commercial property
   b.   Unimproved land
   c.   Mixed-use property
   d.   Residential property

18.5   Which type of commercial lease requires the tenant to pay rent plus all of the operating expenses?

   a.   Net
   b.   Gross
   c.   Percentage
   d.   Loft

18.6   With a gross lease,

   a.   the landlord of storage and warehousing facilities need not provide operating services.
   b.   there is no fixed rent.
   c.   the tenant pays a negotiated rent amount, and the landlord pays operating expenses.
   d.   the rent is based on the gross income generated by the tenant.

18.7   Which of the following is the formula for determining taxable income?

   a.   NOI - reserves – interest – depreciation
   b.   NOI + reserves – interest expense – cost recovery expense x tax rate
   c.   NOI + reserves – interest – depreciation
   d.   Property description potential rental income – vacancy and collection loss + other income

18.8 How does one derive an investment's value?

    a. net operating income ÷ rate of return
    b. income – operating expenses ÷ investment price
    c. cash flow ÷ cash invested
    d. net operating income ÷ equity

18.9 Income tax liability for an income property is based on

    a. cash flow.
    b. net operating income.
    c. after-tax cash flow.
    d. taxable income.

18.10 Which of the following is not included when deriving cash flow?

    a. Vacancy loss
    b. Depreciation
    c. Rental income
    d. Reserves

18.11 Given a value, revenue, expenses, and net operating income, how is an investment's cap rate determined?

    a. net operating income ÷ value or price
    b. income – operating expenses ÷ investment price
    c. cash flow ÷ cash invested
    d. net operating income ÷ equity

18.12 _____ determines cash-on-cash return.

    a. Rate of return x value or price
    b. Market value – current debt principal
    c. Cash flow ÷ cash invested
    d. Net operating income ÷ equity

18.13 The formula for deriving equity is

    a. market value – current debt principal.
    b. net operating income ÷ equity.
    c. income – operating expenses ÷ investment price.
    d. rate of return x value or price.

18.14 A rented facility's load factor is expressed as

    a. only a percentage.
    b. only as square footage.
    c. either a percentage or square footage.
    d. neither a percentage nor square footage.

18.15 An add-on factor is expressed as

    a. a percentage.
    b. square footage.
    c. either a percentage or square footage.
    d. neither a percentage nor square footage.

18.16 Which commercial lease clause protects the property owner against inflationary rises in operating costs?

    a.   Attornment clause
    b.   Use clause
    c.   Proportionate clause
    d.   Escalation clause

18.17 An attornment clause in a commercial lease

    a.   defines what business the tenant may conduct within the leased property.
    b.   defines who is to be paid rent and who is to pay the rent.
    c.   protects the owner against inflationary rises in operation costs.
    d.   defines the tenant's share of operation cost increases.

18.18 When a commercial lease has an escalation clause, the tenant's proportionate share of the cost increase is determined by using the following formula:

    a.   tenant usable area – rentable area
    b.   tenant rentable area ÷ building gross rentable area
    c.   building gross rentable area ÷ number of rented areas
    d.   building gross rental area – tenant's usable area

18.19 The point at which the tenant's liability for increased operational costs begins is defined by

    a.   the proportionate share clause.
    b.   the operating and tax stop.
    c.   the base year.
    d.   a use clause.

18.20 A porters wage index for rent escalation is adjusted every

    a.   year.
    b.   4 years.
    c.   2 years.
    d.   5 years.

UNIT NINETEEN TEST: INCOME TAX ISSUES IN REAL ESTATE TRANSACTIONS

19.1   Which of the following statements is true regarding the Tax Reform Act of 2018?

   a.   The Act created nine income tax brackets.
   b.   The Act removed mortgage interest deduction limits.
   c.   The Act reduced the top corporate tax rate.
   d.   The Act increased the limits on real estate tax deductions.

19.2   Under the Tax Reform Act of 2018, the maximum deduction for homeowner property taxes is

   a. $5,000.
   b. $10,000.
   c. $20,000.
   d. $25,000.

19.3   Interest prepaid to lenders, called points, applies only to

   a.   vacation homes.
   b.   primary residences.
   c.   like-kind exchanges.
   d.   acquisition financing.

19.4   Closing costs are not deductible in the acquisition year for

   a.   investment properties.
   b.   owner-occupied properties.
   c.   commercial properties.
   d.   multiple-unit rental properties.

19.5   Long-term gains apply to property owned for _____ income tax years.

   a.   1 or more
   b.   2 or more
   c.   at least 3
   d.   no more than 5

19.6   The formula for calculating an income property's adjusted basis is

   a.   purchase price plus improvement value minus depreciation.
   b.   purchase price minus improvement value minus depreciation.
   c.   improvement value minus purchase price minus depreciation.
   d.   adjusted basis does not apply to income properties.

19.7   John owns stock in ABC Company and receives monthly dividends from the stock. These dividends are considered _____ income.

   a.   active
   b.   passive
   c.   portfolio
   d.   employment

19.8 The depreciation recovery period for residential property where 80% of the income is from improvements is

    a. 5 years.
    b. 32 ½ years.
    c. 39 years.
    d. 27 ½ years.

19.9 The 39-year depreciation recovery period applies to what kind of property?

    a. Residential property where 80% of the income is from improvements
    b. Commercial income property
    c. Primary residential property
    d. Agricultural property

19.10 The formula for calculating depreciable basis is

    a. total purchase cost plus land value.
    b. total purchase cost minus land value.
    c. land value minus total purchase cost.
    d. purchase cost minus closing costs minus land value.

19.11 Under IRS code 1031, capital gains taxes are

    a. due within the first tax payment year.
    b. eliminated.
    c. deferred.
    d. increased by 20%.

19.12 Which of the following types of property qualifies for a 1031 tax deferral?

    a. Vacant properties held for investment
    b. Leaseholds for 20 or more years
    c. Stocks and bonds.
    d. Non-U.S. properties

19.13 IRS code 1031 applies to

    a. all acquisitions of primary residential properties.
    b. commercial income properties only.
    c. like-kind property exchanges only.
    d. all sales of residential income properties.

19.14 When utilizing IRS code 1031 to exchange like-kind properties, a replacement property must be designated with _____ of the sale of the first property.

    a. 30 days
    b. 45 days
    c. 90 days
    d. 180 days

19.15 Tax credits provided under the Low-income Housing Tax Incentives are applied for

    a. project construction period only.
    b. 5 years.
    c. 10 years.
    d. 30+ years.

UNIT TWENTY TEST: MORTGAGE BROKERAGE

20.1   In a real estate transaction, who originates a mortgage loan?

    a.   The real estate broker
    b.   The mortgage broker
    c.   The mortgage banker
    d.   The borrower

20.2   Who handles the mortgage loan application and approval?

    a.   The mortgage banker
    b.   The mortgage broker
    c.   The borrower
    d.   All of the above

20.3   In a real estate transaction, whose job is it to analyze a borrower's creditworthiness for loan preapproval?

    a.   The mortgage broker
    b.   The mortgage banker
    c.   The borrower
    d.   The credit reporting agency

20.4   Which of the following is not the responsibility of a mortgage broker?

    a.   Issuing the mortgage loan commitment
    b.   Connecting borrowers with the best loan terms based on the borrower's needs and qualifications
    c.   Preparing a fee agreement for the borrower
    d.   Explaining different types of loans to the borrower

20.5   The purpose of a New York mortgage broker obtaining a surety bond is

    a.   to help fund the loan.
    b.   to cover fines the broker may incur for law violations.
    c.   to guarantee the broker's legal compliance.
    d.   to pay mortgage bankers for their cooperation in obtaining a loan.

20.6   Mortgage brokers may do all of the following except

    a.   determine a borrower's financial qualifications for a loan.
    b.   service the loan.
    c.   explain the loan terms to the borrower.
    d.   avoid undisclosed dual agency relationships.

20.7   Mortgage broker licenses are renewed

    a.   every year.
    b.   every 2 years.
    c.   every 3 years.
    d.   They are not renewable.

20.8 Which of the following statements is false?

a. Mortgage brokers solicit residential mortgage loans for others.
b. Mortgage bankers charge brokers a fee for their services.
c. Mortgage brokers negotiate mortgage loans for real estate purchasers.
d. Mortgage bankers advance funds for mortgage loans.

20.9 Documentation required by lenders includes the borrower's tax return(s) from the previous _____.

a. year.
b. 2 years.
c. 3 years.
d. 5 years.

20.10 Which of the following qualifications applies to a mortgage broker license?

a. 5 years of credit analysis experience
b. Obtain liability insurance
c. 3 years of experience as a real estate broker
d. Pass a criminal background check

20.11 When a lender agrees to fund a mortgage loan, the agreement is expressed with a

a. loan guarantee.
b. closing statement.
c. loan commitment letter.
d. loan funding contract.

20.12 Making sure the borrower understands the terms of the loan and payment schedule is the responsibility of

a. the mortgage broker.
b. the mortgage banker.
c. the borrower's attorney.
d. the borrower's real estate broker.

20.13 Both mortgage brokers and mortgage bankers

a. issue loan commitments.
b. advance funds for the loan.
c. work to provide a borrower with a loan that meets his/her needs.
d. assist the borrower with loan preapproval.

20.14 When an individual acts as both real estate agent and mortgage broker for the same client, the individual has entered into

a. a fee agreement.
b. an underwriting agreement.
c. a loan commitment.
d. a dual agency.

20.15 A mortgage broker prequalifies a borrower in a real estate transaction by

a. establishing the borrower will most likely meet the lender's loan requirements.
b. determining the borrower has no credit issues.
c. obtaining a loan commitment letter from the lender.
d. Mortgage brokers do not prequalify borrowers.

UNIT TWENTY-ONE TEST: PROPERTY MANAGEMENT

21.1   Which of the following is a duty specific to landlords and not to property managers?

   a.   Set rents
   b.   Comply with applicable laws
   c.   Maintain financial records
   d.   Find tenants

21.2   Under what circumstances may a property manager hire staff?

   a.   If the management workload is too much for the manager to handle alone
   b.   When the property owner resides out of state
   c.   If the management contract grants that authority to the manager
   d.   If the landlord fails to provide adequate staff

21.3   Which of the following is not a component of a property management agreement?

   a.   The budget
   b.   Allocation of costs
   c.   Owner's authority
   d.   Property description

21.4   What are the functions required of a property manager?

   a.   Managing the property and finances
   b.   Providing monthly reports to the owner
   c.   Any and all functions specified in the management agreement
   d.   Only those functions verbally discussed in the management interview

21.5   A manager may project a property's income based on

   a.   other rents in the immediate area.
   b.   the property's past performance and the current market.
   c.   the property owner's willingness to consistently upgrade the property's amenities.
   d.   the manager's experience and skills.

21.6   When budgeting expenses for a property, the manager does not typically include

   a.   variable and fixed expenses.
   b.   capital expenditures.
   c.   major renovations.
   d.   staff turnover.

21.7   Which of the following statements is true?

   a.   Resident property managers manage properties for multiple owners.
   b.   Property managers must specialize in only one type of property.
   c.   Building managers are employed to manage a single property.
   d.   Property management functions are the same regardless of the type of manager.

21.8 Property managers are required to submit reports to the owner

    a. monthly.
    b. quarterly.
    c. annually.
    d. as determined by the management agreement.

21.9 Property managers who handle property rentals are required to comply with

    a. fair housing laws.
    b. the Americans with Disabilities Act.
    c. the Equal Credit Opportunity Act.
    d. all of the above.

21.10 When financially maintaining property, managers must balance

    a. owner's goals with manager's skills.
    b. cost of services, owner's financial objectives, and tenant needs.
    c. owner's plans for the future, tenants' expectations, and manager's willingness to perform.
    d. operational costs and management salary.

21.11 When a property is leased, New York City and Buffalo's Multiple Dwelling Law requires

    a. tenants to install additional locks on doors.
    b. no more than two pets per apartment.
    c. automatic self-closing and self-locking doors.
    d. multiple generators for each building.

21.12 Which of the following is not a requirement for leased apartments in New York?

    a. Window guards for children under 16 years of age
    b. Guards on public hall windows
    c. Smoke and carbon monoxide detectors
    d. Secure mailboxes in buildings with three or more units

21.13 In New York, rent control applies

    a. to buildings with at least five units.
    b. to properties built after February 1947.
    c. until the unit is vacated.
    d. to buildings in any location.

21.14 In New York City, rent stabilization applies to

    a. communities under the Emergency Tenant Protection Act.
    b. buildings with three or more units built or renovated since 1974 with special tax benefits.
    c. properties with six or more units.
    d. communities that limit the size of the building covered.

21.15 The Rent Act of 2015

    a. changed the method for calculating rents on vacancy leases.
    b. administers rent control on properties within NYC.
    c. monitors rent stabilization on properties outside NYC.
    d. limits a tenant's income while leasing an apartment.

21.16 Effective gross income is determined by

    a.   subtracting the operating expenses from the potential gross income.
    b.   adding rents and revenues.
    c.   subtracting debt service and reserves from the net operating income.
    d.   subtracting uncollected rents, vacancies, and evictions from the potential gross income.

21.17 A basic responsibility of a landlord is to

    a.   provide leased space at market rental rates.
    b.   deliver a habitable property.
    c.   keep the rental space freshly painted.
    d.   refrain from entering the leased space at any time during the lease term.

21.18 How does a constructive eviction occur?

    a.   The landlord obtains a court order to remove the tenant from the property.
    b.   A court officer forceable removes the tenant from the property.
    c.   The landlord declares the tenant in default and takes possession of the property.
    d.   The tenant declares the landlord in default and vacates the property.

21.19 An actual eviction

    a.   requires a 60-day notice to the tenant.
    b.   can only occur when the tenant fails to pay rent.
    c.   requires a New York state court order to remove the tenant.
    d.   occurs when the tenant voluntarily moves out of the unit.

21.20 Variable expenses include

    a.   operating expenses.
    b.   administrative costs.
    c.   regular maintenance costs.
    d.   capital expenditures.

UNIT TWENTY-TWO TEST: REAL ESTATE MATH

22.1 A licensee sells 5/6 of an acre for $28,000, and receives a 6% commission. If she splits with her broker 50-50, what did she receive per square foot?

    a. $.023 / SF
    b. $.046 / SF
    c. $.037/ SF
    d. $.002 / SF

22.2 Lots in the South Hyde subdivision are selling for approximately $.50 / SF. The Grandersons want to build a 2,500 SF home on a 1.5 acre corner lot. The custom builder can build the home for $135 / SF. What will the completed property cost the Grandersons?

    a. $359,170
    b. $370,170
    c. $32,670
    d. $374,070

22.3 Ivan owned a 1/4 acre lot. He wanted to construct a 120' x 80' tennis court on the lot. What approximate percentage of the lot will be left over, if any, when he has completed the construction?

    a. 12%
    b. 88%
    c. 3%
    d. 15%

22.4 A developer wants to develop a 16-acre subdivision. He figures that the streets and common area will take up about 30% of this overall area. If the minimum lot size is to be 12,000 SF, how many lots can the developer have on this property?

    a. 42
    b. 487
    c. 40
    d. 57

22.5 A homeowner wants to insulate the new recreation room in her basement. She has been told that 3" of insulation would do the job. The walls are all 9' high and respectively measure 13', 13', 18', and 18' in length. How many rolls will she need if each roll measures 3" x 2' x 50'?

    a. 6
    b. 56
    c. 5
    d. 9

22.6 Maria plans to mulch the flower area around her house. The house measures 40' x 30', and she figures she'll mulch an area 8' in width to form a big rectangle all around the perimeter. What is the square footage of the resulting mulched area?

    a. 64 SF
    b. 2,576 SF
    c. 1,824 SF
    d. 1,376 SF

22.7. Calculate how many acres are in the Southeastern ¼ of the Western ½ of the Eastern ½ of Section 9.

    a. 20 acres
    b. 40 acres
    c. 60 acres
    d. 5 acres

22.8. Homeowner Savannah owns the Southeastern ¼ of the Southwestern ¼ of the Northwestern ¼ of Section 4. How many acres is that property?

    a. 4 acres
    b. 40 acres
    c. 10 acres
    d. 8 acres

22.9 Yard of Pizza has a percentage lease on its 1,800 SF space in Lincoln Shops. The terms are $1.40 / SF / month rent plus 1.75% of the store's gross income. If monthly sales averaged $41,500 last year, how much annual rent did Yard of Pizza pay last year?

    a. $38,955
    b. $43,420
    c. $30,240
    d. $21,525

22.10 A home appreciated 2 2/3% one year, then 5 1/5% the next year, then 7 1/4% the third year. What was the average appreciation over the 3-year period expressed as a decimal?

    a. 5.04%
    b. 15.24%
    c. 7.56%
    d. 4.8%

22.11 A homeowner paid $185,000 for a house three years ago. The house sells today for $239,000. How much has the property appreciated?

    a. 23 %
    b. 77 %
    c. 29 %
    d. 123 %

22.12 Seller Frank receives an offer of $290,000 on a property he listed at $308,000. How much is the offer as a percent of the listing price?

    a. 87%
    b. 91%
    c. 94%
    d. 106%

22.13 A property is being appraised using the income capitalization approach. Annually, it has potential gross income of $30,000, vacancy and credit losses of $1,500, and operating expenses of $10,000. Using a capitalization rate of 9%, what is the indicated value (to the nearest $1,000)?

    a. $206,000
    b. $167,000
    c. $222,000
    d. $180,000

22.14 If gross income on a property is $75,000, net income is $30,000 and the cap rate is 8%, the value of the property using the income capitalization method is

a. $625,000
b. $375,000
c. $3,750,000
d. $937,500

22.15 The roof of a property cost $16,000. The economic life of the roof is 20 years. Assuming the straight-line method of depreciation, what is the depreciated value of the roof after 3 years?

a. $16,000
b. $13,600
c. $18,400
d. $12,000

22.16 Lee had to report his home office depreciation for the tax year. He has a 2,500 SF home and a 500 SF office area. Lee paid $280,000 for his home, and he figures the land portion carries about 25% of that value. If Lee depreciates on a 39-year basis, how much can he write off for his home office depreciation per year?

a. $1,077
b. $1,436
c. $5,384
d. $2,108

22.17 A property is being appraised by the cost approach. The appraiser estimates that the land is worth $40,000 and the replacement cost of the improvements is $175,000. Total depreciation from all causes is $27,000. What is the indicated value of the property?

a. $148,000
b. $228,000
c. $162,000
d. $188,000

22.18 An apartment owner paid $500,000 for her complex 5 years ago. An appraiser at that time valued the land @ $100,000, but land has appreciated 25% over this period. The investor has used a 40-year straight-line depreciation method to depreciate the property. What is its current value using the cost approach?

a. $437,500
b. $462,500
c. $475,000
d. $546,875

22.19 An apartment building that recently sold for $400,000 had monthly gross rent receipts of $3,200. What is its monthly gross rent multiplier?

a. 80
b. .01
c. 110
d. 125

22.20 A rental home has monthly gross income of $1,100. A suitable gross income multiplier derived from market data is 14.7. What estimated sale price (to the nearest $1,000) is indicated?

a. $99,000
b. $162,000
c. $194,000
d. $173,000

22.21 Amy obtains a 75% LTV loan on her new $200,000 home with an annual interest rate of 6%. What is the first month's interest payment?

a. $900
b. $250
c. $1,000
d. $750

22.22 Emily has an interest-only home equity loan at an annual interest rate of 5.3%. If her monthly payment is $790, how much is the loan's principal balance (to the nearest $1,000)?

a. $222,000
b. $179,000
c. $95,000
d. $146,000

22.23 The loan officer at Sixth Fourth Bank tells Amanda she can afford a monthly payment of $1,000 on her new home loan. Assuming this is an interest-only loan, and the principal balance is $249,000, what interest rate is Amanda getting?

a. 4.82%
b. 5.03%
c. 6.25%
d. 3.69%

22.24 The Keegans obtain a fixed-rate amortized 30-year loan for $280,000 @ 6.25% interest. If the monthly payments are $1,724, how much interest do the Keegans pay in the second month of the loan?

a. $1,748.33
b. $1,456.95
c. $1,458.33
d. $1724.00

22.25 A lender offers the Greys two alternative loan packages for their $60,000 home equity application. One option is an interest-only loan for 5 years @ 6.5% interest with no points, and the second, a 6.25% interest-only loan for 5 years with 1 point to be paid at closing. Which loan will cost the Greys less total interest, and by how much?

a. The first option, by $150.
b. The second option, by 150.
c. The second option, by $750.
d. Both options charge the same amount of interest.

22.26 Jose recently obtained a 90% loan on his $410,000 home, and he had to pay $6,150 for points. How many points did he pay?

a. 1.4 points
b. 1.67 points
c. 2.48 points
d. 1.5 points

22.27 Mack is buying Roy's house for $500,000. Mack's loan amount is $325,000. He has agreed to pay 1.5 points at closing. How much will Mack pay for points?

a. $450
b. $4,500
c. $4,875
d. $7,500

22.28 A lender determines that a homebuyer can afford to borrow $130,000 on a mortgage loan. The lender requires an 80% loan-to-value ratio. How much can the borrower pay for a property and still qualify for this loan amount?

a. $138,000
b. $104,000
c. $162,500
d. $170,000

22.29 Home buyer Janet pays $1,600 / month for the interest-only loan on her new house. The loan's interest rate is 6.75%. If she obtained a 75% loan, what was the purchase price?

a. $313,333
b. $31,604
c. $379,259
d. $256,000

22.30 Loan applicant Taylor has an annual gross income of $76,000. How much will a lender allow Taylor to pay for monthly housing expense to qualify for a loan if the lender uses an income ratio of 30%?

a. $2,160
b. $1,900
c. $1,215
d. $4,433

22.31 An investor paid $80,000 for a lot and $600,000 to have an apartment building constructed on it. He has depreciated the property for the past 10 years on a 39-year straight-line schedule. If he sells the property this year and realizes $780,000, what is his capital gain?

a. $253,846
b. $274,000
c. $100,000
d. $179,000

22.32. A homeowner bought a house five years ago for $250,000. Since then, the homeowner has spent $2,000 to build a screened porch and has added a central air-conditioning system at a cost of $5,000. What is the homeowner's adjusted basis if the house is sold today?

a. $256,000
b. $257,000
c. $244,000
d. $245,000

22.33 A homeowner sold her house and had net proceeds of $265,000. Her adjusted basis in the home was $231,000. She immediately bought another house for $301,000. What was her capital gain?

a. $265,000
b. $36,000
c. $34,000
d. None

22.34 Debra bought a home for $120,000, paying $24,000 down and taking a mortgage loan of $96,000. The following year she had a new roof put on, at a cost of $5,000. What is Debra's adjusted basis in the house if she now sells the house for $150,000?

a. $29,000
b. $96,000
c. $101,000
d. $125,000

22.35 A certain investor wants an 11% return on investment from any real estate investment. A property priced at $360,000 has gross income of $60,000 and expenses of $22,000. Approximately how much too high or too low is the price of this property for the investor to obtain her desired return exactly?

a. $1,000 overpriced.
b. $8,000 underpriced.
c. $15,000 overpriced.
d. $16,000 underpriced.

22.36 An office building investor sees a listing of an office building which is priced at $2 million. He loves the property, but he knows he needs to make a return of at least 8% to satisfy his partners. If the building is 25,000 SF, rents for $10/SF per year, has 5% vacancy, and annual expenses of $70,000, should he buy it? What is his return?

a. No, since he will yield 2.00%.
b. Yes, since he will yield 8.375%.
c. Yes, since he will yield 8%.
d. Yes, since he will yield 9.125%.

22.37 Chad owns a small retail property that he inherited from his father. There are no mortgages or interest expenses connected with the property. Chad takes an annual cost recovery expense of $7,000. The property has a monthly gross income of $1,650 and monthly operating expenses of $600. Chad's taxable income from this property will be taxed at a rate of 30%. What is the tax liability for the year?

a. $1,680
b. $5,940
c. $2,100
d. $7,000

22.38 A property has a net income of $150,000, interest payments of $105,000, principal payments of $30,000, and annual cost recovery of $7,000. The property's tax rate is 28%. What is the property's annual tax on income?

a. $14,550
b. $40,040
c. $10,640
d. $2,240

22.39 An investor bought 4 oversized lots in order to subdivide. He paid $70,000 for the lots. After subdividing, the investor was able to sell each lot for $23,000. Excluding commissions and closing costs, what per cent profit did the investor realize?

a. 0%
b. 45%
c. 23.9%
d. 31.4%

22.40 A school district's tax rate is 10 mills. The school district's required revenue from taxes is $10,000,000. What is the tax base of the area?

a. $10,000,000
b. $100,000,000
c. $1,000,000,000
d. $100,000,000,000

22.41 A homeowner's residence has an assessed valuation of $140,000, and a market value of $170,000. The homestead exemption is $25,000. Tax rates for the property are 7 mills for schools; 3 mills for the city; 2 mills for the county; and 1 mill for the local community college. What is the homeowner's tax bill?

a. $1,495
b. $1,820
c. $1,150
d. $2,210

22.42 The village of Goodsprings has an annual budget requirement of $8,000,000 to be funded by property taxes. Assessed valuations are $400,000,000, and exemptions total $25,000,000. What must the tax rate be to finance the budget?

a. 2.00%
b. 2.13%
c. 1.32%
d. 21.33%

22.43 A property has sold for $127,000. The listing agreement calls for a commission of 7%. The listing broker and selling broker agree to share the commission equally. What will the listing agent receive if the agent is scheduled to get a 40% share from his broker?

a. $4,445
b. $3,556
c. $2,667
d. $1,778

22.44 Kevin, who works for selling broker Paul, sells a house listed by listing broker Adams. The house sells for $325,000. The co-brokerage split between Paul and Adams is 50-50. Kevin is on a 65% commission schedule with Paul. If the total commission rate is 6.5%, what is Kevin's commission?

a. $6,866
b. $5,282
c. $10,563
d. $13,731

22.45. A sale transaction closes on April 1, the ninety-first day of the tax year. The day of closing belongs to the seller. Real estate taxes for the year, not yet billed, are expected to be $3,150. According to the 365-day method, what should appear on the closing statement?

a. A debit to the buyer and credit to the seller for $2,364.62
b. A debit to the buyer and credit to the seller for $785.34
c. A credit to the buyer and debit to the seller for $785.34
d. A credit to the buyer and debit to the seller for $2,364.62

22.46 Alexis is buying Jack's house. The closing date (day belongs to seller) of the sale transaction is September 1 (day 244 of the year). Her loan has a monthly payment of $577.84, with $525 going to interest in the first month. At closing, Alexis must pre-pay interest for the period of Sept. 2-Sept. 30. Use the 365-day method for prorating. What is her prepaid interest amount?

a. $507.50
b. $525.00
c. $543.10
d. $558.58

22.47 A sale transaction on rental property closes on December 16. The landlord received the December rent of $1,380 on December 1. Assuming the closing day is the buyer's, and that the 365-day method is used for prorating, which of the following entries would appear on the settlement statement?

a. Debit seller $667.74.
b. Credit seller $1,380.00.
c. Debit buyer $712.26.
d. Credit buyer $712.26.

22.48 A home sells for $322,600 in Primm County. Here, transfer taxes are set at $1.00 per $500 of the sale price. Title insurance runs $450, and the attorney costs $550. The agent's commission is 7%, and the mortgage balance is $210,000. Annual real estate taxes are estimated to be $4,000, half of which will have to be charged to the seller. If the seller pays all of these expenses, what will she net at closing?

a. $86,873
b. $88,371
c. $81,372
d. $86,372

22.49 A farmer wants to net at least $5,000/acre on the sale of his 300-acre property. If he allows for 10% commissions and closing costs, and to allow for negotiating room, he wants to get 95% of the listing price as the selling price, what should his listing price be per acre?

a. $5,750
b. $5,882
c. $4,250
d. $5,848

22.50. The Wildes have purchased a $740,000 home. The land is worth 25%, and they insure the improvements @ 75% of their replacement value. If the Wildes suffer damage estimated at $500,000, and they have an 80% co-insurance clause, what will their recovery be from the policy?

a. Zero
b. $531,915
c. $500,000
d. $468,750

22.51 The Uptons carry a $140,000 property insurance policy which covers 75% of the replacement cost of their insurable property, valued at $190,000. They have an 80% co-insurance requirement in the policy. If the family incurs a $150,000 loss, what if any amount will the Uptons recover?

a. $159,999
b. $140,625
c. $140,000
d. $187,500

Section III: New York License Examination Sample Test

S 1. Applicants for a broker license must complete 152 hours of broker education coursework, _____ hours of which are the broker course.

    a.   22 ½
    b.   75
    c.   55
    d.   100

S 2. Licensees are required to meet continuing education requirements as part of their license maintenance every

    a.   year.
    b.   2 years.
    c.   3 years.
    d.   4 years.

S 3. The existence of an uncapped natural gas well on a property for sale must be disclosed to the property buyer

    a.   prior to accepting a purchase offer.
    b.   at transaction closing.
    c.   prior to transferring the property title.
    d.   prior to entering into a purchase contract.

S 4. Unlicensed assistants may not

    a.   collect rents.
    b.   place signs on property.
    c.   gather information for a property appraisal.
    d.   obtain loan status reports.

S 5. If a property seller fails to provide the buyer with a property condition statement, the buyer can

    a.   rescind the purchase contract.
    b.   file a civil lawsuit against the seller.
    c.   receive a monetary credit against the purchase.
    d.   require the seller to pay for repairs discovered after the closing.

S 6. An agency disclosure form

    a.   may be written or oral.
    b.   must be presented to prospective clients upon signing a listing agreement.
    c.   allows clients to give advanced consent to dual agency.
    d.   is to be presented only to a seller client.

S 7. Under which type of listing may a seller contract with multiple brokers?

    a.   Open listing
    b.   Exclusive right-to-sell
    c.   Exclusive agency
    d.   Net listing

S 8. A designated agent is a

   a. subagent.
   b. single agent.
   c. cooperative agent.
   d. dual agent.

S 9. The type of agency wherein the principal uses a power of attorney to empower the agent to perform actions the principal delegates to the agent is a

   a. universal agency.
   b. limited agency.
   c. special agency.
   d. general agency.

S 10. A farmer temporarily installs produce coolers in a leased farm stand in order to prevent spoilage. The coolers would be considered which of the following?

   a. Trade fixtures that are real property.
   b. Trade fixtures that are personal property.
   c. Temporary real property.
   d. Emblements.

S 11. Property can be converted from real to personal property and from personal property to real property by means of which processes, respectively?

   a. Assemblage and plottage.
   b. Application and dissolution.
   c. Severance and affixing.
   d. Planting and harvesting.

S 12. The highest form of ownership interest one can acquire in real estate is the

   a. legal life estate.
   b. conventional life estate.
   c. defeasible fee simple estate.
   d. absolute fee simple estate.

S 13. Who are the essential parties involved in an estate in trust?

   a. Owner, trustor and lawyer.
   b. Owner, trustor and trustee.
   c. Trustee, title company, and beneficiary.
   d. Trustor, trustee and beneficiary.

S 14. A property owner may sue for compensatory damages from

   a. an encroachment.
   b. an appurtenant easement.
   c. a gross easement.
   d. all of the above.

S 15. Which of the following is utilized when a government takes over the use of part or all of a landowner's property?

    a.   Easement by prescription
    b.   Encroachment
    c.   Power of eminent domain
    d.   Appurtenant easement

S 16. Lienors voluntarily lowering the priority of a junior lien is an action called

    a.   lien modification.
    b.   subordination.
    c.   inferiorizing the lien.
    d.   insubordination.

S 17. A mortgage lien is

    a.   Involuntary/general/superior
    b.   Involuntary/specific/junior
    c.   Voluntary/general/superior
    d.   Voluntary/specific/junior

S 18. When knowledge of ownership is acquired directly through inspecting a deed, this is called

    a.   research.
    b.   transfer notice.
    c.   constructive notice.
    d.   actual notice.

S 19. Which of the following is a means of voluntary title transfer?

    a.   Escheat
    b.   Public grant
    c.   Descent
    d.   Eminent domain

S 20. To accomplish an involuntary title transfer through adverse possession, one must

    a.   take possession of land as a result of the land owner's loan default.
    b.   exercise the right of eminent domain.
    c.   show claim of right as the reason.
    d.   claim ownership after non-hostile possession.

S 21. A deed clause that assures the grantor's ownership interest is called the

    a.   warrant of seisin.
    b.   warranty forever.
    c.   warrant of further assurance.
    d.   warranty against grantor's acts.

S 22. The purpose of RESPA is to

    a.   transfer residential property.
    b.   assure mortgage loans are awarded based strictly on the borrower's creditworthiness.
    c.   clarify and disclose costs associated with mortgage loans.
    d.   make mortgage lending more difficult for lenders.

S 23. Debits and credits are determined and prorated during the

   a. inspection process.
   b. settlement process.
   c. process of proving marketability of the title.
   d. valuation process.

S 24. Sam is selling his house to Charley for $350,000 after he has paid $3,000 for heating oil for 1 year in advance. The closing date is set for March 15. If the 30-day, 12-month method is used to prorate the heating oil cost, how much will Charlie owe for the heating oil? (Assume the oil will deplete on the last day of the year.)

   a. $2250.00
   b. $2138.63
   c. $133.43
   d. $2383.44

S 25. A duplicate set of property records which are maintained by a private company, such as a title company, are called a

   a. chain of title.
   b. cloud on the title.
   c. title plant.
   d. abstract of title.

S 26. A leasehold estate with a specific lease term is an

   a. estate for years.
   b. estate from period-to-period.
   c. estate at will.
   d. estate at sufferance.

S 27. One way a residential lease differs from commercial leases is that it has

   a. includes unimproved property to be developed with land ownership staying with the owner.
   b. longer lease terms.
   c. shorter lease terms and non-negotiable lease clauses.
   d. greater common area expenses.

S 28. A contract that may be rescinded is referred to as a _____ contract.

   a. valid.
   b. valid but unenforceable.
   c. void.
   d. voidable.

S 29. A sales contract is created by

   a. a seller signing a listing agreement with a real estate broker.
   b. a borrower signing a loan agreement with a mortgage lender.
   c. a buyer submitting an offer to purchase a seller's property.
   d. a seller accepting a purchaser's offer to purchase the seller's property.

S 30. In a contract for deed, the buyer actually gets the legal title to the property

    a.   when the seller agrees to the sale terms.
    b.   when the buyer takes possession of the property.
    c.   after the buyer makes the first installment payment of the purchase price.
    d.   when the buyer pays the balance owed on the purchase price.

S 31. In New York, a satisfaction of mortgage document must be recorded within

    a.   60 days of the mortgage payoff.
    b.   45 days of the request.
    c.   30 days of removal of the lien.
    d.   10 days of the last submitted loan payment.

S 32. Which of the following organizations is considered to be part of the secondary mortgage market?

    a.   Investment firms
    b.   Commercial banks
    c.   Savings and loans
    d.   Mortgage bankers

S 33. Which of the following statements is true?

    a.   RESPA prohibits discrimination in lending based on protected classes.
    b.   RESPA requires lenders to provide the Consumer Financial Protection Bureau Closing Disclosure 5 days before loan execution.
    c.   Borrowers of "federally-related loans" must obtain flood insurance if property is in designated flood-hazard area.
    d.   Under the ECOA, applicants who are denied a loan must be notified of the denial within 45 days.

S 34. Regulation Z implements which of the following laws?

    a.   Equal Credit Opportunity Act
    b.   Real Estate Settlement Procedures
    c.   Truth-in-Lending Simplification and Reform Act
    d.   National Flood Insurance Act

S 35. The extent to which a loan applicant's total assets exceed total liabilities is called his or her

    a.   loan-to-value ratio.
    b.   cash qualification.
    c.   income qualification.
    d.   net worth.

S 36. If a lender holds a borrower in default, which mortgage clause provides the borrower with the right to reinstatement by performing certain actions, usually paying overdue payments plus expenses to the lender?

    a.   Acceleration clause
    b.   Defeasance clause
    c.   Redemption clause
    d.   Escalation clause

S 37. A school built in an area zoned as residential is an example of

    a.   an amendment.
    b.   eminent domain.
    c.   a special exception.
    d.   an illegal nonconforming use.

S 38. Which of the following is not a goal of land use control?

    a.   Preserve property values
    b.   Justify property tax increases
    c.   Incorporate community consensus
    d.   Control growth

S 39. Which zone type includes sub-zones that stipulate the allowable types of structures?

    a.   Residential
    b.   Commercial
    c.   Agricultural
    d.   Industrial

S 40. John Chestnut is a commercial builder who is building a ten-unit apartment building within an area zoned for single-family residential homes. Which of the following statements is true?

    a.   The apartment building is an example of legal nonconforming use.
    b.   The apartment building will be allowed as a variance to the existing zoning ordinance.
    c.   The apartment building will be considered a special exception to the area's existing zoning ordinance.
    d.   The apartment building is an example of an illegal nonconforming use.

S 41. The design purpose of a planned unit development (PUD) is to

    a.   accommodate demand for services and infrastructure.
    b.   safeguard public health, safety and welfare.
    c.   achieve optimum space efficiency and maximize open space.
    d.   incorporate community consensus.

S 42. A county or municipal authority usually grants a certificate of occupancy for new construction only after

    a.   all contractors' work has been inspected.
    b.   all work has been completed for at least sixty days.
    c.   the construction conforms to building codes.
    d.   the tax assessor has valued the improvement.

S 43. The New York Smoke Detector Law requires

    a.   all smoke detectors to be hardwired.
    b.   smoke detectors to be powered by 5-year sealed batteries.
    c.   smoke alarms in new home construction to be hardwired with battery backup.
    d.   smoke detectors for sale to be powered by a 10-year removable battery.

S 44. The New York New Home Warranty applies to which of the following types of dwellings?

    a.   High-rise condominiums
    b.   Mobile homes
    c.   Apartment buildings with more than five stories
    d.   Single-family houses

S 45. A scaled drawing of a building and its components is called

    a.   a blueprint.
    b.   a rendering.
    c.   a sketch.
    d.   a plan.

S 46. The New York Home Improvement Law

   a.   applies only to improvements under $500.
   b.   imposes fines up to $10,000 for non-compliance.
   c.   requires contractors to provide a written contract for the home improvement work.
   d.   requires customers to deposit their payments for home improvement work into an escrow account to be
        transferred to the contractor when the work is completed.

S 47. Termite extermination and damage repair must be done by

   a.   a construction contractor.
   b.   an EPA employed contractor.
   c.   a pest control specialist.
   d.   an appropriately licensed professional.

S 48. The city recently installed a drainage ditch along the edge of Derrick's property line, resulting in a loss of
      value to Derrick's house. This is an example of

   a.   functional obsolescence.
   b.   economic obsolescence.
   c.   deterioration.
   d.   incurability.

S 49. Steps in which of the following include estimating total depreciation of the property?

   a.   Cost approach
   b.   Income approach
   c.   Sales comparison approach
   d.   Comparative market analysis

S 50. Which of the following is based on the principle of anticipation?

   a.   Cost approach
   b.   Income approach
   c.   Sales comparison approach
   d.   Comparative market analysis

S 51. In the cycle of supply and demand, what typically occurs immediately after construction has resulted in an
      oversupply?

   a.   Demand absorbs the supply
   b.   Cycle repeats itself
   c.   Construction stops
   d.   Market equilibrium

S 52. Plottage value is when

   a.   a property's form and use are consonant with the surrounding properties and uses.
   b.   a property's value is influenced by the values of neighboring properties.
   c.   division of a single property into smaller properties results in a higher total value.
   d.   conjoining adjacent properties create a combined value in excess of the values of the unassembled
        properties.

S 53. The only acceptable defense against being accused of an act of illegal discrimination is providing proof that

   a.   the offender was not familiar with the laws.
   b.   the offender was exercising freedom of speech.
   c.   the act was not intentional.
   d.   the act never happened.

S 54. Is sexual orientation a protected class?

   a.   Yes, but only under the New York City Human Rights Law
   b.   Yes, within sex as a protected class under Federal and New York laws
   c.   Yes, but only under Federal law
   d.   No, not under any anti-discrimination or human rights laws

S 55. Which law or ruling first included families with children as a protected class?

   a.   Civil Rights Act of 1968
   b.   Title VIII
   c.   Jones v. Mayer
   d.   Fair Housing Amendments Act of 1988

S 56. Barbara owns a two-family home in New York and occupies one of the units. Because she refuses to rent the other unit to single men, she is violating which law?

   a.   The New York Human Rights Law which protects gender
   b.   The New York City Human Rights Law which protects gender
   c.   The Fair Housing Amendments Act of 1988 which protects sex
   d.   No law because her two-unit home is exempt

S 57. Jones v. Mayer prohibits anti-discrimination exemptions based on

   a.   race.
   b.   sexual orientation.
   c.   religion.
   d.   national origin.

S 58. When a property owner tells a real estate agent not to show the property to buyers of certain ethnicities and the agent goes along with that, who is liable for the anti-discrimination law violation?

   a.   Owner
   b.   Agent
   c.   Neither owner nor agent
   d.   Both owner and agent

S 59. The Home Mortgage Disclosure Act

   a.   allows loan exemptions for specific protected classes.
   b.   applies only to loans for active military personnel.
   c.   requires lenders to report the locations of housing loans.
   d.   prohibits blockbusting.

S 60. Which NY agency enforces building, electrical, and zoning codes and standards?

   a.   Village Board of Trustees
   b.   Conservation Advisory Council
   c.   Planning Department
   d.   Department of Building

S 61. On which board do members serve terms that are equal to the number of members on the board?

    a. Village Board of Trustees
    b. Planning Board
    c. City Council
    d. Conservation Advisory Council

S 62. What is a land use that conflicts with current zoning but is authorized for certain reasons, including undue hardship to comply and minimal negative impact to leave it alone?

    a. Eminent condemnation
    b. Master plan exemption
    c. Variance
    d. Restriction

S 63. Municipality tax rates are based on

    a. homestead or non-homestead.
    b. taxing district.
    c. net deficit to be covered.
    d. all of the above.

S 64. Which of the following would NOT be handled by an independent insurance agent?

    a. Comparison shopping for policy terms and prices
    b. Providing loss prevention advice
    c. Helping with a loss or claim
    d. Offering coverage from a company who only employs its own agents

S 65. If a homeowner wanted coverage for his home and all structures on the property as well as coverage in case a visitor is injured on his property, what type of policy should he buy?

    a. Dwelling
    b. Monoline
    c. Package
    d. Liability

S 66. A limitation of coverage on an insurance policy is called a(n)

    a. deductible.
    b. condition.
    c. exclusion.
    d. package.

S 67. When should an agent only meet a client at the office?

    a. To prepare for an open house
    b. When the client is new
    c. To identify items that should be removed or secured prior to an open house or showing
    d. When no technology applications are available to track the agent's whereabouts

S 68. When conducting an open house, which of the following steps should an agent take?

    a. Allow all visitors and groups to wander freely through the house.
    b. Do not communicate with neighbors so as to avoid problems.
    c. Have visitors follow the agent through the house.
    d. Have the office call the agent at a specified time.

S 69. Which of the following is not a good idea when protecting an agent's safety?

    a.   Advertise when a house is vacant prior to showing it.
    b.   Wear practical clothing.
    c.   Know self-defense strategies.
    d.   Limit personal information shared with clients.

S 70. The New York STaR program allows homeowners to apply for permanent reduction in

    a.   annual property taxes.
    b.   school taxes.
    c.   veteran owned property taxes.
    d.   none of the above.

S 71. The veterans cold war exemption is provided to veterans who served

    a.   in a war zone.
    b.   from September 1945 to December 1991.
    c.   in a combat zone.
    d.   from January 1956 to December 2000.

S 72. New York special tax exemptions and reductions do not include

    a.   veteran homeowners.
    b.   agricultural land.
    c.   the disabled.
    d.   the elderly.

S 73. If a property's assessed value is $150,000 with a tax rate of 50 mills, what is the resulting tax bill?

    a. $5,000
    b. $1,500
    c. $7,500
    d. $3,000

S 74. One mill equals

    a.   1 cent.
    b.   1/2 cent.
    c.   1/10 cent.
    d.   1 dollar.

S 75. Which of the following sets up covenants, conditions, and restrictions for condominium residents?

    a.   New York Condominium Act
    b.   Real Property Act
    c.   Condominium Owners Association By-laws
    d.   State Fair Housing laws

S 76. When rental units are converted to condominiums, which of the following are permanently exempt from eviction?

    a.   Residents 50 years and older
    b.   Disabled tenants
    c.   Non-purchasers
    d.   All existing tenants

S 77. Who determines who may occupy cooperative units?

    a.   Shareholders
    b.   The financial nonprofit corporation
    c.   Board of Directors
    d.   Members of the co-op

S 78. Dividing the tenant's rentable area by the building's gross rentable area determines

    a.   the tenant's usable area.
    b.   the tenant's proportionate share of operational cost increases.
    c.   the tenant's loss factor.
    d.   the add-on factor which is reciprocal of the loss factor.

S 79. A commercial tenant's annual rent is calculated based on the

    a.   space's usable area.
    b.   building's gross rentable area.
    c.   space's rentable area.
    d.   the number of tenants in the building.

S 80. The formula for determining the return on investment

    a.   income – operating expenses ÷ investment price.
    b.   rate of return x value or price.
    c.   cash flow ÷ cash invested.
    d.   market value – current debt principal.

S 81. In a commercial gross lease,

    a.   a single tenant pays rent plus all operating expenses and taxes.
    b.   a tenant pays a fixed rent and the landlord pays operating expenses.
    c.   the landlord does not need to provide operating services.
    d.   the rent amount is based on the gross income generated by the tenant.

S 82. Purchase price plus improvement value minus depreciation is used as the formula to calculate

    a.   a property's adjusted basis.
    b.   a property's depreciation recovery amount.
    c.   a property's passive income amount.
    d.   a property's depreciable basis.

S 83. The total purchase price to include realtor commission, legal fees, appraisals, etc. minus land value is used as the formula to calculate

    a.   a property's adjusted basis.
    b.   a property's depreciation recovery amount.
    c.   a property's passive income amount.
    d.   a property's depreciable basis.

S 84. IRS code 1031 includes time limits for designating a replacement property and closing on the purchase of the replacement property. What happens if the time limits are not met?

    a.   The exchange will be denied.
    b.   The involved parties will be fined.
    c.   The entire capital gain will be taxed.
    d.   The gain tax will be deferred.

S 85. A mortgage broker does not

    a.   negotiate residential mortgage loans.
    b.   solicit mortgage loans for others.
    c.   issue letters of loan commitment.
    d.   handle loan applications.

S 86. Which of the following statements is true?

    a.   Mortgage brokers service mortgage loans.
    b.   Mortgage brokers are responsible for analyzing a borrower's creditworthiness.
    c.   Mortgage brokers do not establish a borrower's preapproval for a loan.
    d.   Mortgage brokers help gather documents for a loan application, including 5 years of the borrower's tax returns.

S 87. To qualify as a mortgage broker in New York, one must

    a.   obtain an umbrella insurance policy.
    b.   provide proof of 5 years of NY residency.
    c.   renew the license and registration semi-annually.
    d.   obtain a NY mortgage broker surety bond.

S 88. Property managers have a _____ relationship with the property owner.

    a. non-binding
    b. partnership
    c. fiduciary
    d. subagency

S 89. One of the property manager's fundamental responsibilities is

    a. obtaining construction loans for the principal.
    b. financial reporting to the principal.
    c. finding a buyer for the property.
    d. maintaining good standing in a managers' professional association.

S 90. What are the three kinds of maintenance a manager has to carry out for a managed property?

    a. Constructive, deconstructive, and reconstructive
    b. Routine, preventive, and corrective
    c. Scheduled, planned, and improvised
    d. Emergency, elective, and optional

S 91. Mr. Ignacio is employed as a property manager for Fairview Apartments. The property owner requires Mr. Ignacio to live on site. What type of property manager is Mr. Ignacio?

    a.   Individual manager
    b.   Building manager
    c.   Resident manager
    d.   Special manager

S 92. Jennifer advised her clients they needed to paint their living room before showing the property. The walls of these rooms were all 8' high. The wall lengths were 14', 18', 16', and 18'. If a gallon of paint covers 200 SF, how many whole gallons would the home sellers have to buy?

a. 1
b. 2
c. 3
d. 6

S 93. An investor just purchased a rectangular 2-acre retail lot for $250 a frontage foot. If she paid $100,000 total, what was the depth of the lot?

a. 400'
b. 250
c. 871'
d. 218'

S 94. Andra can afford to spend $5,000 in closing costs to refinance her home. The lender quotes closing costs of $800 plus 2 points. The house appraised out at $240,000, and she can get an 80% loan. Can Annika afford to refinance?

a. No, she is short by $64.
b. No, she is short by $1,600.
c. Yes, with $360 left over.
d. Yes, she in fact breaks even.

S 95. A lender offers an investor a maximum 70% LTV loan on the appraised value of a property. If the investor pays $230,000 for the property, and this is 15% more than the appraised value, how much will the investor have to pay as a down payment?

a. $93,150
b. $79,350
c. $90,000
d. $69,000

S 96. A house is being appraised using the sales comparison approach. The house has three bedrooms, two bathrooms, and a patio. The appraiser selects a comparable house that has three bedrooms, 2.5 bathrooms, and no patio. The comparable house just sold for $500,000. A half-bath is valued at $5,000, and a patio at $1,000. Assuming all else is equal, what is the adjusted value of the comparable?

a. $500,000
b. $504,000
c. $496,000
d. $506,000

S 97. A family purchased a $90,000 lot to build a custom home. At the date of closing, the lot was assessed at $84,550 and the tax rate was $1.91 / $100 assessed valuation. When they completed the home, the assessment increased by $235,000 to include the new construction. If the monthly tax escrow is based on the assessed value, what will the monthly tax escrow be?

a. $517
b. $6096
c. $508
d. $367

S 98. The James family purchased a home for $180,000 five years ago and obtained an 80% LTV loan. Now the property has appreciated 25%. In addition, the loan has been paid down $11,000. What is the James's current equity in the home?

    a. $47,000
    b. $81,000
    c. $45,000
    d. $92,000

S 99. George and Mary have owned a rental house for 10 years. They bought it for $240,000 and estimated the land value @ 25%. If the property is depreciated on a 39-year schedule, and appreciation totals 50% over the period, what is their gain if they sell the property today?

    a. $159,230
    b. $166,150
    c. $181,538
    d. $120,000

S 100. Adelpha's home is valued at $250,000. She has insurance coverage of $160,000 with an 80% co-insurance clause. If Adelpha has a damage claim amounting to $100,000, how much will she receive from her policy?

    a. $32,000
    b. $60,000
    c. $80,000
    d. $100,000

Section IV: Answer Key

UNIT ONE TEST: LICENSE LAW AND REGULATIONS

1.1 (b) To maintain professional standards
The purpose of licensing real estate practitioners is to protect the general public's welfare, safety, and health; to prevent economic loss resulting from dishonest and incompetent brokerage practices for a fee or other valuable consideration; and to maintain high professional standards.

1.2 (d) Broker, associate broker, salesperson
The three types of licenses for real estate practitioners are broker, associate broker, and salesperson. The associate broker is a licensed broker who chooses to work under the name and supervision of a licensed broker, just as a salesperson does.

1.3 (c) Supervision, guidance, training
Supervision, guidance, training of affiliated licensees is a responsibility of the sponsoring broker, not a salesperson.

1.4 (a) 18
Applicants for a salesperson license must be at least 18 years old.

1.5 (c) 77
Applicants for a real estate salesperson license must successfully complete 77 hours of salesperson education coursework and pass the end-of-course exams.

1.6 (c) He must have the Secretary of State determine whether his conviction bars or does not bar his licensure
Since Antoine is a convicted criminal, he is not eligible for a real estate license unless the Secretary of State deems the conviction is not a bar to his licensure.

1.7 (b) 75
Applicants for a broker's license must complete a 152-hour broker education course, 77 hours of which are the salesperson course and 75 hours of which are the broker course.

1.8 (b) 2 years of salesperson experience.
An applicant for a broker's license must have 2 years of experience as a licensed salesperson or 3 years of experience in general real estate field or a combination of both.

1.9 (b) Negotiating residential loans that are secured by a mortgage
An individual who negotiates residential loans that are secured by a mortgage does not need to be licensed as a real estate professional. However, one who negotiates commercial loans that are secured by a mortgage do need to be licensed.

1.10 (b) An attorney acting as a broker
A New York licensed attorney who is acting as a broker and supervising salespersons must obtain a real estate broker license.

1.11 (b) The licensee's sponsoring broker
The licensee holds the pocket card and must always carry it with him/her. However, the sponsoring broker holds the license itself and can choose to display it within the brokerage office.

1.12 (a) File a change of association notice with the Department of State
When a salesperson's association with the current sponsoring broker is terminated, the current broker should return the license to the salesperson, file a termination notice with the DOS, and collect all client and transaction related

documents from the salesperson. Filing a change of association notice with the DOS is the responsibility of the new sponsoring broker.

1.13 (b) Reciprocity agreement
Applicants seeking a nonresident license in NY are not required to take additional education or testing because states with reciprocity agreements have similar licensure requirements. For licensure under mutual recognition, the state recognizes the licensee's education and experience in the other state but may still require additional education to compensate for fewer hours required by the other state and may require the applicant to pass the law section of the NY licensing exam.

1.14 (c) Maintain a place of business in NY and in home state
Applicants seeking a nonresident license in NY must meet NY's licensing and exam requirements and must file an irrevocable consent form. However, if the applicant maintains a place of business in the home state, the applicant does not need to maintain one in NY.

1.15 (d) dual licensure.
When a broker holds multiple NY licenses or a salesperson holds licenses under multiple brokers, it is called dual licensure.

1.16 (b) 2 years.
Licensure periods for NY real estate licenses is 2 years.

1.17 (d) 90%
Continuing education can be completed in a classroom with a minimum 90% attendance requirement or online distance learning, or a combination of both.

1.18 (c) 22 ½
22 ½ hours of continuing education must be completed every 2-year licensure period.

1.19 (b) fair housing.
Continuing education for NY real estate licensees must include 3 hours of fair housing or discrimination or both in the sale or rental of real property.

1.20 (c) the licensee retaking the state licensure exam.
Licenses must be renewed every 2 years. Failure to renew the license within 2 years of the expiration date results in the licensee having to retake the state licensure exam.

1.21 (c) Secretary of State.
Each branch office must hold its own license separate from the main office license. It must be supervised by the broker owner and approved by the Secretary of State.

1.22 (b) Manager license
Branch offices must be supervised by the broker owner but can be operated by an associate broker under the broker owner's supervision if the associate broker has a manager license.

1.23 (b) All email ads must include the brokerage name and identify the advertiser as a real estate broker.
Initial emails are to include all advertising required information, such as the name of the brokerage, but subsequent emails do not need to include all of this same information.

1.24 (c) Ads that include team names must also include the word "team" in the name.
Ads that include team names may or may not include the team members' names, but when they do, they should include both the licensed members and the unlicensed members of the team. The ad must include the word "team" in the team's name. Nicknames are allowed in ads.

1.25 (a) the listing broker's consent is required.
When advertising another broker's exclusive listing, the consent of the listing broker is required, the listing broker's name must be conspicuously included in the ad, and the ad must include words that identify the listing broker.

1.26 (b) Broker Dan hired unlicensed Sue to relocate tenants.
Relocating tenants is an activity that requires a real estate license. When Dan hired unlicensed Sue to perform an activity that requires licensure, he violated NY license law and is subject to receiving a sanction for the violation.

1.27 (c) is paid on a per-transaction basis.
Anyone being paid om a per-transaction basis must be licensed. Performing activities that require licensure when the individual is not licensed is a violation of NY license law.

1.28 (b) Seller
The Property Condition Disclosure Act requires sellers to complete a property condition disclosure statement and provide it to the buyer prior to the buyer signing a contract for the purchase of the property.

1.29 (c) When a property condition disclosure statement is provided to the buyer, there is no need for a property inspection.
A property condition disclosure statement is no substitute for a property inspection and no warranty for the property's condition.

1.30 (c) A transfer to the owner's unrelated roommate
Transfers to relatives, beneficiaries, and lenders are all exempt from the requirement to provide a property condition disclosure statement. However, transferring the property to a roommate who is not a relative would require the disclosure statement to be completed and provided to the roommate buyer.

UNIT TWO TEST: LAW OF AGENCY AND DISCLOSURE

2.1 (b) client.
The principal in a real estate transaction is the party who hires the agent. It can be the seller, buyer, landlord, or tenant who becomes the client once the agent is hired.

2.2 (a) Universal agency
With a universal agency, the principal utilizes a power of attorney to empower the agent to perform any and all actions legally delegated to an agency representative.

2.3 (d) General agency
In a general agency, the principal delegates ongoing tasks and duties to the agent within a particular business or enterprise. This agency may include the agent's authority to enter into contracts on behalf of the principal.

2.4 (c) Special
Real estate brokerage is typically based on special agency wherein the principal hires the broker to procure a buyer or seller with the relationship terminating when the objective is achieved.

2.5 (a) an implied agency
An implied agency is intentionally or unintentionally established by implication when the involved parties behave as though there is an agreement even though one has not been specifically discussed. An implied agency obligates the agent to fiduciary duties and standards of care for which the agent can be held liable for failure to fulfill.

2.6 (c) dual agent.
A dual agent represents both the buyer and seller in the same transaction as long as both parties provide written informed consent for the agency.

2.7 (d) A designated agent works as a single agent within the broker's dual agency.
Designated sales agents work for the same broker who is engaged in a consented dual agency. Each agent is designated to represent either the buyer or the seller as a single agent.

2.8 (b) Confidentiality
An agent owes a customer the duties of honesty and fair dealing, reasonable care and skill, and proper disclosure. The agent does not owe a customer confidentiality.

2.9 (d) Confidentiality
An agent has the duty of confidentiality to the client and must hold the client's personal and business information in confidence during the agency relationship and after the relationship terminates.

2.10 (a) Compensation
A principal owes the agent availability, information, and compensation.

2.11 (a) Agents can be held liable for breaching fiduciary duties to a client.
Agents can be held liable for a breach of duty and can face forfeiture of any earned compensation, a lawsuit by the client for damages, a recission of the listing agreement, and disciplinary sanctions.

2.12 (b) negligent misrepresentation.
Negligent misrepresentation occurs when an agent fails to disclose facts the agent is unaware of but should have known.

2.13 (c) practices that create monopolies.
The Clayton Act of 1914 prohibits practices that create monopolies, such as price discrimination against competing companies, conditioning sales on exclusive dealing, mergers and acquisitions that reduce competition, and serving on board of directors for competing companies.

2.14 (a) market allocation.
Market allocation occurs when competing brokerages agree to divide a market area and restrict their competitive activities to their own designated market area. Market allocation is an illegal activity and an antitrust violation.

2.15 (d) the sale of one product or service is contingent upon the sale of another, less desirable product or service.
Tie-in agreements restrict competition and limit consumers' freedom by making the sale of one product or service contingent upon the sale of another, less desirable product or service. Tie-in agreements are illegal and antitrust violations.

2.16 (b) fines up to $350,000.
Antitrust violations by an individual can result in fines up to $350,000, up to 3 years in prison, both fines and prison, or other penalties imposed by the DOJ and the FTC.

2.17 (c) separate DOJ fines.
When a business entity violates antitrust laws, the entity can be penalized by fines up to $10,000,000, separate DOJ fines, or a combination of both types of fines. Unlike individuals who violate the laws, business entities cannot be sent to prison, so their fines are much higher than an individual's fines.

2.18 (c) a single agent.
Single agents represent one party in a transaction.

2.19 (c) Brokerage without subagency
In a brokerage without subagency, the listing broker splits the commission with the broker who provides a buyer without a subagency relationship, thereby eliminating the seller's liability for the agent's actions.

2.20 (d) subagent.
Subagents are agents of the broker who is the agent of the client. Subagents work with the listing broker to procure a buyer for the property.

2.21 (d) results in a conflict of interest.
Because a broker in a dual agency relationship represents both the buyer and the seller, the broker is unable to put both clients' interest above the others, thereby resulting in a conflict of interest for the broker.

2.22 (a) full disclosure.
An agent in a dual agency relationship still owes each client the duties of skill, care, diligence, obedience, and accounting. However, the agent does not owe either client the duties of confidentiality or full disclosure.

2.23 (b) agent's undivided loyalty.
Dual agencies require the written informed consent of all parties, an agency disclosure to all parties, and confidentiality of each party's pricing strategy and other designated information. The relationship does not include the agent's undivided loyalty as the agent cannot give both clients undivided loyalty.

2.24 (b) Barry's representation changes from a single agency to a dual agency, requiring both parties' consent.
Barry is experiencing an in-house sale wherein he is the listing broker whose salesperson has found and is representing a buyer. The result is that a dual agency has been created. Consequently, Barry must obtain voluntary written consent from both parties.

2.25 (a) designated single agents.
When a broker in a dual agency designates one salesperson to represent the seller and another salesperson to represent the buyer, the broker remains the dual agent and the two salespersons become designated agents in single agencies.

2.26 (d) Net
Net listings are illegal in New York and most other states because they not only create a conflict of interest for the broker, but the violate the broker's fiduciary duties to the client by not putting the client's interests first.

2.27 (a) Exclusive right-to-sell
Exclusive right-to-sell listings are the most commonly used listings because they are the only listing type that guarantees the broker is paid commission regardless of who actually sells the property, as long as it is sold during the listing term.

2.28 (a) Exclusive right-to-sell
Exclusive right-to-sell listings are the most commonly used listings because they are the only listing type that guarantees the broker is paid commission regardless of who actually sells the property, as long as it's sold during the listing term.

2.29 (c) Open listing
Open listings are not favored by brokers because they allow sellers to contract with multiple brokers so that no one broker has an assurance of compensation for his or her marketing efforts.

2.30 (c) The listing broker and the cooperating broker who procured the buyer
MLS allows multiple brokers to cooperate in the property sale in exchange for a share of the commission for the broker who finds the buyer.

2.31 (a) Automatic extension clause
While the term of the broker's employment is required in the listing agreement, automatic extension clauses in exclusive listings are prohibited in NY.

2.32 (b) Agency disclosures must be presented to prospective clients after a listing agreement is signed.
Agency disclosures forms must be presented to prospective clients or customers at the first substantive meeting.

2.33 (c) residential property with five units.
Agency disclosures are required for residential property with four or fewer units. A property with five or more units does not require an agency disclosure.

2.34 (c) When all parties to the transaction consent
Brokers may accept compensation from more than one party only if all parties consent.

2.35 (c) 3 years.
All records pertaining to a transaction must be maintained for at least 3 years.

2.36 (a) seller.
Property condition statements are to be completed by the seller with no help from the seller's agent.

2.37 (b) each year
NYC requires landlords to annually inspect for lead hazards when children under 6 years are involved in the rental.

2.38 (c) 2 years
When requested in writing, the seller is to provide a buyer with 2-years heating and cooling statements for one or two-family properties.

2.39 (a) when the property is listed and again before closing or lease signing.
Lead disclosures are to be made at the time of property listing and again before the closing or lease signing.

2.40 (c) year.
Landlords are to provide prospective tenants with the rental unit or building's bedbug infestation history for the past year, using state required form.

UNIT THREE TEST: ESTATES AND INTERESTS

3.1 (a) Wells, driveways, and signs on a parcel of land.
The legal concept of real estate encompasses land and all man-made structures that are "permanently" attached to the land. The phrase "permanently attached" refers primarily to one's intention in attaching the item. Obviously, very few if any man-made structures can be permanently attached to the land in the literal sense. But if a person constructs a house with the intention of creating a permanent dwelling, the house is considered real estate. By contrast, if a camper affixes a tent to the land with the intention of moving it to another camp in a week, the tent would not be considered real estate.

3.2 (a) enjoyed by the owner of a property.
This group of rights includes the right to Possess, Use, Transfer, Encumber, and Exclude others from using the property. (Remember: "PUTEE") Transfer rights include the right to sell, rent, donate, assign, or bequeath. The owner may also encumber the item by mortgaging it as collateral for debt.

3.3 (b) Any item of property that is not definable as real property.
Personal property is any owned item which is not real estate, and the rights associated with owning the personal property item. Items of personal property are also called chattels or personalty.

3.4 (d) Yes. The drones infringe on his air rights.
Air rights apply to the space above the surface boundaries of the parcel, as delineated by imaginary vertical lines extended to infinity. Since the advent of aviation, property owners' air rights have been curtailed to allow aircraft to fly over one's property provided the overflights do not interfere with the owner's use and enjoyment of the property. The issue of violation of air rights for the benefit of air transportation is an ongoing battle between aircraft owners, airlines, airports, and nearby property owners.

3.5 (c) Navigable lakes, seas, and oceans.
Littoral rights concern properties abutting bodies of water that are not moving, such as lakes and seas. Owners of properties abutting a navigable, non-moving body of water enjoy the littoral right of use, but do not own the water nor the land beneath the water. The legal premise underlying the definition of littoral rights is that a lake or sea is a navigable body of water, therefore, public property owned by the state. By contrast, a body of water entirely contained within the boundaries of an owner's property is not navigable. In such a case, the owner would own the water as well as unrestricted rights of usage.

3.6 (a) the high water mark of the body of water at the shoreline.
Ownership extends to the high-water mark of the body of water. The low water mark would imply that the owner owned the water itself at times of high water levels!

3.7 (c) Streams and rivers.

Riparian rights concern properties abutting moving water such as streams and rivers. If a property abuts a stream or river, the owner's riparian rights are determined by whether the water is navigable or not navigable. If the property abuts a non-navigable stream, the owner enjoys unrestricted use of the water and owns the land beneath the stream to the stream's midpoint. If the waterway in question is navigable, the waterway is considered to be a public easement. In such a case, the owner's property extends t the water's edge as opposed to the midpoint of the waterway.

3.8 (b) An item of personal property that has been converted to real property.

A personal property item that has been converted to real property by attachment to real estate is called a fixture. Typical examples are chandeliers, toilets, water pumps, septic tanks, and window shutters. The owner of real property inherently owns all fixtures belonging to the real property. When the owner sells the real property, the buyer acquires rights to all fixtures.

3.9 (a) the owner originally intended to remove it after a period of time.

One's original intention can override the test of movability in determining whether an item is a fixture or not. If someone attached an item to real property, yet intended to remove it after a period of time, the article may be deemed personal property. If a person intended an article to be a fixture, even though the item is easily removable, the article may be deemed a fixture. For example, an apartment renter installs an alarm system, fully intending to remove the system upon lease expiration. Here, the alarm system would be considered personal property.

3.10 (c) Fifty percent of the estate consisting of the indivisible whole of the real property.

An undivided interest is an owner's fractional interest in an entire (undivided) estate, but not in a physical portion of the real property itself. An owner who has an undivided equal interest with another cannot exercise exclusive rights over a portion of the real estate, which is an indivisible whole.

3.11 (a) an estate in land.

Interests are principally distinguished by whether they include possession. If the interest-holder enjoys the right of possession, the party is considered to have an estate in land, or, familiarly an estate. Freehold and leasehold estates in land are further distinguished by whether the duration of the owner's rights can be determined.

3.12 (c) a freehold estate.

In a freehold estate, the duration of the owner's rights cannot be determined: the rights may endure for a lifetime, for less than a lifetime, or for generations beyond the owner's lifetime. By contrast, leasehold estates have expirations.

3.13 (d) that the estate is limited by a lease term.

A leasehold estate is distinguished by its specific duration, as represented by the lease term. Further, leasehold tenants only enjoy limited property rights: use; temporary possession, and limited exclusion.

3.14 (d) Fee simple defeasible.

The defeasible fee estate is perpetual, provided the usage conforms to stated conditions. Essential characteristics are that the property must be used for a certain purpose or under certain conditions, and, if the use changes or if prohibited conditions are present, the estate reverts to the previous grantor of the estate.

3.15 (c) An ordinary life estate.

A life estate is limited in duration to the life of the owner or other named person. Upon the death of the owner (ordinary life estate) or other named individual (pur autre vie life estate), the estate passes to the original owner (a reversionary interest) or another named party (a remainder interest). Thus with the life estate, the owner enjoys full ownership rights during the estate period, and holders of the future interest own either a reversionary or a remainder interest.

3.16 (b) The boat, house, and motorcycle.

Separate property consists of: property owned by either spouse at the time of the marriage; property acquired by either spouse through inheritance or gift during the marriage; property acquired with separate-property funds; and income from separate property. Community property consists of all other property earned or acquired by either party during the marriage. A spouse owns separate property free and clear of claims by the other spouse. He or she can transfer it without the other spouse's signature. Upon the death of the separate property owner, the property passes to heirs by will or laws of descent. Community property cannot be transferred or encumbered without the signatures of both spouses. Upon the death of either spouse, half of the deceased's community property passes to the surviving spouse, and the other half passes to the decedent's heirs.

3.17 (a) the tenant makes, and landlord accepts, regular rent payments.
In an estate from period-to-period, also called a periodic tenancy, the tenancy period automatically renews as long as the tenant pays rent in a timely manner and the landlord accepts it. At the end of a tenancy period, if the landlord accepts another regular payment of rent, the leasehold is considered to be renewed for another period. A conveyance of leased property does not cancel a leasehold interest.

3.18 (a) an estate at sufferance.
In an estate at sufferance, a tenant occupies the premises without consent of the landlord or other legal agreement with the landlord. Usually such an estate involves a tenant who fails to vacate at the expiration of the lease, continuing occupancy without any right to do so. For example, a tenant violates the provisions of a lease and is evicted. The tenant protests and refuses to leave despite the eviction order.

3.19 (b) Estate from period to period.
In an estate from period-to-period, also called a periodic tenancy, the tenancy period automatically renews for an indefinite period of time, subject to timely payment of rent. At the end of a tenancy period, if the landlord accepts another regular payment of rent, the leasehold is considered to be renewed for another period.

3.20 (a) tenancy in severalty.
If a single party owns the fee or life estate, the ownership is a tenancy in severalty. Synonyms are sole ownership, ownership in severalty, and estate in severalty.

3.21 (c) tenancy in common.
The tenancy in common, also known as the estate in common, is the most common form of co-ownership when the owners are not married (though tenants in common can be married). The defining characteristics are: two or more owners; identical rights; interests individually owned; electable ownership shares; no survivorship; and no unity of time. With "identical rights", co-tenants share an indivisible interest in the estate, i.e., all have equal rights to possess and use the property subject to the rights of the other co-tenants.

3.22 (a) Parties must acquire respective interests at the same time.
To create a joint tenancy, all owners must acquire the property at the same time, use the same deed, acquire equal interests, and share in equal rights of possession. These are referred to as the four unities.

3.23 (b) cannot will their interest to a party outside the tenancy. The survivorship feature of joint tenancy presents an advantage to tenancy in common, in that interests pass without probate proceedings. On the other hand, joint tenants relinquish any ability to will their interest to parties outside of the tenancy.

3.24 (c) Legal life estate.
A legal life estate is created by state law as opposed to being created by a property owner's agreement. The focus of a legal life estate is defining and protecting the property rights of surviving family members upon the death of the husband or wife.

3.25 (c) If they are married.
Tenancy by the entireties is a form of ownership reserved exclusively for husband and wife. It features survivorship, equal interests, and limited exposure to foreclosure. In some states it now applies to same-sex couples.

UNIT FOUR TEST: LIENS AND EASEMENTS

4.1 (a) They involve the property that contains the easement and a non-owning party. An easement is an interest in real property that gives the holder the right to use portions of the legal owner's real property in a defined way. One cannot own an easement over one's own property. Easement rights may apply to a property's surface,

subsurface, or airspace, but the affected area must be defined. An easement may be affirmative, allowing a use, such as a right-of-way, or negative, prohibiting a use, such as an airspace easement that prohibits one property owner from obstructing another's ocean view.

4.2 (d) An easement appurtenant.

An easement appurtenant gives a property owner a right of usage to portions of an adjoining property owned by another party. The property enjoying the usage right is called the dominant tenement, or dominant estate. The property containing the physical easement itself is the servient tenement, since it must serve the easement use.

4.3 (c) easement by necessity.

An easement by necessity is an easement appurtenant granted by a court of law to a property owner because of a circumstance of necessity, most commonly the need for access to a property. Since property cannot be legally landlocked, or without legal access to a public thoroughfare, a court will grant an owner of a landlocked property an easement by necessity over an adjoining property that has access to a thoroughfare.

4.4 (b) an unauthorized physical intrusion of one property into another.

An encroachment is the unauthorized, physical intrusion of one owner's real property into that of another. Examples of encroachments are: a tree limb extending into the neighbor's property, violating his or her airspace; a driveway extending beyond the lot line onto the neighbor's land; and a fence built beyond the property line.

4.5 (c) a trespasser has been using an owner's property for a certain period with the owner's knowledge but without permission.

If someone uses another's property as an easement without permission for a statutory period of time and under certain conditions, a court order may give the user the easement right by prescription, regardless of the owner's desires. For a prescriptive easement order to be granted, the following circumstances must be true: the use has been occurring without permission or license; the owner knows or is presumed to have known of the use; and the use has been generally uninterrupted over the statutory prescriptive period.

4.6 (d) how a property may be used and what improvements may be built on it.

A deed restriction is a limitation imposed on a buyer's use of a property by stipulation in the deed of conveyance or recorded subdivision plat. A deed restriction may apply to a single property or to an entire subdivision. A developer may place restrictions on all properties within a recorded subdivision plat. Subsequent re-sales of properties within the subdivision are thereby subject to the plat's covenants and conditions.

4.7 (c) the creditor's claim against the property as collateral security for the loan.

A lien is a creditor's claim against personal or real property as security for a debt of the property owner. If the owner defaults, the lien gives the creditor the right to force the sale of the property to satisfy the debt. For example, a homeowner borrows $5,000 to pay for a new roof. The lender funds the loan in exchange for the borrower's promissory note to repay the loan. At the same time, the lender places a lien on the property for $5,000 as security for the debt. If the borrower defaults, the lien allows the lender to force the sale of the house to satisfy the debt.

4.8 (a) Payment of the debt that is the subject of the lien and recording of the satisfaction.

A lien terminates on payment of the debt and recording of documents. Payment of the debt and recording of the appropriate satisfaction documents ordinarily terminate a lien. If a default occurs, a suit for judgment or foreclosure enforces the lien. These actions force the sale of the property.

4.9 (a) Real estate tax lien.

The category of superior, or senior, liens ranks above the category of inferior, or junior, liens, meaning that superior liens receive first payment from the proceeds of a foreclosure. The superior category includes liens for real estate tax, special assessments, and inheritance tax. Other liens, including income tax liens, mortgage liens and judgment liens, are inferior.

4.10 (d) subordinate the lien.

A lienor can change the priority of a junior lien by voluntarily agreeing to subordinate, or lower, the lien's position in the hierarchy. This change is often necessary when working with a mortgage lender who will not originate a mortgage loan unless it is senior to all other junior liens on the property. The lender may require the borrower to obtain agreements from other lien holders to subordinate their liens to the new mortgage.

4.11 (d) A license, which terminates upon the owner's death.
A license is a personal right that a property owner grants to another to use the property for a specific purpose (to reach the kindergarten school bus). Unlike a personal easement in gross, which terminates only on the death of the grantee (Betty Luanne, in this instance), a license is revocable at any moment, is not transferable and does not attach to the land. It ceases on the death of either party, or on the sale of the property.

4.12 (b) a deed restriction.
A private party who wants to control the quality and standards of a property can establish a deed restriction. Deed restrictions take precedence over zoning ordinances if they are more restrictive.

4.13 (a) It involves a monetary claim against the value of a property.
A lien is a creditor's claim against personal or real property as security for a debt of the property owner. If the owner defaults, the lien gives the creditor the right to force the sale of the property to satisfy the debt. Liens do not necessarily alter the property value. Liens can be involuntary as well as voluntary. Finally, liens attach to the property, but so do other encumbrances.

4.14 (d) involuntary general lien.
A general lien is one placed against any and all real and personal property owned by a particular debtor. An example is an inheritance tax lien placed against all property owned by the heir. A specific lien attaches to a single item of real or personal property and does not affect other property owned by the debtor. In addition, judgment liens are junior, involuntary liens.

4.15 (c) A third party's interest in a real property that limits the interests of the freehold property owner.
An encumbrance is an interest in and right to real property that limits the legal owner's freehold interest. In effect, an encumbrance is another's right to use or take possession of a legal owner's property, or to prevent the legal owner from enjoying the full bundle of rights in the estate.

4.16 (c) ownership reverting to the previous owner.
Breaches of deed covenants may result in an injunction to force compliance or payment of compensatory damages, but violations of the deed conditions may result in the ownership reverting back to the previous owner.

4.17 (b) the deed restriction is more restrictive than the zoning ordinance.
If a deed restriction is more restrictive than a related zoning ordinance, the deed restriction takes precedence over the ordinance.

4.18 (a) Mortgage lien
While real estate tax liens, state inheritance tax liens, and federal estate tax liens are all superior liens, mortgage liens are junior liens.

4.19 (b) use.
Easements affect a property's use by allowing a non-owner to use a section of the property for his/her own use.

4.20 (c) An owner may sue to have an encroachment removed from his/her property.
An encroachment is an unauthorized intrusion by one property owner onto another owner's property. The intruder may be sued to remove the encroachment or may be ordered to pay compensatory damages.

UNIT FIVE TEST: DEEDS AND CONVEYANCES

5.1 (d) It is knowledge received or imparted through direct experience.
The term "notice" is synonymous with "knowledge." A person who has received actual notice has actual knowledge of something. Receiving actual notice means learning of something through direct experience or communication. Thus, a document in itself cannot be actual notice. It is the seeing of the document that makes it actual notice.

5.2 (b) It is knowledge one could have or should have obtained. Constructive notice, or legal notice, is knowledge of a fact that a person could have or should have obtained. The foremost method of imparting constructive notice is by recordation of ownership documents in public records, specifically, title records. Since public records are open to everyone, the law generally presumes that when evidence of ownership is recorded, the public at large has received constructive notice of ownership.

5.3 (a) grant, deed, and will.
Voluntary transfer, or voluntary alienation, is an unforced transfer of title by sale or gift from an owner to another party. If the transferor is a government entity and the recipient is a private party, the conveyance is a public grant. If the transferor is a private party, the conveyance is a private grant. A living owner makes a private grant by means of a deed of conveyance, or deed. A private grant that occurs when the owner dies is a transfer by will.

5.4 (c) It gives constructive notice of ownership.
Recording is not necessary to make a deed valid. However, it is in the grantee's best interests to do so. Recording the deed gives the public constructive notice of the grantee's ownership.

5.5 (b) granting clause.
The granting, or premises, clause is the only required clause. It contains the conveyance intentions; names the parties; describes the property; and indicates a nominal consideration.

5.6 (a) general warranty deed.
The general warranty deed, or warranty deed for short, contains the fullest possible assurances of good title and protection for the grantee. The deed is technically a bargain and sale deed in which the grantor promises to defend against any and all claims to the title. The overall general warranty covenant is: "I own and will defend."

5.7 (a) A transfer tax based on the price of the property being conveyed.
State law usually requires payment of a documentary stamp tax on a conveyance of real property. The tax is based on the actual price of the property conveyed, thus enabling taxing authorities to ascertain current market value for ad valorem tax purposes. Payment of the tax is evidenced on the deed.

5.8 (b) probate.
A court proceeding called probate generally settles a decedent's estate, whether the person has died testate (having left a valid will) or intestate (having failed to do so).

5.9 (a) It will escheat to the state or county.
If an intestate decedent has no heirs, the estate escheats, or reverts, to the state or county after all claims and debts have been validated and settled.

5.10 (d) Eminent domain.
Various government and public entities can transfer private property to the public sphere by the power of eminent domain. The transfer is involuntary, even though the owner receives compensation. For example, a city government wants to widen a highway to accommodate growth. The government uses eminent domain to condemn and purchase all properties abutting the thoroughfare in order to complete the construction project.

5.11 (a) openly possessing and claiming the property without the owner's consent.
To claim legal title, the adverse possessor must be able to show a claim of right or color of title as reason for the possession; have notorious possession, which is possession without concealment; maintain a consistent claim of hostile possession, which is a claim to ownership and possession regardless of the owner's claims or consent; occupy the property continuously for a statutory period of time; in some states, pay taxes.

5.12 (d) A quitclaim deed.
A quitclaim deed transfers real and potential interests in a property, whether an interest is known to exist or not. The grantor makes no claim to any interest in the property being conveyed and offers no warrants to protect the grantee. Where there is a possibility that prior errors in deeds or other recorded documents might cloud (encumber) the title, the relevant parties execute a quitclaim deed to convey "any and all" interest to the grantee.

5.13 (d) declined because possession was secretive.
One of the preconditions for a claim of ownership based on adverse possession is notorious possession, or possession without concealment. Even if the length of possession in this case meets the statutory requirement, the drifter's secretiveness would invalidate the claim.

5.14 (b) A legal instrument used to transfer a real estate title voluntarily to another party
A deed of conveyance is defined as a legal instrument that is used by an owner (grantor) to transfer title to real estate voluntarily to another party, the grantee.

5.15 (a) The grantee must sign the deed.
For a title to pass from the grantor to the grantee, the grantor must be competent and intend to deliver the deed beyond the act of physical delivery. In other words, the grantor must intend to convey the title and property to the grantee. The grantee must then receive delivery of the title and accept it so that he/she has physical possession of the deed or its record.

5.16 (c) Escheat
Deeds, wills, and public grants are all used when a title is voluntarily being transferred. However, an escheat is a means of involuntarily transferring a title to the state when the land owner dies with no will and no heirs.

5.17 (c) To provide evidence of the land's ownership to the public
The purpose of a notice, whether actual or constructive, is to provide evidence to the public as to who owns the land.

5.18 (a) deed of conveyance.
A deed of conveyance is the legal instrument used by an owner, the grantor, to transfer title to real estate voluntarily to another party, the grantee.

5.19 (b) Warrant of seisin clause
There are six covenant or warrant clauses that can be found in a deed, one of which is the warrant of seisin which is the grantor's assurance that he/she actually owns the land and has the right to convey it.

5.20 (d) Special purpose
A tax deed is a special purpose deed that is used to convey property that is being sold at a tax sale when the land owner has not paid required taxes on the property.

UNIT SIX TEST: TITLE CLOSING AND COSTS

6.1 (b) title closing process.
There are several steps in the title closing process, the first of which is for the buyer and seller to verify all of the terms of the sales contract have been met.

6.2 (c) residential property.
The Real Estate Settlement Procedures Act was put into place to protect consumers by clarifying and disclosing costs and to eliminate kickbacks and undisclosed fees in residential real estate transactions.

6.3 (d) 3 days
Under RESPA, mortgage lenders must provide the CFPB H-24 Loan Estimate of settlement costs within 3 days of the loan application.

6.4 (a) settlement process.
During the settlement process, prorated and non-prorated debits and credits are identified, the closing statement is completed, and funds are disbursed.

6.5 (a) Title insurance
Sellers are responsible for the stamp tax on the deed, brokerage fees, inspection fees, and title insurance costs, all of which are non-prorated items.

6.6 (c) Utilities bill
Attorney fees, mortgage fees, and title insurance are all non-prorated items at closing. However, property utilities, if paid in advance, would be prorated at closing.

6.7 (c) 365-day
The 365-day method determines proration amount by multiplying the daily amount of the expense by the number of days within in the time period the expense belongs to each party.

6.8 (d) $682.50
$2700 ÷ 12 months = $225 monthly
$225 ÷ 30 days = $7.50 daily
$225 x 3 months (January – March) = $675
$7.50 x 1 day (April 1) = $7.50
$675 + $7.50 = $682.50, seller John's share

6.9 (c) Truth-in-Lending Integrated Disclosures Rule
The Truth-in-Lending Integrated Disclosures Rule combines the financial disclosure requirements of RESPA and the Truth-in-Lending Act, replaces the Good Faith Estimate and HUD-1 forms, and uses the Loan Estimate and Closing Disclosure forms.

6.10 (b) 3 business days before consummation.
To provide the borrower with advance notice of loan closing terms, the closing disclosure must be provided to the borrower 3 business days before loan consummation.

6.11 (d) construction loans.
Transactions which are covered by the Truth-in-Lending Integrated Disclosures Rule include most closed-end consumer mortgages, including: construction loans, loans secured by vacant land, loans to trusts.

6.12 (b) Sales contract
Costs, such as brokerage fees, mortgage-related fees, title-related expenses, real estate taxes, settlement of buyer and seller debits and credits, prorated and non-prorated items, and who will be responsible for paying each are first identified in the sales contract.

6.13 (d) settlement process
During the settlement process, selling terms and costs are identified, debits and credits are determined as prorated or non-prorated, the closing statement is completed, and funds are disbursed.

6.14 (c) No, RESPA prohibits them.
The Real Estate Settlement Procedures Act prohibits both referral fees and kickbacks and requires disclosure of business relationships between firms involved in the transaction.

6.15 (d) $0.0 as Charlie is responsible for the non-prorated brokerage fee
Brokerage fees are non-prorated expenses which are paid by the seller, in this case, by Charlie. Consequently, Sue does not pay any amount of the brokerage fee.

6.16 (c) A notary stamp on the title
When transferring land ownership, one must produce evidence of the title. Producing proof of a title insurance policy, and attorney's opinion of the title abstract, or a title certificate satisfies that requirement. A notary stamp does not qualify as the evidence required.

6.17 (b) unrecorded claims.
Unrecorded claims result in a cloud on the title and need to be resolved prior to the title transfer.

6.18 (d) abstract of title.
Although a chain of title is the successive property owners from the original grant to the present, an abstract of title is a written chronology of recorded owners, transfers, and encumbrances. When an attorney provides a written opinion of the abstract, that serves as evidence of the title.

6.19 (a) a suit to quiet title.
Whether recorded or not, a claim on the title needs to be resolved prior to title transfer. In some cases, to have the claim settled, a suit to quiet title is filed.

6.20 (c) loan estimate costs are based on the best information available.
Under TRID/TILA, good faith estimates are created based on the best information available at the time the estimate is written. While the estimate should match the actual costs, there are tolerance limits for variances.

UNIT SEVEN TEST: CONTRACTS, CONTRACT OF SALE AND LEASE

7.1 (b) The tenant pays a fixed rent, and the landlord pays all operating expenses.
In a gross lease, the tenant pays an established, fixed rent, and the landlord pays all property operating expenses, such as taxes, insurance, utilities, and other services. This is the arrangement commonly used in residential leases. If the tenant pays some of the operating expenses, the lease is a form of net lease.

7.2 (d) the landlord does not have to maintain it.
The lease should set forth items that are excluded or included in the leased property. For instance, a residential lease may include built-in appliances such as dishwashers but exclude freestanding ones, such as refrigerators. At issue for the landlord is the cost of maintenance. If a refrigerator is not included, it does not have to be maintained by the property manager.

7.3 (b) deliver a habitable property.
The landlord (by way of the property manager), is expected to deliver a property that is habitable. This means keeping heating, plumbing, cooling, and electrical systems in good repair as well as maintaining serviceability of floors, stairways, railings, roofs, and windows.

7.4 (c) A tenant declares a landlord in default and vacates the leased premises.
A constructive eviction occurs when a tenant vacates the leased premises and declares the lease void, claiming that the landlord's actions have made the premises unfit for the purpose described in the lease. The tenant must prove that it was the landlord's actions that were responsible and may be able to recover damages.

7.5 (c) percentage lease A percentage lease allows the landlord to share in the income generated from the use of the property. A tenant pays percentage rent, or an amount of rent equal to a percentage of the tenant's periodic gross sales.

7.6 (d) net lease.
A net lease requires a tenant to pay for utilities, internal repairs, and a proportionate share of taxes, insurance, and operating expenses in addition to rent.

7.7 (b) The leased property is foreclosed.
A foreclosure extinguishes all prior interests in a property, including a leasehold.

7.8 (c) Estate at will.
Three of the four principal types of leasehold estate are: the estate for years, which has a specific lease term; the estate from period-to-period, where the lease term of a specific period automatically renews; and the estate at will, which has no specified lease term. The fourth principal type, the estate at sufferance, is a tenancy without consent that therefore also has no specific term.

7.9 (a) compliance with the rules and regulations of the building.
The lease defines the tenant's obligations, which principally are to pay the rent on time; maintain the property's

condition; and comply with the rules and regulations of the building.

7.10 (d) the tenant's estate is still obligated under the lease.
A valid lease creates obligations that survive the death of the landlord or tenant, with certain exceptions. A tenant's estate remains liable for payment of rent if the tenant dies; the landlord's estate remains bound to provide occupancy despite the landlord's death.

7.11 (a) The remaining tenant is responsible for the full rent obligation.
Multiple tenants who sign a single lease are jointly and severally responsible for fulfilling lease obligations. Thus, if one renter abandons an apartment, the other renters remain liable for rent.

7.12 (c) sublease.
Subletting (subleasing) is the transfer by a tenant, the sublessor, of a portion of the leasehold interest to another party, the sublessee, through the execution of a sublease. The sublease spells out all of the rights and obligations of the sublessor and sublessee, including the payment of rent to the sublessor. The sublessor remains primarily liable for the original lease with the landlord. The subtenant is liable only to the sublessor

7.13 (d) net lease.
A net lease requires a tenant to pay for utilities, internal repairs, and a proportionate share of taxes, insurance, and operating expenses in addition to rent. In effect, the landlord "passes through" actual property expenses to the tenant rather than charging a higher rent level. Net leases vary as to exactly what expenses the tenant is responsible for. The purest form of net lease requires tenants to cover all expenses, including major repairs and property taxes.

7.14 (a) gross lease.
A gross lease, or full-service lease, requires the landlord to pay the property's operating expenses, including utilities, repairs, and maintenance, while the tenant pays only rent. Rent levels under a gross lease are higher than under a net lease, since the landlord recoups expense outlays in the form of added rent.

7.15 (b) An owner-developer wants to retain ownership of the land portion of the improved real property.
Ground leases are primarily used when an owner wishes to lease raw land to an agricultural or mining interest; when unimproved property is to be developed and the owner wants to retain ownership of the land; when the developer or future users of the property do not want to own the land; or when the owner of an improved property wishes to sell an interest in the improvements while retaining ownership of the underlying land.

7.16 (c) When either party gives proper notice.
In the absence of an explicit term with beginning and ending date, a court will generally construe the lease to be a tenancy at will, cancelable upon proper notice.

7.17 (b) A sale contract before closing.
An executory contract is one in which performance is yet to be completed. A sales contract prior to closing is executory: while the parties have agreed to buy and sell, the buyer has yet to pay the seller and the seller has yet to deed the property to the buyer

7.18 (a) both parties promise to do something in exchange for the other party's performance.
A bilateral contract is one in which both parties promise to perform their respective parts of an agreement in exchange for performance by the other party. An example of a bilateral contract is an exclusive listing: the broker promises to exercise due diligence in the efforts to sell a property, and the seller promises to compensate the broker when and if the property sells.

7.19 (d) the failure of a party to perform according to the terms of the contract.
A breach of contract is a failure to perform according to the terms of the agreement.

7.20 (b) The act of declaring that a contract is no longer in effect for a given party.
Parties to a contract may rescind a contract by mutual consent, or a damaged party may rescind the contract unilaterally. This act of rescission cancels the contract and returns the parties to their pre-contract condition, including the refunding of any monies already transferred.

7.21 (a) reflect a mutual understanding or agreement.

Mutual consent, also known as offer and acceptance and meeting of the minds, requires that a contract involve a clear and definite offer and an intentional, unqualified acceptance of the offer.

7.22 (c) unenforceable.

A valid contract that is in writing is enforceable within a statutory time period. A valid contract that is made orally is also generally enforceable within a statutory period, with the exception that some contracts are enforceable only if they are in writing. These laws apply in particular to the transfer of interests in real estate. A void or voidable contract was not a truly valid contract.

7.23 (b) require certain conveyance-related contracts to be in writing.

The statute of frauds requires that certain contracts must be in writing to be enforceable. Real estate contracts that convey an interest in real property fall in this category, with the exception that a lease of one year's duration or less may be oral.

7.24 (b) implied agreement.

One of the reasons contracts need to be in writing is to avoid implied agreements, ones where the agreement is unintentional based on one party's actions.

7.25 (c) A 6-month lease

The Statute of Frauds requires that certain contracts be in writing. One exemption is a lease for a duration of 1 year or less.

7.26 (c) attorney

Contracts may only be prepared/written by an attorney or a party to the contract.

7.27 (a) A sales contract after transaction closing

An executed contract is one that has been fully performed. Of the choices give, only the sales contract after the transaction is complete and closed is a fully performed contract.

7.28 (b) On a date and time indicated by the offeror

Offers are initially created by the offeror, the buyer, who provides a date and time the offer will expire so as to limit the amount of time the offeree, the seller, has to respond to the offer.

7.29 (a) a unilateral contract requiring the seller to perform.

With an option-to-buy contract, only the seller is required to perform by allowing the buyer to purchase at some point in time. The buyer is not required to perform by purchasing the property. Consequently, the contract is a unilateral contract.

7.30 (c) a five-year lease must be in writing to be enforceable.

Generally, a lease for a period exceeding one year cannot be oral but must be in writing to be enforceable because of the statute of frauds.

UNIT EIGHT TEST: REAL ESTATE FINANCE

8.1 (b) Promissory note and mortgage

The elements of a mortgage transaction are the promissory note, which is a promise to repay the loan, and the mortgage, which pledges the property as collateral for the loan.

8.2 (c) equity.

At closing, the borrower's cash that has been invested in the property is called equity; after closing, equity is the difference between the property's market value and the balance of the loan.

8.3 (d) A clause covering the escrow payment for principal, interest, taxes, and insurance

PITI stands for principal, interest, taxes, and insurance which are paid into an escrow account and subsequently used to pay these expenses.

8.4 (a) It protects the lender against monetary loss if the borrower defaults.
PMI is private mortgage insurance that is used to protect lenders against loss in case the borrower defaults on the loan. It is typically required for loans with down payments of less than 20%.

8.5 (d) The ratio of the loan amount and the value of the property expressed as a percent
The relationship of the loan amount to the property value, expressed as a percentage, is called the loan-to-value ratio, or LTV. If the lender's loan to value ratio is 80%, the lender will lend only $80,000 on a home appraised at $100,000. The difference between what the lender will lend and what the borrower must pay for the property is the amount the borrower must provide in cash as a down payment.

8.6 (b) private mortgage insurance.
Mortgage insurance protects the lender against loss of a portion of the loan (typically 20-25%) in case of borrower default. Private mortgage insurance generally applies to loans that are not backed by the Federal Housing Administration (FHA) or Veterans Administration (VA) and that have a down payment of less than 20% of the property value. The FHA has its own insurance requirement for loans with a down payment of less than 20%.

8.7 (c) buyer's down payment.
Price less loan is the down payment. Generally, this is also the buyer's initial equity.

8.8 (a) refusing a loan because the borrower does not match the lender's target market.
The Equal Credit Opportunity Act (ECOA) requires a lender to evaluate a loan applicant on the basis of that applicant's own income and credit rating, unless the applicant requests the inclusion of another's income and credit rating in the application. In addition, ECOA has prohibited a number of practices in mortgage loan underwriting, including refusing a loan based on an applicant's demographic characteristics.

8.9 (b) $1680.
Monthly income qualification is derived by multiplying monthly income by the income ratio. Thus (72,000 / 12) x .28 = $1680. Remember to first derive the monthly income.

8.10 (b) adjust the applicant's debt ratio calculation and lower the loan amount.
Since a lender lends only part of the purchase price of a property according to the lender's loan-to-value ratio, a lender will verify that a borrower has the cash resources to make the required down payment. If someone is lending an applicant a portion of the down payment with a provision for repayment, a lender will consider this another debt obligation and adjust the debt ratio accordingly. This can lower the amount a lender is willing to lend.

8.11 (c) All loans secured by a residence.
Regulation Z applies to all loans secured by a residence. It does not apply to commercial loans or to agricultural loans over $25,000. Its provisions cover the disclosure of costs, the right to rescind the credit transaction, advertising credit offers, and penalties for non-compliance with the act.

8.12 (d) the borrower has a limited right to cancel the transaction within a certain period.
A borrower has a limited right to cancel the credit transaction, usually within three days of completion of the transaction. The right of rescission does not apply to "residential mortgage transactions," that is, to mortgage loans used to finance the purchase or construction of the borrower's primary residence. It does, however, apply to refinancing of mortgage loans, and to home equity loans. State law may require a rescission period and notice on first mortgage loan transactions as well.

8.13 (b) ask the buyer/borrower about his/her religion or national origin.
ECOA prohibits discrimination in extending credit based on race, color, religion, national origin, sex, marital status, age, or dependency upon public assistance. A creditor may not make any statements to discourage an applicant on the basis of such discrimination or ask any questions of an applicant concerning these discriminatory items. A real estate licensee who assists a seller in qualifying a potential buyer may fall within the reach of this prohibition.

8.14 (d) not FHA-insured or VA-guaranteed.
A conventional mortgage loan is a permanent long-term loan that is not FHA-insured or VA-guaranteed. FNMA does not "back" loans; FHA only insures FHA loans; and the VA, not GNMA guarantees loans.

8.15 (a) The borrower gives the lender a note and a mortgage in exchange for loan funds.

When a borrower gives a note promising to repay the borrowed money and executes a mortgage on the real estate for which the money is being borrowed as security, the financing method is called mortgage financing.

8.16 (c) The trustor conveys title to a trustee in exchange for loan funds from the beneficiary.

A deed of trust conveys title to the property in question from the borrower (trustor) to a trustee as security for the loan. The trustee is a third-party fiduciary to the trust. While the loan is in place, the trustee holds the title on behalf of the lender, who is the beneficiary of the trust.

8.17 (d) may be required to execute a release of mortgage document.

Lenders may be required to release the mortgage or trust document to the borrower when the borrower has paid off the loan and all other sums secured by the document. The release clause, also known as a defeasance clause, may specify that the mortgagee will execute a satisfaction of mortgage (also known as release of mortgage and mortgage discharge) to the mortgagor.

8.18 (b) consider the income of a spouse in evaluating a family's creditworthiness.

The Equal Credit Opportunity Act (ECOA) requires a lender to evaluate a loan applicant on the basis of that applicant's own income and credit rating, unless the applicant requests the inclusion of another's income and credit rating in the application. In such a case, a lender may not discount or disregard income from part-time work, a spouse, child support, alimony, or separate maintenance.

8.19 (a) insure the borrower has the earning power to make the loan payments.

Both the income and debt ratios in borrower qualification quantify how much a borrower can safely afford to pay on a mortgage loan. The income ratio focuses on the borrower's earning power.

8.20 (c) the parties complete all loan origination documents and the loan is funded.

Closing of a mortgage loan normally occurs with the closing of the real estate transaction. At the real estate closing, the lender typically has deposited the funded amount with an escrow agent, along with instructions for disbursing the funds. The borrower deposits necessary funds with the escrow agent, executes final documents, and receives signed copies of all relevant documents.

8.21 (b) Truth-in-Lending laws and Regulation Z.

Regulation Z, which implements the Truth-in-Lending Act, applies to all loans secured by a residence. It does not apply to commercial loans or to agricultural loans over $25,000. It prescribes requirements to lenders regarding the disclosure of costs, the right to rescind the credit transaction, advertising credit offers, and penalties for non-compliance with the Truth-in-Lending Act.

8.22 (a) The Equal Credit Opportunity Act.

ECOA prohibits discrimination in extending credit based on race, color, religion, national origin, sex, marital status, age, or dependency upon public assistance.

8.23 (c) the Real Estate Settlement and Procedures Act.

RESPA is a federal law which aims to standardize settlement practices and ensure that buyers understand settlement costs. RESPA applies to purchases of residential real estate (one- to four-family homes) to be financed by "federally related" first mortgage loans. In addition to imposing settlement procedures, RESPA provisions prohibit lenders from paying kickbacks and unearned fees to parties who may have helped the lender obtain the borrower's business.

8.2 (a) Fannie Mae, Freddie Mac, and Ginnie Mae.

As major players in the secondary market, the Federal National Mortgage Association (FNMA, "Fannie Mae"), Government National Mortgage Association (GNMA, "Ginnie Mae), and Federal Home Loan Mortgage Corporation (FHLMC, "Freddie Mac") tend to set the standards for the primary market. FHA, VA, and the Federal Reserve are not organizations in the secondary mortgage market.

8.25 (a) It cycles funds back to primary lenders so they can make more loans.

Secondary mortgage market organizations buy pools of mortgages from primary lenders and sell securities backed by these pooled mortgages to investors. By purchasing loans from primary lenders, the secondary market returns funds to the primary lenders, thereby enabling the primary lender to originate more mortgage loans.

8.26 (c) It purchases FHA-backed and VA-backed loans.
Fannie Mae buys conventional, FHA-backed and VA-backed loans; gives banks mortgage-backed securities in exchange for blocks of mortgages; and sells bonds and mortgage-backed securities. It does not guarantee, insure, or originate loans.

8.27 (b) acceleration.
A mortgage clause that allows the lender to require the borrower to repay the loan before the scheduled due date is called an acceleration clause.

8.28 (b) the lender to execute a satisfaction of mortgage document.
When a borrower pays a loan in full, a release or defeasance clause may require the lender to execute a satisfaction of mortgage to show the loan is paid in full and the lien can be removed.

8.29 (c) VA
While conventional and FHA-insured loans require a down payment, typically 20%, VA loans have no down payment requirement and can offer 100% financing.

8.30 (d) Assignment of mortgage
If the note and mortgage contain an assignment clause, the lender may sell the loan to a third-party investor, which is considered a member of the secondary mortgage market.

UNIT NINE TEST: LAND USE REGULATIONS

9.1 (d) Zoning ordinances are a primary means of keeping land use in harmony with the master plan.
The master plan fuses state and regional land use laws with local land use objectives that correspond to the municipality's social and economic conditions. The completed plan becomes the overall guideline for creating and enforcing zones, building codes, and development requirements.

9.2 (c) specify usage for every parcel within the zoning authority's jurisdiction.
The intent of zoning ordinances is to specify land usage for every parcel within the jurisdiction. In some areas, state laws permit zoning ordinances to apply to areas immediately beyond the legal boundaries of the city or county.

9.3 (b) To separate land uses so that they do not interfere with each other.
One of the primary applications of zoning power is the separation of residential properties from commercial and industrial uses. Proper design of land use in this manner preserves the aesthetics and value of neighborhoods and promotes the success of commercial enterprises through intelligently located zones. Six common types of zone are: residential; commercial; industrial; agricultural; public; and planned unit development (PUD).

9.4 (c) The public interest
The principal forms of exceptions to a conforming use is legal nonconforming use (grandfathered in); variance based on hardship; and special exception based on the public interest.

9.5 (d) The area of a commercial or industrial facility in relation to the size of the site.
Commercial zoning regulates intensity of usage by limiting the area of store or office per site area. Intensity regulation is further achieved by minimum parking requirements, setbacks, and building height restrictions.

9.6 (c) It requires that multiple tracts of land be developed according to a single design.
Planned unit development zoning restricts use to development of whole tracts that are designed to use space efficiently and maximize open space. A PUD zone may be for residential, commercial, or industrial uses, or combinations thereof.

9.7 (a) A homeowner in a residential zone converts her residence to a private school.
A legal nonconforming use can be illustrated as follows. A motel is situated in a residential area that no longer allows commercial activity. The zoning board rules that the motel may continue to operate until it is sold, destroyed

242

or used for any other commercial purpose. An illegal nonconforming use is one that conflicts with ordinances that were in place before the use commenced. For instance, if the motel in the previous example is sold, and the new owner continues to operate the property as a motel, the motel is now an illegal, nonconforming use.

9.8 (b) A variance is granted by the zoning board if the owner has a justifiable reason.
A nonconforming use is one that clearly differs from current zoning and is subject to change upon conveyance. A zoning variance allows a use that differs from the applicable ordinance for a variety of justifiable reasons.

9.9 (c) certificate of occupancy.
Building inspectors inspect a new development or improvement for code compliance. If the work complies, the municipality or county issues a certificate of occupancy which officially clears the property for occupation and use.

9.10 (c) It conveys legal title to the acquiring entity.
Eminent domain allows a government entity to purchase a fee, leasehold, or easement interest in privately owned real property for the public good, regardless of the owner's desire to sell or otherwise transfer any interest. In exchange for the interest, the government pays the owner a "just" compensation. To acquire a property, the public entity initiates a condemnation suit. Transfer of title extinguishes all existing leases, liens, and other encumbrances on the property.

9.11 (a) Individual property rights and the public's interest.
The optimum management of real property usage must take into account both the interests of the individual and the interests of the surrounding community. While maintaining the value of an individual estate is important, the owner of an estate must realize that unregulated use and development can jeopardize the value not only of the owner's estate but of neighboring properties.

9.12 (c) police power.
At the local level, county and city governments control land use through the authority known as police power. The most common expressions of police power are county and municipal zoning.

9.13(d) The owner must sell the property in exchange for market-value compensation.
Eminent domain allows a government entity to purchase a fee, leasehold, or easement interest in privately owned real property for the public good, regardless of the owner's desire to sell or otherwise transfer any interest. In exchange for the interest, the government pays the owner a "just" compensation.

9.14 (a) reasonably promote community health, safety and welfare.
Local planners do not have unlimited authority to do whatever they want. Their zoning ordinances must be clear in import, apply to all parties equally, and promote health, safety, and welfare of the community in a reasonable manner.

9.15 (d) To ensure that improvements comply with codes.
Local governments enforce zoning ordinances by issuing building permits to those who want to improve, repair, or refurbish a property. To receive a permit, the project must comply with all relevant ordinances and codes.

9.16 (b) To regulate the density of dwellings in the residential zone.
Residential zoning regulates density, by limiting the number and size of dwelling units and lots in an area.

9.17 (a) a special exception.
A special exception grant authorizes a use that is not consistent with the zoning ordinance in a literal sense, yet is clearly beneficial or essential to the public welfare and does not materially impair other uses in the zone.

9.18 (c) a legal nonconforming use.
An illegal nonconforming use is one that conflicts with ordinances that were in place before the use commenced. For instance, if a motel that was allowed as a legal nonconforming use is sold, and the new owner continues to operate the property as a motel, the motel is now an illegal, nonconforming use.

9.19 (c) concurrency.
Developers are held responsible to the impact of their projects on the local infrastructure under a policy called concurrency. The developer must make accommodations concurrently with the project development, not when the

project is completed.

9.20 (b) building codes.
Building codes protect the public against hazards caused by unregulated construction by establishing standards for every aspect of the construction project. New development is inspected for compliance to the codes.

9.21 (b) National Environmental Policy Act
Major legislation has been implanted to protect the environment based on how land is developed and used. One such law, the National Environmental Policy Act, sets standards for land use planning and has implemented environmental impact surveys to assure land uses are in compliance with environmental protection laws.

9.22 (c) Deed condition
Deed conditions restrict certain uses of property. When a condition is violated, the grantor may re-take possession of the property and sue for legal title.

9.23 (a) air quality.
When exposed and disturbed, asbestos adversely impacts air quality and can cause serious health conditions.

9.24 (c) The property title is ultimately transferred in exchange for the property's market value.
When an entity is taking possession of a property under eminent domain, the title is ultimately transferred to the entity in exchange for just compensation. There is no contingency that compensation must meet market value.

9.25 (d) amendment.
In a coding appeal, a property owner may seek and amendment to the code by petitioning the zoning board for a change to the zone.

9.26 (b) legal nonconforming use.
An illegal nonconforming use occurs when the use conflicts with ordinances that were already in place when the use began. However, a legal nonconforming use occurs when a new ordinance is put into place and causes the existing use of properties to be in violation of the new ordinance.

9.27 (b) Retail
Residential, commercial, industrial, and agricultural are the zone types. Retail falls under commercial.

9.28 (a) promote community health, safety, and welfare.
For a zoning ordinance to be valid, it must be clear in import, apply to all parties equally, and promote community health, safety, and welfare in a reasonable manner.

9.29 (c) the master plan.
Master plans are often required by state law. Local plans fuse municipal goals and needs with state and regional laws and include long term growth and usage strategies.

9.30 (b) police power.
The definition of police power is a government's legal authority to create, regulate, tax, and condemn real property in the interest of the public's health, safety, and welfare.

UNIT TEN TEST: CONSTRUCTION AND ENVIRONMENTAL ISSUES

10.1 (a) specifications.
When planning a construction project, the contractor needs to submit the project plans, blueprints, and specifications. While the plans and blueprints are scale drawings of the building and its components, the specifications are the written narrative of the materials and techniques to be used.

10.2 (c) the building is in compliance with building codes and is ready for occupancy.
After the plans, blueprints, and specifications have been submitted for construction approval, after the construction is completed, and after the final inspection has confirmed the building is in compliance with all building codes, a certificate of occupancy is issued to show the building is ready for occupancy. People may now move in and occupy the building.

10.3 (b) New York new home warranty
Under the New York New Home Warranty, also called the Housing Merchant Implied Warranty, which is the exclusive warranty for a new construction home, is an implied warranty and is not required to be in writing. The warranty is required by law and applies to single-family houses and units in multi-unit residential buildings of five stories or less.

10.4 (c) every 3 years.
The National Electric Code, which provides national standards for electricity installation and service, is renewed every 3 years.

10.5 (d) 6-year
The New York Housing Merchant Implied Warranty is a legally required warranty on all new construction homes which provides a 1-year warranty for construction defects; a 2-year warranty for plumbing, electrical, heating, cooling, and ventilation systems; and a 6-year warranty for material defects.

10.6 (a) carbon monoxide alarms in specific dwellings.
Amanda's Law was named after a teenager whose life was tragically ended by a carbon monoxide leak from a defective boiler while she was sleeping at a friend's house. As a result, the standards were changed to require carbon monoxide detectors in all one- and two-family dwellings, townhouses, condominiums, cooperatives, multiple dwellings regardless of construction date or sale date if the dwelling has appliances, devices, or systems that may emit carbon monoxide. The law also applies to dwellings with attached garages.

10.7 (c) the building's roof, walls, doors, windows, and foundation.
A building envelope is the structural barrier between the interior and exterior of a building. The building envelope structure includes the roof, walls, foundation, doors, and windows.

10.8 (b) Carpeting
Construction components are those items used to actually build and support the building. They include many materials and purposes. Doors, downspouts, and termite shields are all used in the actual construction of the building. Carpeting, on the other hand, is not an actual component of the building's construction, just as paint and wallpaper are not.

10.9 (a) is metal piping used to carry flexible wiring.
Circuit breakers and fuses interrupt a circuit when an overload or fault occur on the line. Amperage is the measure of overall capability of household supply, and the service entrance panel is the main control box for the electrical system. A conduit is metal piping used to carry flexible wiring.

10.10 (a) Jamb
A jamb is the vertical sides of a door frame. Louvers, mullions, and sashes are all parts of windows, not doors.

10.11 (c) roof.
A cross gable is a type of roof that has two or more gable rooflines which add more interior space and visual dynamics to the house.

10.12 (d) exterior covering.
Along with brick, clapboard, redwood, and shiplap, stucco is a type of exterior covering on buildings.

10.13 (c) When disturbed and dust is released
If asbestos is left undisturbed, it is harmless. However, if disturbed with its dust released into the air, it can cause lung disease and cancer.

10.14 (c) No, John does not lease to anyone with children.
New York City requires lead dust testing on homes built before 1978 when the occupants have children under 7 years old. Because John does not lease to tenants with children, he does not need to have the testing performed.

10.15 (d) Through foundation cracks and floor drains
Radon is a detectable radioactive ground gas that enters homes through foundation cracks and floor drains. It is known to cause lung cancer.

10.16 (a) on structures built before 1978.
Lead-based paint was banned in 1978, so any home built prior to that date could have a potential lead-based paint hazard. Consequently, whether renting or selling a pre-1978 dwelling, the potential hazard must be disclosed and the occupant must be provided a copy of the "Protect Your Family from Lead in Your Home" pamphlet.

10.17 (b) mold.
Mold in a home is typically caused by moisture or water damage. If it is present, it may cause allergy and respiratory problems and must be disclosed to renters and buyers.

10.18 (b) 1979.
Polychlorinated Biphenyls are man-made chemicals that are used in electrical and hydraulic equipment, plastics, and paints. Because they can cause cancer, neurological problems, and other health issues, manufacturing Polychlorinated Biphenyls has been banned since 1979.

10.19 (c) cleaning up uncontrolled hazardous waste dumps and spills.
Comprehensive Environmental Response, Compensation, and Liability Act (CERCLA) addresses contamination and cleanup of hazardous materials. The Act established the Superfund to cover the cost of cleaning up uncontrolled hazardous waste dumps and spills.

10.20 (c) remediates, cleans up, and performs follow-up monitoring of the site.
CERCLA employs audits in three phases: Phase I to identify users and materials; Phase II to analyze the substances; and Phase III to remediate and clean up the contamination and then perform follow-up monitoring of the site.

10.21 (d) All of the above
Depending on the circumstances, current and previous landowners may be held responsible for site contamination and cleanup, as can real estate licensees for improper disclosure of the contamination and tenants if their operations are linked to the contamination.

10.22 (b) 1985
The original Superfund expired in 1985.

10.23 (b) innocent landowners.
The Superfund Amendments and Reauthorization Act of 1986 removed liability from innocent landowners who had no link to or knowledge of the cause of contamination.

10.24 (c) provided higher funding than CERCLA's original Superfund.
The Superfund Amendments and Reauthorization Act of 1986 reauthorized the original Superfund with stricter standards for contamination cleanup and higher funding than CERCLA's original Superfund.

10.25 (c) allow only treated wood to touch the ground.
Termites live in the ground and eat wood foundations and structures. To prevent their damage, when constructing new homes, only treated wood should touch the ground where termites have access.

10.26 (a) require reporting, testing, and restrictions on Polychlorinated Biphenyls.
Polychlorinated Biphenyls are man-made organic chemicals used in electrical and hydraulic equipment, plastics, and paints. Manufacturing the chemicals was banned in 1979. Consequently, under the Toxic Substances Control Act of 1976, the EPA has the authority to require reporting, testing, and restrictions on use of the chemicals.

10.27 (b) industrial site cleanup.
There is extensive legislation in place to regulate and restrict environmental issues. Brownfields is one such

legislation in place since 2002 to specifically regulate industrial site cleanup.

10.28 (a) Resource Conservation and Recovery Act
The Resource Conservation and Recovery Act gives the EPA the authority to control hazardous solid waste from the "cradle-to-grave." This includes the generation, transportation, treatment, storage, and disposal of hazardous waste.

10.29 (d) National Environmental Policy Act
President Nixon signed into law the National Environmental Policy Act in 1970. That bill formed the Council on Environmental Quality which then led to the formation of the EPA that same year. The EPA's mission is to protect human health by safeguarding the air we breathe, water we drink, and the land on which we live.

10.30 (d) 1989

In 1977, asbestos was banned in artificial fireplace embers and wall patching compounds, but it was still allowed for other uses. In 1989, the manufacture of asbestos was banned in the U.S.

10.31 (b) Pressed wood products
Urea formaldehyde is used in foam insulation, adhesives, and pressed wood products, such as particle board.

10.32 (c) Depletion of earth's ozone layer
Chlorofluorocarbons are gases that are used in solvents, refrigerants, and aerosol sprays. The gases have been found to deplete the earth's ozone layer and add to the greenhouse effect.

10.33 (a) Junction box
Fuses and circuit breakers interrupt the circuit when an overload or fault occurs. The service entrance panel is the main control box for all electrical systems. It is the junction box that contains wire splices or cable connections.

10.34 (b) swings out at the bottom.
Awning windows swing out at the bottom.

10.35 (d) blueprint preparation.

Site preparations include clearing and grading the land, providing drainage and building location for construction of legal improvement with landscaping considerations, but do not include blueprint preparation.

UNIT ELEVEN TEST: VALUATION PROCESS AND PRICING PROPERTIES

11.1 (b) demand for the item is increasing in relation to supply of the item.
In a market economy, the primary interactions between supply, demand and price are: if supply increases relative to demand, price decreases; if supply decreases relative to demand, price increases; if demand increases relative to supply, price increases; and if demand decreases relative to supply, price decreases.

11.2 (d) Supply and demand are equal, and price and value are equal.
A market tends toward a state of equilibrium in which supply equals demand, and price, cost, and value are identical. According to this principle, market demand moves to meet supply, and supply moves to meet demand. If there is an extreme shortage of an item for which there is normally a strong demand, suppliers will rush to increase production to close the gap. If inventories of an item are very high, suppliers will stop production until the oversupply has been depleted.

11.3 (c) the uniqueness of every parcel.
In comparison with other economic products and services, real estate has certain unique traits. Traits of real estate include: inherent product value; uniqueness of every property; demand must come to the supply; illiquidity; slow to respond to changes; and a decentralized local market.

11.4 (d) Prices rise.
If demand is increasing and a moratorium slows supply, demand will begin to outpace supply, forcing prices to rise as the product becomes scarcer in relation to demand.

11.5 (b) an increase in demand for all types of real estate.
New businesses will arise to support the new company. They will hire new employees, some from out of town. The new employees will need housing. Hence the demand for residential real estate, as well as for commercial and industrial, will intensify, and it will also stimulate new construction.

11.6 (b) will increase.
If there is no longer a supply to meet the increasing demand of a growing population, prices for existing supply will rise.

11.7 (d) the market tending toward equilibrium.
A market tends toward a state of equilibrium in which supply equals demand, and price, cost, and value are identical. Thus, if supply is scarce, construction will increase to stabilize the imbalance.

11.8 (c) the market is over-supplied.
Falling prices indicate an oversupply of commercial properties in relation to demand. In this case, construction of new supply will also slow down.

11.9 (a) have been increasing.
A rise in prices is a market signal that there is an undersupply of product in relation to demand. As the market moves toward equilibrium, builders construct more buildings to meet the unmet demand.

11.10 (b) anticipation.
Anticipation is the value principle that a buyer will pay a price based on the benefits the buyer expects to derive from a property over a holding period. For example, if an investor anticipates an annual rental income from a leased property to be one million dollars, this expected sum has a direct bearing on what the investor will pay for the property.

11.11 (b) A homeowner adds a third bathroom to a house and thereby increases the appraised value by $10,000.
The principle of contribution focuses on the degree to which a particular improvement affects market value of the overall property. In essence, the contribution of the improvement is equal to the change in market value that the addition of the improvement causes. For example, adding a bathroom to a house may contribute an additional $15,000 to the appraised value. Thus the contribution of the bathroom is $15,000.

11.12 (a) assemblage.
Assemblage, or the conjoining of adjacent properties, sometimes creates a combined value that is greater than the values of the unassembled properties. The excess value created by assemblage is called plottage value.

11.13 (d) Market value is an estimate; market price is the price at which a property sold.
Market value is an estimate of the price at which a property will sell at a particular time. The market price, as opposed to market value, is what a property actually sells for. Market price should theoretically be the same as market value if all the conditions essential for market value are present. Market price, however, may not reflect the analysis of comparables and of investment value that an estimate of market value includes.

11.14 (d) define the appraisal problem and the purpose of the appraisal.
The first step in the process is to define the appraisal problem and the purpose of the appraisal. This involves identifying the subject property by legal description; specifying the interest to be appraised; specifying the purpose of the appraisal; specifying the date for which the appraisal is valid; and identifying the type of value to be estimated.

11.15 (c) weighing the applicability of the approaches and considering the quality of data supporting each approach.
The final step in the appraisal process is to reconcile the value estimates produced by the three approaches to value into a final value estimate. To do this, an appraiser must weigh the appropriateness of a particular approach to the

type of property being appraised and take into account the quality and quantity of data obtained in each method.

11.16 (b) Make dollar adjustments to the sale prices of comparable properties to account for competitive differences with the subject. The sales comparison approach consists of comparing sale prices of recently sold properties that are comparable with the subject, and making dollar adjustments to the price of each comparable to account for competitive differences with the subject. After identifying the adjusted value of each comparable, the appraiser weights the reliability of each comparable and the factors underlying how the adjustments were made. The weighting yields a final value range based on the most reliable factors in the analysis.

11.17 (d) takes into account the competitive value of specific amenities of the subject property.
The sales comparison approach is widely used because it takes into account the subject property's specific amenities in relation to competing properties. In addition, because of the currency of its data, the approach incorporates present market realities.

11.18 (a) adds value to a comparable that is inferior to the subject property.
If the comparable is inferior to the subject in some characteristic, an amount is added to the price of the comparable. If the comparable is better than the subject in some characteristic, an amount is deducted from the sale price of the comparable. This neutralizes the comparable's competitive advantage or disadvantage in an adjustment category. For example, a comparable has a swimming pool and the subject does not. To equalize the difference, the appraiser deducts an amount, say $6,000, from the sale price of the comparable.

11.19 (b) requires the fewest and smallest adjustments.
As a rule, the fewer the total number of adjustments, the smaller the adjustment amounts, and the less the total adjustment amount, the more reliable the comparable.

11.20 (c) $195,000.
Since the comparable has an extra bath, it is adjusted downward to equalize with the subject. Conversely, since it has no patio, the appraiser adds value to the comparable. Thus, $200,000 minus $7,000 plus $2,000 equals $195,000.

11.21(d) Add the estimated land value and cost of improvements and subtract the accrued depreciation of the improvements.
The cost approach consists of estimating the value of the land "as if vacant;" estimating the cost of improvements; estimating and deducting accrued depreciation; and adding the estimated land value to the estimated depreciated cost of the improvements.

11.22 (b) is very accurate for a property with new improvements that represent the highest and best use.
The strengths of the cost approach are that it: provides an upper limit for the subject's value based on the undepreciated cost of reproducing the improvements. It is also very accurate for valuing a property with new improvements which are the highest and best use of the property.

11.23 (c) a property loses the same increment of value each year over the economic life of the property.
All property improvements have an economic life, which becomes incrementally shorter year after year as physical deterioration takes its toll. The property as a whole does not lose value, since land itself does not depreciate. Similarly, an improvement can regain value if it is repaired or updated. Finally, not all properties lose value from economic obsolescence.

11.24 (d) $115,000.
To appraise value using the cost approach, add the land value to the value of the depreciated improvement. Thus you have $30,000 + ($95,000 - 10,000), or $115,000.

11.25 (b) Divide the income a property generates by a rate of return.
An appraiser obtains an indication of value from the income capitalization method by dividing the estimated net operating income for the subject by the rate of return, or capitalization rate. The formula is: NOI / Cap rate = Value.

11.26 (c) uses a method that is also used by investors to determine how much they should pay for an investment property.
The strength of the income approach is that it is used by investors themselves to determine how much they should

pay for a property. Thus, in the right circumstances, it provides a good basis for estimating market value. The approach, however, does not project what an income property's future income will be. Moreover, it is not an applicable method for estimating value if the subject is a non-income producing property.

11.27 (a) $370,000.
First, identify net income by subtracting out vacancy and expenses. Then divide by the capitalization rate. Thus, ($60,000 –3,000 – 20,000) ÷ 10% = $370,000.

11.28 (d) 150.
The monthly gross rent multiplier for a property is equal to the price divided by the monthly rent. Thus, ($450,000 ÷ $3,000) = 150.

11.29 (a) if two similar properties are for sale, a buyer will purchase the cheaper of the two.
According to the principle of substitution, a buyer will pay no more for a property than the buyer would have to pay for an equally desirable and available substitute property. For example, if three houses for sale are essentially similar in size, quality and location, a potential buyer is unlikely to choose the one that is priced significantly higher than the other two.

11.30 (a) is physically and financially feasible, legal, and the most productive.
This valuation principle holds that there is, theoretically, a single use for a property that produces the greatest income and return. A property achieves its maximum value when it is put to this use. The use must however be legal.

11.31 (d) $200,000. Market value is an opinion of the price that a willing seller and willing buyer would probably agree on for a property at a given time if: the transaction is for cash; the property is exposed on the open market for a reasonable period; buyer and seller have full information about market conditions ; there is no abnormal pressure on either party; it is an "arm's length" transaction; title is marketable; and the price does not include hidden influences such as special financing deals. The amount Lynne actually paid is the market price. The previous listing price and Ken's offer might be interesting data for the appraiser, but the appraisal must also consider other market data, such as comparable sales.

11.32 (a) there may be no recent sale price data in the market.
The sales comparison approach is limited in that every property is unique. As a result, it is difficult to find good comparables, especially for special-purpose properties. In addition, the market must be active; otherwise, sale prices lack currency and reliability.

11.33 (b) the seller offers below-market seller financing.
The principal factors for comparison and adjustment are time of sale, location, physical characteristics, and transaction characteristics. An adjustment may be made for such differences as mortgage loan terms, mortgage assumability, and owner financing.

11.34 (b) weights the comparables.
The last step in the approach is to perform a weighted analysis of the indicated values of each comparable. The appraiser, in other words, must identify which comparable values are more indicative of the subject and which are less indicative. However, all comparables are taken into account, not simply the nearest comparable.

11.35 (b) market value is not always the same as what the property cost.
The limitations of the cost approach are that: the cost to create improvements is not necessarily the same as market value; and depreciation is difficult to measure, especially for older buildings.

11.36 (b) incurable economic obsolescence.
Economic (or external) obsolescence is the loss of value due to adverse changes in the surroundings of the subject property that make the subject less desirable. Since such changes are usually beyond the control of the property owner, economic obsolescence is considered an incurable value loss.

11.37 (c) depreciation.
Depreciation is the loss of value in an improvement over time. The loss of an improvement's value can come from any cause, such as deterioration, obsolescence, or changes in the neighborhood.

11.38 (a) estimates depreciation, subtracts depreciation from cost, and adds back the land value.
The steps in the costs approach are: (1) estimate land value; (2) estimate reproduction or replacement cost of improvements; (3) estimate accrued depreciation; (4) subtract accrued depreciation from reproduction or replacement cost; and (5) add land value to depreciated reproduction or replacement cost.

11.39 (b) Objectivity and comprehensiveness
CMAs are prepared by real estate agents and are not to be confused with appraisals which are prepared by licensed or certified appraisers. The main differences in the two are objectivity and comprehensiveness, as the appraiser has no personal stake in the results.

11.40 (c) Sale prices for homes sold in the previous year
When preparing a CMA, agents should not use comparison information for homes sold longer ago than the last 6 months as older data is typically not relevant due to market changes.

UNIT TWELVE: HUMAN RIGHTS AND FAIR HOUSING

12.1 (a) Civil Rights Act of 1866.
The original fair housing statute, the Civil Rights Act of 1866, prohibits discrimination in housing based on race. The prohibition relates to selling, renting, inheriting, and conveying real estate.

12.2 (c) race, color, religion, and national origin.
Title VIII of the Civil Rights Act of 1968, known today as the Fair Housing Act, prohibits discrimination in housing based on race, color, religion, or national origin.

12.3 (c) Advertising a property as available to individuals of a particular race. The prohibition against discriminatory advertising states that an agent may not advertise residential properties in such a way as to restrict their availability to any prospective buyer or tenant.

12.4 (c) An agent persuades a family to put their house on the market because Jewish families are beginning to move into the neighborhood.
Blockbusting, a prohibited activity, is the practice of inducing owners in an area to sell or rent to avoid an impending change in the ethnic or social makeup of the neighborhood that will cause values to go down.

12.5 (a) The Home Mortgage Disclosure Act.
The Home Mortgage Disclosure Act requires lenders involved with federally guaranteed or insured loans to exercise impartiality and non-discrimination in the geographical distribution of their loan portfolio. In other words, the act is designed to prohibit redlining, the practice of restricting loans by geographical are(a)

12.6 (c) privately owned single-family residences listed with a broker.
Among the circumstances where the Fair Housing Act might allow for an exemption is: a privately owned single-family home where no broker is used, with certain additional conditions. In other words, as soon as a broker is used in the sale, the law applies.

12.7 (a) illegal, because the agent changed the terms of the sale to discourage this particular couple.
The Fair Housing Act prohibition against discriminatory misrepresentation states that an agent may not conceal available properties, represent that they are not for sale or rent, or change the sale terms for the purpose of discriminating.

12.8 (d) The owner of a duplex who resides in one of the units refuses to rent the other unit to a non-Christian.
The Fair Housing Act would exempt the owner in this situation because it involves rental of an apartment in a 1-4 unit building where the owner is also an occupant and there is no discriminatory advertising.

251

12.9 (b) File a complaint with HUD and/or file suit against the offending parties in a state or federal court within the prescribed time period.
The Fair Housing Amendments Act of 1988 prohibits discrimination based on sex. If May feels she has been discriminated against in this way, she may file a complaint with the Office of Fair Housing and Equal Opportunity (OFHEO) in HUD within one year or file suit in a federal or state court within two years of the alleged violation.

12.10 (a) Inform Scott that the condition is illegal and that she cannot comply with it.
Scott is not allowed to discriminate based on race, color, religion, national origin, sex, family status, or handicap. If an agent goes along with a client's discriminatory act, the agent is equally liable for violation of fair housing laws. It is thus imperative to avoid complicity with client discrimination. Further, an agent should withdraw from any relationship where client discrimination occurs.

12.11 (c) require families without children to pay the same security deposit that families with children must pay.
Fair housing laws prohibit discriminatory advertising, discrimination on the basis of national origin, discrimination based on age in dwellings of more than four units, and discrimination against families with children. The fact that the owner is requiring the same deposit from tenants with and without children does not discriminate against families with children but actually favors them.

12.12 (d) It is a single-family house, and the owner owns only one other rental home in addition to his own residence.
Federal fair housing laws do not prohibit age and family status discrimination in residential dwellings of four units or less and in single family houses if sold or rented by owners who have no more than three houses.

12.13 (c) the Fair Housing Amendments Act of 1988.
The Fair Housing Amendments Act of 1988 prohibited discrimination based on sex and discrimination against handicapped persons and families with children. Executive Order 11063 concerned racial discrimination in housing where federal funding was involved; the Civil Rights Act of 1968 concerned discrimination based on race, color, religion, and national origin; Jones v Mayer concerned racial discrimination.

12.14 (c) steering.
Steering is the illegal practice of limiting customers' choices by encouraging or discouraging them about the suitability of an area and directing them only to areas the agent deems suitable for them.

12.15 (a) providing unequal services.
The agent may be illegally providing unequal services by altering the nature or quality of brokerage services to a party based on race, color, sex, national origin, or religion.

12.16 (a) discriminatory misrepresentation by omission.
Discriminatory misrepresentation is the concealing of available properties, representing that they are not for sale or rent, or changing the sale terms for the purpose of discriminating.

12.17 (b) the principal has proposed an illegal act, which should not be obeyed.
An agent must comply with the client's directions and instructions, provided they are legal. If the directive is illegal, the agent must also immediately withdraw.

12.18 (c) The agent and the owner.
The owner has illegally discriminated, and the agent, by going along with the owner, is equally guilty of violating fair housing laws.

12.19 (b) public accommodations and employees.
Real estate agents are most likely to encounter Title I Employment concerns and Title III Public Accommodations concerns for public and commercial facilities.

12.20 (a) induces owners in a particular area to sell to avoid an impending change in the ethnic makeup of the neighborhood.
Blockbusting is inducing owners in a particular area to sell or rent to avoid impending change in ethnic or social makeup of the area that will result in lower home values. It is a form of illegal discrimination.

12.21 (c) Jones v. Mayer.
Jones v. Mayer ruled that discrimination in selling/renting residential housing based on race is prohibited without exception or exemption. Consequently, no anti-discrimination exemption may include race.

12.22 (c) federally guaranteed or insured loans.
Home Mortgage Disclosure Act applies to federally guaranteed or insured loans, prohibits redlining, and is enforced by tracking the location of lender loans.

12.23 (b) NYC Human Rights Law
The NYC Human Rights Law adds partnership status, citizenship, and victims of domestic violence, sex offenses, and stalking as protected classes in the city.

12.24 (b) real estate agents.
Exemptions to the NY Human Rights Law do not apply if the rentals are being conducted by real estate agents. Agents are not exempt from anti-discrimination laws.

12.25 (a) Military status
The NY Human Rights Law recognizes all federally mandated protected classes and adds lawful source of income and military status to those classes. While the NY City Human Rights Law also recognizes the federal protected classes and lawful source of income, it does not recognize military status as a protected class, making military status only recognized by the NY state law.

12.26 (d) agricultural real estate.
The NY Human Rights Law provides anti-discrimination protection for renting, selling, leasing, and advertising housing, vacant land, commercial real estate, public housing, and membership in real estate boards, but does not include agricultural real estate in its protection.

12.27 (a) Apartment rentals in five-unit buildings with the owner occupying one unit
If an individual owns a two-unit apartment, lives in one unit, and rents out the other unit, the owner is exempt from the NY Human Rights Law regarding anti-discrimination.

12.28 (b) Advertisements for rental of an owner-occupied two-family house
NY City Human Rights Law does not include or recognize an anti-discrimination exemption for the advertised rental of an owner-occupied two-family house.

12.29 (c) Being a victim of domestic violence is not a protected class in Albany.
Federal and NY state anti-discrimination laws do not include victims of domestic violence as a protected class. Only NY City includes victims of domestic violence, sexual offenses, and stalking as a protected class. Therefore, the landlord did not violate any anti-discrimination law in Albany.

12.30 (d) U.S. Department of Justice.
Titles II and III of the Americans with Disabilities Act are enforced by the U.S. Department of Justice who will impose penalties for violations.

12.31 (b) Installation of an elevator inside a two-story apartment building
The Americans with Disabilities Act and Fair Housing laws require owners and landlords to make reasonable accommodations to provide accessibility to those with disabilities. While installing ramps and widening doorways are reasonable both in effort and cost, installing an elevator would not be considered reasonable. Instead, the landlord could possibly offer the disabled person a ground floor apartment.

12.32 (a) restricting access to market.
Blockbusting, redlining, and steering are all illegal forms of discrimination, as is discriminatorily restricting participation in an MLS bad on any protected class, called restricting access to market.

12.33 (c) 62 years old.
Restricting residents to those 62 and older is an exemption allowed under the Fair Housing Amendments Act of 1988. Consequently, landlords may refuse to rent to families with children when the rental property is one that falls

under this age restriction.

12.34 (d) redlining.
Federal law prohibits lending institutions from refusing to provide residential loans within certain areas based strictly on the area and not the borrower's qualifications. Institutions that do so are practicing redlining.

12.35 (c) Race
The Civil Rights Act of 1866 prohibited discrimination in housing based on race. Other protected classes and exemptions were added through later laws. However, Jones v. Mayer prohibited discrimination based on race in any and all situations, with no exemptions.

12.36 (d) Banning black people from attending the same public schools as white people
The Jim Crow laws were recognized in southern states at the time and banned black people from living in some of the same towns as white people, attending the same public schools as white people, and using the same public facilities as white people.

12.37 (b) 1954
Segregation in public schools became illegal in 1954 when the court declared it violated the equal protection clause of the 14th Amendment.

12.38 (b) at first substantive contact.
While landlords are given 30 days after residency to provide the form to tenants, real estate licensees are required to provide the form to prospective tenants at the first substantive contact.

12.39 (c) The landlord must modify the rules to accommodate the disabled tenant's need for the service dog.
The laws covering reasonable accommodations for disabled people require landlords to modify rules, policies, practices, and/or services for disabled tenants, including allowing service dogs when pets are not allowed.

UNIT THIRTEEN TEST: MUNICIPAL AGENCIES

13.1 (b) The purpose is to assure the highest and best use of property.
The purpose of public and private control of land is the preservation of property values, assurance of the highest and best use of property, the balance of individual property rights with public good, and the control of growth within infrastructure capabilities.

13.2 (a) two 4-year terms.
The New York City Council is made up of 51 elected members who each may serve a maximum of two 4-year terms

13.3 (d) New York City Council.
The New York City Council works as an equal to the mayor in governing the city.

13.4 (c) village mayor.
The Village Board of Trustees is made up of elected officials who serve 4-year terms. The Board meetings are presided over by the village mayor.

13.5 (a) Municipal Home Rule Law
While the State Constitution grants the power to enact local laws, the Municipal Home Rule Law sets the scope of power and procedures for implementation of the laws.

13.6 (c) 30 days
When a zoning board member refers a new law or amendment proposal to the planning agency for review, if the agency does not respond within 30 days, the zoning board may finalize the law without the agency's input.

13.7 (a) Secretary of State
The zoning commission votes on proposed laws and then files the final report with the municipal clerk. The municipal clerk then has 5 days to file the final report with the Secretary of State.

13.8 (c) 12 months.
New budgets are developed and adopted every 12 months to meet the financial needs of taxing districts.

13.9 (b) collecting real property taxes.
When a new budget is created, expenditures and income are estimated and the tax rate is determined so sufficient real property taxes can be collected to cover the deficit in the municipality's finances.

13.10 (c) 6 years
Members of the Planning Board are appointed either by the town board or the mayor and serve terms equal to number of members on the board (7 members, 7 years, etc.) or until appointing board removes or replaces them. Consequently, the members on this particular board would serve 6-year terms.

13.11 (a) subdivision plat review.
State statute or the local governing board provides the Planning Board with regulatory powers only to review subdivision plats and other specific documents. The Board's powers related to master plan development, land use regulations, and capital budgets are advisory powers, not regulatory powers.

13.12 (a) the owner's situation is unique.
The Zoning Board of Appeals may grant a use variance based on several conditions, one of which is if the owner's situation is unique. Whether or not the variance will harm conditions of in the surrounding environment, there is an alternative way to achieve the same benefit, or the variance is substantial are factors weighed for area variances, not use variances.

13.13 (c) using specific land in a way other than as it is zoned.
A use variance is used for a structure that is being used in a way other than how it is zoned, but an area variance is needed when using land in a way other than how it is zoned to be used.

13.14 (b) building signs.
The Architectural Review Board approves new construction and remodeling and provides regulation and guidance for maintaining quality of building exteriors and signs for either new buildings and signs or modifications to existing structures.

13.15 (d) Conservation Advisory Council
The Conservation Advisory Council provides environmental perspective on land use proposals, master plans, stewardship of natural areas, etc. and assists with land use decisions with consideration of environmental issues related to development, management, and protection of natural resources.

13.16 (c) tidal and freshwater.
The NY Department of Environmental Conservation protects tidal wetlands and freshwater wetlands.

13.17 (c) NY Office of Parks, Recreation, and Historic Preservation.
The New York Office of Parks, Recreation, and Historic Preservation handles applications the for National Register of Historic Places listings. Once a structure is placed on a registry, it is automatically listed on both the National and State registers.

13.18 (a) Department of Building.
Department of Building enforces building, electrical, and zoning codes and standards along with NY labor law and multiple dwelling law and issues building and demolition permits; performing inspections; issuing trade licenses, certificates of occupancy, and public assembly permits.

13.19 (a) Four classes of property
Taxes are assessed differently depending on the area of the state. For example, some areas use full value assessment; some use uniform percentage of value; but NYC and Long Island use four classes of property for assessment.

13.20 (b) County Health Department
The County Health Department is responsible for protecting, improving, and promoting health, productivity, and well being of all New Yorkers. In light of that mission, the Department is responsible for reviewing plans submitted by engineers and architects for septic system approvals.

UNIT FOURTEEN TEST: PROPERTY INSURANCE

14.1 (a) The mortgage lender will place coverage on the home.
Mortgage lenders require borrowers to maintain homeowners' insurance coverage on the mortgaged property. If the insurance is allowed to lapse, the lender will force place insurance on the property.

14.2 (d) flood insurance.
If a mortgaged property is located in a flood zone, lenders will require the homeowner to carry flood insurance on the home.

14.3 (d) HO-6
HO-6 policies provide condominium and cooperatives coverage for personal property and interior structures such as cabinets, no coverage for structure itself; the HOA carries coverage for the actual structure.

14.4 (c) HO-8
HO-8 policies provide coverage for older homes where replacement costs are higher than the home's market value. The policy covers repairs or replacements of damaged property with cheaper materials, referred to as functional replacement.

14.5 (c) HO-4
An HO-4 policy is a renters' policy that covers personal property and liability for damage to the property or injuries to third parties within the rented unit.

14.6 (b) If insured for less than 80% of replacement cost, a home's coverage will include a deduction for depreciation.
According to the 80% rule, policies are to cover at least 80% of home's replacement cost, minus the deductible. Not having 80% coverage results in only the cash value of the property being paid based on depreciation and the home's age.

14.7 (d) Damage caused by earthquakes
HO-1 policies cover basic perils and do not include earthquakes.

14.8 (d) 60 days.
When a commercial property has been vacant for 60 days, coverage for water damage, theft, and vandalism are excluded.

14.9 (b) monoline
The two types of policies are monoline that includes one type of coverage or package that includes two or more types of coverage.

14.10 (a) flood and homeowners.
Real estate deals with real property, as do homeowners and flood insurance. Consequently, they are the most common types of insurance related to real estate.

14.11 (b) A fence
Dwelling policies cover the home and attached structures and major systems. Since fences are not an attached structure, they are not covered under dwelling policies.

14.12 (c) Theft
Casualty policies cover vandalism, theft, burglary, machinery damage, and not fire or weather-related damage.

14.13 (b) adds coverage for property or perils that are not included in the base policy.
When a policy excludes certain perils or property, an endorsement can add coverage for specific perils at an additional cost.

14.14 (c) peril policies because they add specific perils to HO-1 policies.
HO-2 policies are peril policies that add specific perils to HO-1 policies.

14.15 (d) The home buyer must first obtain a homeowners', auto, or liability policy.
Because the umbrella policy adds protection to base policies, the base policies must be obtained prior to obtaining the umbrella policy.

UNIT FIFTEEN TEST: LICENSEE SAFETY

15.1 (d) Agents should rely strictly on their GPS in unfamiliar areas.
Agents should know the exact address and note landmarks near the location as well as use their GPS.

15.2 (c) let the office know the agent is in trouble.
Agents should let the office know their location and client information, let the client know the offices has the client's personal information, and establish a subtle code word to use to let the office know if they're in trouble.

15.3 (c) To be aware of situations that may result in a medical emergency
With a record of the agent's health conditions, the broker can alert emergency responders of any condition that may result in a serious and dangerous situation.

15.4 (d) Expensive jewelry
To prevent valuables such as jewelry from potential theft during an open house, the agent should advise the client to remove or secure such items prior to the house showing.

15.5 (a) The agent locking his/her cell phone in the vehicle
The agent should keep the cell phone with him/her at all times in case of a problem.

15.6 (b) Agents should bring a second person along for a house showing.
For safety, agents should practice the buddy system and never show a property alone.

15,7 (b) print an agent's personal address on business cards.
Agents' personal contact information should not be printed on business cards.

15.8 (d) advise the client to refer all inquiries about the home to the agent.
Clients should not talk to other agents or buyers, should not show the home to buyers without an appointment, should be reminded that strangers will be walking through their home, and should refer all inquiries to the agent.

15.9 (c) Two things: she met the client alone and then turned off her cell phoner.
For Marie's safety, she should always use the buddy system and not show or view properties alone. She also should have her cell phone on and ready for use in case of emergency.

15.10 (a) The agents' personal contact information should not be included on business cards.
The safety issue Jose has incorporated into his procedures is putting agents' personal contact information on their business cards.

15.11 (b) Carry a gun.
While wearing practical clothing, not turning your back on clients, and establishing a code word with the office as a safety alert, there are no recommendations for carrying a gun.

15.12 (c) To provide critical information to first responders in case of an emergency
Among other safety protocols a broker can implement, keeping a record of agents' health conditions allows Sherri to provide relevant information to first responders in case an agent is injured or experiencing a health emergency.

15.13 (c) Instead of providing potential buyers information about the home, refer all inquiries Alex.
Rather than talking to other agents or potential buyers, clients should refer all inquiries to the agent.

15.14 (a) A large screen television from the family room
Medications, jewelry, and guns should all be removed, but it's not necessary to remove large televisions as they are too big to be stolen during an open house.

15.15 (d) Open all of the blinds in the house.
While it's recommended not to show a property after dark, if it is necessary to do so, the agent should turn on all of the lights and open all of the blinds in the house.

UNIT SIXTEEN TEST: TAXES AND ASSESSMENTS

16.1 (c) ad valorem taxes.
General taxes levied on homeowners based on the value of the property are known as ad valorem taxes.

16.2 (a) court-ordered sale of the property.
Non-payment of property taxes results in a priority lien on the property enforced by a court-ordered sale of the property.

16.3 (c) only properties that will benefit from the specific improvements.
Special assessments are levied on specific real estate that will benefit from area improvements with the assessment based on how each land parcel will benefit from the improvement.

16.4 (b) New construction
Assessments differ between municipalities and between properties, with lower assessments due to older construction, lower land values, or a combination of both. However, new construction has the opposite effect.

16.5 (c) made with no building permit.
Undeclared improvements are those made without a building permit, thereby denying the taxing authority the opportunity to assure the improvements are in compliance with local laws and building codes.

16.6 (c) Special assessment tax
New York City sales require examination of the sale year tax base, the transitional tax, and the target assessment.

16.7 (a) 15%
New York City assessments may not increase more than 20% in a tax year.

16.8 (b) Equalization factor
Uniformity among taxing districts that use different rates to assess property value is accomplished through an equalization factor.

16.9 (a) full-value assessments.
An equalization factor is only used with less than full-value assessments and is not used with full-value assessments.

16.10 (c) Through real estate taxes
Additional income needed to cover expenses not covered by the anticipated income is raised through real estate taxes.

16.11 (d) Apartment buildings with more than four units
Homesteads include dwellings with four or fewer units, owner-occupied mobile homes, condominiums, farms, and some vacant lands.

16.12 (c) 3.5%
Tax rates may be stated in mills, or 1 tenth of a cent, or in mills-per-dollar ration. Consequently, 35 mills would equal 3.5% or $3.50 per $100 of assessed value.

16.13 (b) appropriation.
Appropriation is authorizing expenses and providing the sources of funds to cover the expenses.

16.14 (d) at different times with varying due dates.
Different tax districts bill at different times with varying due dates, with some districts allowing installment payments.

16.15 (c) Hospitals
Tax exempt properties include those used for tax-exempt purposes and owned by city, state, and federal governments; schools, parks, playgrounds; religious organizations and corporations, hospitals, and educational institutions.

16.16 (a) New York special exemptions and reductions.
New York special exemptions and reductions include veteran homeowners, agricultural land, disabled homeowners, and construction of low-income or multi-family housing, among others.

16.17 (b) $50,000.
While the income limit to qualify for a 50% reduction is $29,000 for the state, the income limit for a 50% reduction is $50,000 for New York City.

16.18 (b) 15%
One choice of exemption for veterans is the alternative veteran's exemption which provides a 15% assessed value reduction for the veteran's service during war. There is also an added 10% reduction if the veteran's service was in a combat zone.

16.19 (d) commercial properties.
Properties eligible for STaR include houses, condos, co-ops, manufactured homes, farm houses, and mixed-use properties, but not commercial properties.

16.20 (a) is March 1.
An assessment grievance and protest must be submitted by Grievance Day which varies from community to community. However, Grievance Day in New York City is March 1.

UNIT SEVENTEEN TEST: CONDOMINIUMS AND COOPERATIVES

17.1 (b) Condominiums are only created by converting rental properties into condos.
Condominiums can be created by converting rental properties or by new construction.

17.2 (c) Condominium Owners Association By-laws
The New York Condominium Act and the Real Property Act regulate condominiums in several ways, but it is the Condominium Owners Association By-laws that set up covenants, conditions, and restrictions for condo residents and provide rules and regulations for condo activities.

17.3 (b) 51%
Conversions from rentals to condos in specific areas requires 51% of tenants to agree to purchase units with conditions for purchases and exemptions from eviction set by law.

17.4 (a) 3 years.
Non-purchasers are exempt from eviction for 3 years with tenants who are disabled or 62 years or older being exempt from eviction for an unlimited timeframe.

17.5 (d) condo sponsor.
The condominium sponsor (condo developer/seller) creates the initial offering plan to be approved by the attorney general prior to the units being sold.

17.6 (d) include the terms of the transaction between the sponsor and a potential buyer.
Letters of intent are provided in the early stages of construction, are nonbinding offers to reserve a unit for purchase, show lenders the potential success of the project to induce project funding, and include the terms of the transaction between the condo sponsor and the potential buyer.

17.7 (c) Sponsor-seller
When selling condominiums, deed preparation as well as title and tax transfers are paid by sponsor-seller.

17.8 (a) asset details.
Condominium board packages are required to include verification of income, asset details, and financing information.

17.9 (c) Appliances
Common elements are those portions of the property that are necessary for condominium existence, operation, and maintenance such as elevators, operating systems, recreational facilities, hallways, building structures. Areas inside the interior walls of individual units, such as appliances and kitchen cabinets, are property belonging to the unit owner and are not common elements.

17.10 (b) the Department of Buildings.
The certificate of occupancy is obtained from the Department of Buildings to confirm compliance with building codes and readiness for occupancy.

17.11 (d) Initial Offering Plan
The initial offering plan is to be approved by the attorney general prior to units being sold. It is then provided to purchasers as disclosure of property tax issues, the unit square footage and floor plan, any hidden fees, and the applicable closing date.

17.12 (b) Sponsor
The sponsor retains financial liability after unit sellout but must turn over control of the board to the unit owner. Further, the sponsor appoints the board of directors and manager to limit the sponsor's involvement in the property.

17.13 (b) Shareholders jointly own the units.
A co-op is a developer-formed associations that buys a housing property which becomes jointly owned and controlled by a group of individuals who hold shares. Shareholders do not own their individual units but have equal shares in the whole complex and proprietary leases.

17.14 (c) Mr. Flemming – 1 vote; Ms. Johnson – 1 vote
New York cooperatives allow one vote per member, regardless of member's number of shares or amount of capital invested. Consequently, these shareholders each are allowed one vote.

17.15 (a) A proprietary lease
A group of individuals hold shares, membership, and occupancy rights to the housing complex through proprietary leases which attach to the unit and are transferred to the new shareholders when one shareholder sells his or her stock in the cooperative.

UNIT EIGHTEEN TEST: COMMERCIAL AND INVESTMENT PROPERTY ANALYSIS

18.1 (b) to acquire a cash flow.
While property ownership does afford tax shelters and earns noncash deductions from the property's taxable revenue, the predominant goal of property investment is to acquire a cash flow from the rent proceeds.

18.2 (c) static risk
Business risks include dynamic risk, which is an uninsurable risk based on changes in economy, income taxes, supply and demand. Static risk is an insurable business risk based on specific events, such as theft or fire.

18.3 (a) The degree to which an asset is convertible to cash in a market transaction
Liquidity relates to converting an asset's value to its cash value. Historically, real estate is illiquid, since it is not readily salable as is a blue-chip stock or a treasury bill.. The latter however is very liquid, since a blue-chip stock can be sold in the stock market instantly.

18.4 (d) Residential property
There is a greater demand for residential properties as investments than any other type of property, with multifamily properties producing rental income.

18.5 (a) Net
Net leases have a single tenant paying rent plus all operating expenses and taxes that apply to the rented premises.

18.6 (c) the tenant pays a negotiated rent amount, and the landlord pays operating expenses.
With gross leases, the tenant pays a fixed rent with the landlord paying the operating expenses. The lease may include a rent escalation clause; also called modified gross lease..

18.7 (c) NOI + reserves – interest – depreciation
Taxable income is the net operating income minus allowable deductions, such as depreciation and loan interest, plus the amount allocated for reserves. The formula is NOI + reserves – interest – depreciation.

18.8 (a) net operating income ÷ rate of return
An investment's value is generally the net operating income divided by an investor's required rate of return, or the rate prevailing in the market for that type of income property.

18.9 (d) taxable income.
Tax liability of an income property is based on taxable income, not cash flow. It is derived by adding the reserves to the NOI, subtracting interest and cost recovery expense, then multiplying the result by the tax rate.

18.10 (b) Depreciation
When determining cash flow, identify cash flowing into the investment as revenue, and out of the investment for expenses, debt service, and other cash items. As depreciation is a non-cash item, it is not used in deriving cash flow.

18.11 (a) net operating income ÷ value or price
The cap rate is the expected rate of return on investment and is determined by dividing the NOI by the investment's value or price.

18.12 (c) Cash flow ÷ cash invested
The cash-on-cash return, or the investment's return inclusive of financing, is determined by dividing the cash flow by the amount of cash invested.

18.13 (a) market value – current debt principal.
Equity is derived by subtracting the current debt principal from the market value, or market value – current debt principal.

18.14 (c) either a percentage or square footage.
The load factor is the difference between the interior usable area and the rentable area and can be expressed as a percentage or as square footage.

18.15 (a) a percentage.
An add-on factor is the difference between usable and rental square footage when added to the usable square footage. It is considered reciprocal of the loss factor.

18.16 (d) Escalation clause
A commercial lease escalation clause protects the property owner against inflationary rises in operation costs by passing the increased costs on to the tenant.

18.17 (b) defines who is to be paid rent and who is to pay the rent.
An attornment clause defines who is to be paid rent and who is to pay the rent; can be defined in letter of attornment instead of lease clause.

18.18 (b) tenant rentable area ÷ building gross rentable area
When determining a tenant's proportionate share of increased operation costs, the tenant's space percentage of gross rentable area of the entire building is used by dividing the tenant's rentable area by the building gross rentable area.

18.19 (c) the base year.
The base year is used in commercial leases to pass increased operations costs to the tenant. It defines when the tenant's liability for property taxes and increased operational costs begins.

18.20 (b) 4 years.
A porters wage escalation clause changes every four years, as this is the index's periodic cycle for increases or decreases..

UNIT NINETEEN TEST: INCOME TAX ISSUES IN REAL ESTATE TRANSACTIONS

19.1 (c) The Act reduced the top corporate tax rate.
The Tax Reform Act of 2018 added alternative minimum tax exemptions, created seven income tax brackets, limits interest deduction on mortgage amounts, limits real estate tax deductions, and reduced the top corporate tax rate.

19.2 (b) $10,000.
The Tax Reform Act of 2018 set a maximum $10,000 deduction from homeowners' total property tax bill during the year the tax is paid.

19.3 (d) acquisition financing.
Points, which is the interest prepaid to lenders, provides a conditional deduction in the payment year only for acquisition financing.

19.4 (b) owner-occupied properties.
Closing costs, which are included in depreciable basis for income properties, are not deductible in the acquisition year for owner-occupied properties.

19.5 (b) 2 or more
Long-term capital gains are the property's appreciation of value when the property has been owned for 2 or more income tax years.

19.6 (a) purchase price plus improvement value minus depreciation.
Income property gains are calculated based on the property's adjusted basis, which is calculated by adding the improvement value to the purchase price and then subtracting the depreciation.

19.7 (c) portfolio
When income is received as a salary or commission, the income is considered active. When it is received as rent or investment income that does not require the owner's day-to-day involvement, it is considered passive income. Income is considered portfolio income when it is received from ownership stock dividends, royalties on intellectual property, or interest from any source.

19.8 (d) 27 ½ years.
The depreciation recovery period is 27 ½ years for residential income property wherein 80% of the income is from property improvements.

19.9 (b) Commercial income property
The 39-year depreciation recovery period is specifically for commercial income properties such as office buildings, retail shopping centers, industrial parks, and professional buildings such as medical offices.

19.10 (b) total purchase cost minus land value.
Depreciable basis is used to calculate the annual allowable deductions. It is calculated by adding specific closing costs such as real estate commissions, legal fees, appraisals, inspections, etc. to the purchase price and then subtracting the land value which is not included in depreciation calculations.

19.11 (c) deferred.
Investment properties use IRS code 1031 as tax shelter for tax-deferred exchanges of like-kind property. This code allows capital gains taxes to be deferred but not forgiven or eliminated.

19.12 (a) Vacant properties held for investment
Properties that qualify for a 1031 tax deferral include investment real properties only; commercial, industrial, income residential, hotels, motels, leaseholds for 30+ years, and vacant property held for investment.

19.13 (c) like-kind property exchanges only.
Investment properties use IRS code 1031 as tax shelter for tax-deferred exchanges of like-kind property. The code applies only to like-kind property exchanges.

19.14 (b) 45 days
When exchanging like-kind properties under IRS code 1031, the replacement property must be designated and identified within 45 days of the sale of the first property. Closing must then take place within 180 days of the sale of the first property.

19.15 (c) 10 years.
When a developer qualifies for Low-income Housing Tax Incentives, the tax credits cover most of the tax expenses for the property and are applied for 10 years.

UNIT TWENTY TEST: MORTGAGE BROKERAGE

20.1 (c) The mortgage banker
Mortgage bankers originate mortgage loans, issue loan commitments, and advance loan funds.

20.2 (b) The mortgage broker
Mortgage brokers find lenders and loans for borrowers, handle loan application and approval, and charge a fee for their services.

20.3 (a) The mortgage broker
Mortgage brokers analyze the borrower's financial potential and creditworthiness to establish preapproval and prequalification for a mortgage loan.

20.4 (a) Issuing the mortgage loan commitment
Only a mortgage banker issues a loan commitment.

20.5 (c) to guarantee the broker's legal compliance.
One of the licensing requirements a mortgage broker must meet is to obtain a surety bond to guarantee legal compliance.

20.6 (b) service the loan.
Mortgage bankers may service loans even after the loan is sold on the secondary market.

20.7 (a) every year.
Once obtained, mortgage broker licenses are renewed annually.

20.8 (b) Mortgage bankers charge brokers a fee for their services.
Mortgage brokers charge borrowers a fee for their services and have the borrower sign a fee agreement.

20.9 (b) 2 years.
Lenders require 2 or more years of the borrower's tax returns.

20.10 (d) Pass a criminal background check
Mortgage broker licensing requires the applicant to pass a criminal and state background check.

20.11 (c) loan commitment letter.
When a lender agrees to fund a mortgage, the lender issues a loan commitment letter to the borrower.

20.12 (a) the mortgage broker.
One of the mortgage broker's responsibilities is to explain the terms of the loan and payment schedule to the borrower.

20.13 (c) work to provide a borrower with a loan that meets his/her needs.
Mortgage brokers and bankers negotiate the terms of mortgage loans with the mutual goal of providing the borrower with a loan that meets his/her needs.

20.14 (d) a dual agency.
A dual agency occurs when a licensee acts as both a real estate agent and a mortgage broker for the same client in the same transaction. If the licensee does not disclose the dual agency to the client and obtain the client's signature on the disclosure form, the dual agency is illegal.

20.15 (a) establishing the borrower will most likely meet the lender's loan requirements.
Mortgage brokers analyze a borrower's financial potential and creditworthiness to determine if the borrower prequalifies for the loan.

UNIT TWENTY-ONE TEST: PROPERTY MANAGEMENT

21.1 (a) Set rents
Both landlords and property managers are responsible for complying with applicable laws. Property managers are responsible for maintaining financial records and finding tenants, but landlords set rent amounts.

21.2 (c) If the management contract grants that authority to the manager
While many management responsibilities are common to the job, the management contract determines exactly what

duties the manager must perform and provides the manager with the authority to perform those duties, such as hiring and firing staff and employees. Without that authority, the manager has no right to hire staff, regardless of the circumstances.

21.3 (c) Owner's authority
Management agreements include the involved parties' names; property description; contract term; owner's purpose; owner's responsibilities; manager's authority and responsibilities; budget; allocation of costs; reporting; compensation; HUD Equal Opportunity statement. The owner's authority is a given and not specified as a component of the agreement.

21.4 (c) Any and all functions specified in the management agreement
A property manager's specific functions are determined by and included in the management agreement.

21.5 (b) the property's past performance and the current market.
The best indicator of future performance and subsequent income is the property's past performance and the current market.

21.6 (d) staff turnover.
When budgeting, managers should include variable and fixed expenses, capital expenditures, outlays for major renovations and construction, and cash reserves set aside for variable expenses. While staff turnover may or may not be a financial consideration, it is not typically a specific expense to be included in the property's budget. Instead, it may fall under variable expenses.

21.7 (c) Building managers are employed to manage a single property.
Resident property managers live on the property they are managing. Building managers are employed to manage a single property but are not required to live on site.

21.8 (d) as determined by the management agreement.
A property manager's responsibilities and functions, including reporting schedules, are determined by the management agreement and may vary from property to property.

21.9 (d) all of the above.
Property managers are required to comply with all laws related to housing, protected classes, and equal opportunities, including the ADA, ECOA, and fair housing.

21.10 (b) cost of services, owner's financial objectives, and tenant needs.
Effective property maintenance requires the manager to balance the owner's financial objectives with the costs of services and tenant needs.

21.11 (c) automatic self-closing and self-locking doors.
The Multiple Dwelling Law requires automatic self-closing and self-locking doors and allows, but does not require, tenants to install additional locks; two-way voice buzzers; landlord-provided heat during certain months; mirrors in self-service elevators in buildings with eight or more units, and chain guards and peepholes on apartment doors in buildings with eight or more units.

21.12 (a) Window guards for children under 16 years of age
While window guards are required, they are for children under 11 years of age, not 16 years.

21.13 (c) until the unit is vacated.
NY rent regulation, administered by Office of Rent Administration of the New York State Division of Housing and Community Renewal, administers rent control which is based on location and applies to buildings with three or more units, properties built before February 1947, tenant occupying unit since July 1, 1971, and until the unit is vacated.

21.14 (b) buildings with three or more units built or renovated since 1974 with special tax benefits.
Rent stabilization is based on location with limited annual rent increase and tenants renew for 1 or 2 years. In NYC, the stabilization applies to buildings with six or more units built between February 1, 1947 and January 1, 1974 and to buildings with three or more units built or renovated since 1974 with special tax benefits.

21.15 (a) changed the method for calculating rents on vacancy leases.
The Rent Act of 2015, which was effective June 15, 2015 through June 15, 2019, changed the method for calculating rents on vacancy leases by allowing landlords to request the unit's rent control or stabilization be removed based on the tenant's income or a vacant unit's registered rent.

21.16 (d) subtracting uncollected rents, vacancies, and evictions from the potential gross income.
To determine the effective gross income, rents and revenues are combined to total the potential gross income. Then uncollected rents, vacancies, and evictions are subtracted from that total to equal the effective gross income.

21.17 (b) deliver a habitable property.
When a property is leased, the landlord's primary responsibility is to provide the property in a habitable condition by maintaining heat and cooling, electrical and plumbing, and keeping the property clean and in repair.

21.18 (d) The tenant declares the landlord in default and vacates the property.
A constructive eviction occurs when a tenant vacates the leased property because the landlord fails to maintain the premises as required.

21.19 (c) requires a New York state court order to remove the tenant.
An actual eviction occurs only when the landlord obtains a New York State court order to remove the tenant for failure to comply with the terms of the lease.

21.20 (d) capital expenditures.
Capital expenditures are costs associated with major renovations and construction or repairs. These costs are variable expenses because they are not consistent from month to month.

UNIT TWENTY-TWO TEST: REAL ESTATE MATH

22.1 (a) $.023 / SF
5/6ths of an acre = (5 x 43,560 SF) / 6, or 36,300 SF. Her commission was (.06 x $28,000) x .50, or $840. $840 / 36,300 SF = $.023 / SF.

22.2 (b) $370,170
The land costs $.50 x 43,560 SF/ac. x 1.5 ac, or $32,670. The home will cost $135 / SF x 2,500, or $337,500. The total property will cost $370,170.

22.3 (a) 12%
The lot measures 43,560 / 4, or 10,890 SF. The tennis court will take up 9,600 SF, leaving 1,290 SF. This amount is 11.8% of the total lot area.

22.4 (c) 40
The total area available for lots is 11.2 acres (16 acres x 70% for houses), or 487,872 SF (11.2 x 43,560). Dividing this area by 12,000 SF / lot = 40.66. Thus he can have a 40-lot subdivision.

22.5 (a) 6
First, the requirement = 2(13'x 9') +2 (18'x 9') =558 SF. Each roll is 2'x 50', or 100 SF. Thus she will need 6 rolls.

22.6 (d) 1,376 SF
First figure the area to be mulched. If the home is 40 x 30, the flower area adds 8' to each side of the house. Thus the outside perimeter of the flowered area is (40+8+8) by (30+8+8), or 46' by 56'. The area of the flowered area is (46' x 56') minus the house area of 1,200 SF. This is 1,376 SF.

22.7 (b) 40 acres
First, remember that a section contains 640 acres. The area in question is a forth of a half of a half of the total section. So divide 640 by (4 x 2 x 2). 4 x 2 x 2 is 16 and 640/16= 40 acres.

22.8 (c) 10 acres
This key to this question is to recall that a section has 640 acres. Theresa's property only is a ¼ of a ¼ of a ¼ of the entire section. Multiply 4 x 4 x 4 which equals 64. Savannah owns 1/64 of the section. Divide 640 by 64 and you get the answer of 10 acres.

22.9 (a) $38,955
Their fixed rent is (1,800 SF x $1.40/SF) x 12 months, or $30,240. The percentage rent is ($41,500 x .0175) x 12, or $8,715. Total rent is ($30,240 + 8,715), or $38,955.

22.10 (a) 5.04%
First, convert to decimals: 2 2/3 % = 2.67%; 5 1/5% = 5.2%; 7 1/4% = 7.25%. Thus total appreciation = (2.67% + 5.2% + 7.25%), or 15.12%. Divide by 3 to derive the average: 15.12% / 3 = 5.04%

22.11 (c) 29 %.
Appreciation as a per cent can be estimated by (1) subtracting the estimated current market value from the price originally paid (239,000 - 185,000 = 54,000) and (2) dividing the result by the original price (54,000 / 185,000 = . 29 or 29%).

22.12 (c) 94%
To find the percent of listing price the offer is, divide the offer by the listing price. In this question the offer is $290,000 and the listing price is $308,000. $$\frac{\$290,000}{\$308,000} = 94\%$$

22.13 (a) $206,000.
Remember the formula V = I / R where V is value, I is annual income, and R is the cap rate. Variations of this are: R = I / V in solving for the cap rate, and I = V x R in solving for income. Here, first identify net income by subtracting out vacancy and expenses. Then divide by the capitalization rate. Thus, ($30,000 – 1,500 – 10,000) / 9% = $205,555, or $206,000 rounded.

22.14 (b) $375,000.
Value = Income / Cap rate. Thus, V= $30,000 / .08 = $375,000.

22.15 (b) $13,600.
First derive the annual depreciation which is the cost divided by the economic life. Then multiply annual depreciation times the number of years to identify total depreciation. Remember to subtract depreciation from the original cost if the question asks for the ending value. Thus, ($16,000 / 20 years x 3 years) = $2,400 total depreciation. The ending value is $16,000 –2,400, or $13,600.

22.16 (a) $1,077
First, Lee's depreciable basis, without the land, is $280,000 x 75%, or $210,000. The annual depreciation for the entire home is ($210,000 / 39 years), or $5,384.61. Second, his office is 20% of the house (500 sf / 2,500 sf). Therefore Lee can take annual depreciation of ($5,384.61 x 20%), or $1,076.92.

22.17 (d) $188,000.
Cost Approach formula: Land + (Cost of Improvements + Capital Additions – Depreciation) = Value. Thus you have $40,000 + ($175,000 - 27,000), or $188,000.

22.18 (c) $475,000
Use the same Cost Approach formula: Land + (Cost of Improvements + Capital Additions – Depreciation) = Value. The land is worth (100,000 x 125%), or $125,000. Remember, you cannot depreciate the land, only the cost of the improvements. Therefore, annual depreciation is ($400,000 / 40), or $10,000. Total depreciation is ($10,000 x 5 years), or $50,000. Thus the value is ($125,000 + 400,000 – 50,000), or $475,000.

22.19 (d) 125.
Use the formula: GRM = Price / Monthly Rent. Thus, $400,000 / $3,200 = 125.

22.20 (c) $194,000.
Use the formula: GIM = Price / Annual Income. To solve for price convert the formula to Price = GIM x Annual Income. Thus, ($1,100 x 12) equals $13,200 annual income. ($13,200 x 14.7 GIM) = $194,040, or $194,000 rounded.

22.21 (d) $750
The loan amount is $200,000 x .75, or $150,000. The first month interest equals ($150,000 x 6%) / 12 months, or $750.

22.22 (b) $179,000.
The equation for the loan amount is (annual interest divided by the interest rate) = loan amount. Thus, ($790 x 12) / .053 = $178,868 or $179,000 rounded.

22.23 (a) 4.82%.
The equation for the interest rate is (annual payment / loan amount) = interest rate. Thus ($1,000 x 12) / $249,000 = 4.82%.

22.24 (b) $1,456.95
In the first month they pay interest of ($280,000 x 6.25%) / 12, or $1,458. If their fixed payment is $1,724, they paid down the principal by $266 ($1,724 - 1,458). Now they must pay 6.25% interest on the new principal balance of $279,734. This equals (279,734 x .0625) / 12, or $1,456.95.

22.25 (b) The second option, by 150.
The first option's interest total is (6.5% x $60,000) x 5 years, or $19,500. The second option will charge (6.25% x $60,000) x 5 years, plus $600, or a total of $19,350. The 2nd option is $150 cheaper.

22.26 (b) 1.67 points
A discount point is one percent of the loan amount. Jose's loan is ($410,000 x 90%), or $369,000. If he paid $6,150, he paid 1.67% of the loan amount ($6,150 / 369,000), or 1.67 points.

22.27 (c) $4,875.
$325,000 x .015 = $4,875. Remember, one point = 1% of the loan amount.

22.28 (c) $162,500
Use the formula: Price x LTV Ratio = Loan. Then plug in the figures and calculate: Price x .80 = $130,000. Therefore, Price = $130,000 / .80 = $162,500.

22.29 (c) $379,259
First, the annual interest paid is $1,600 x 12, or $19,200. The interest rate is 6.75%. Using the formula (Loan = Interest / Rate), the loan amount is $19,200 / 6.75%, or $284,444. As this is 75% of the price, the price is ($284,444 / .75), or $379,259.

22.30 (b) $1,900.
Monthly income qualification is derived by multiplying monthly income by the income ratio. Thus (76,000 / 12) x .30 = $1,900. Remember to first derive the monthly income.

22.31 (a) $253,846
Total depreciation on this property = ($600,000 / 39 years) x 10 years, or $153,846. His adjusted basis is therefore ($680,000 original price – 153,846 depreciation taken), or $526,154. The gain is then ($780,000 – 526,154), or $253,846.

22.32 (b) $257,000.
Adjusted basis = beginning basis ($250,000) + capital improvements ($2,000 + $5,000) – depreciation (0) = adjusted basis ($257,000).

22.33 (c) $34,000.
Capital gain = amount realized (net sales proceeds, $265,000) - adjusted basis ($231,000) = ($34,000).

22.34 (d) $125,000.
The basic formula for adjusted basis is: Beginning Basis + Capital Improvements - Exclusions and Credits = Adjusted Basis. Debra's adjusted basis is therefore $120.000 + $5,000 = $125,000. The financing terms and subsequent selling price are not relevant.

22.35 (c) $15,000 overpriced.
Use the same formula V = I / R where V is the price and R is the rate of return. Then plug in the numbers to solve for V. The NOI of this property is ($60,000 - $22,000), or $38,000. The return is 11%. Therefore, the value to get this return must be $38,000 / .11, or $345,455. Since the price is $360,000, the price exceeds the amount needed for an 11% return by approximately $15,000 ($360,000 - $345,455 = $14,545).

22.36 (b)   Yes, since he will yield 8.375%
Use the same formula R = I / V where V is the $2 million price, and R is the cap rate or rate of return. To identify income: (25,000 SF x $10/SF) = $250,000 gross income, minus 5% vacancy (.05 x $250,000), or $12,500, minus expenses of $70,000 = $167,500 net income. ($250,000 – 12,500 – 70,000)   Now divide net income of $167,500 by $2,000,000 to derive the return of 8.375%.

22.37 (a) $1,680.
Annual gross operating income ($1,650 x 12 = $19,800) - annual operating expenses ($600 x 12 = $7,200) = annual net operating income ($12,600); annual net operating income ($12,600) - cost recovery expense ($7,000) = taxable income ($5,600); taxable income ($5,600) x tax rate (30%) = tax liability ($1,680).

22.38 (c) $10,640
The basic formula for tax liability is: Taxable Income x Tax Rate = Tax Liability. Taxable Income is Net Operating Income - Interest Expense - Cost Recovery Expense. Therefore, the annual tax is $150,000 (NOI) - $105,000 (Interest Expense) - $7,000 (Cost Recovery Expense) x 28% = $10,640. Note that the principal payment is not deductible in calculating taxable income.

22.39 (d)   31.4%
The formula for profit % is (profit / initial investment). The profit made was ($23,000 x 4) – 70,000 initial investment, or $22,000. Dividing this by the amount invested derives a profit percent of 31.4%.

22.40 (c) $1,000,000,000.
The mill rate = (tax requirement / the tax base). A mill is one one-thousandth of a dollar ($.001). To solve for the tax base, reconfigure this formula to be: Base = Tax Requirement / Mill Rate. Thus the Base = $10,000,000 / .010, or $1,000,000,000.

22.41 (a) $1,495
First, always use the assessed valuation, not the market value. Subtract out the homestead exemption to derive taxable value, or $140,000 – 25,000 = $115,000. As a shortcut to calculating the tax bill, simply add up all the mills, multiply them times .001 to convert mills to decimals, then multiply this number times the taxable value. Thus (7 + 3 + 2 + 1) x .001 x $115,000 = $1,495.

22.42 (b)   2.13%
The rate = budget / tax base. Thus, $8,000,000 / (400,000,000 – 25,000,000) = 2.13%

22.43 (d) $1,778.
First calculate the total commission, then the co-brokerage splits, then the agent-broker split. Thus: $127,000 x 7% = $8,890 total commission. ($8,890 x 50%) = $4,445 total listing broker share. ($4,445 x 40% = $1,778 agent's share.

22.44 (a) $6,866
Figure the total commission, then the co-brokerage splits, then the broker-agent splits. Thus, ($325,000 x 6.5%) = $21,125. ($21,125 x 50%) = $10,563. ($10,563 x .65) = $6,866.

22.45 (c)   A credit to the buyer and debit to the seller for $785.34.
The daily tax expense, first, is ($3,150 / 365) or $8.63. Since the buyer will pay the taxes after closing, the seller must pay the buyer his or her portion of the tax bill at closing, which is the 91 days from the beginning of the year through closing. Therefore, credit the buyer and debit the seller ($8.63 x 91), or $785.34.

22.46 (a) $507.50.
If the buyer pays $525 interest for 30 days, the daily expense is ($525 / 30), or $17.50. If there are 29 days of pre-paid expense, the buyer's charge is ($17.50 x 29), or $507.50.

22.47 (d)   Credit buyer $712.26.
For the monthly proration using the 365-day method, solve first for the daily rent amount: ($1,380 / 31), or $44.52. Since the landlord received the rent and owes the buyer portions of the rent, the buyer will be credited. The owed amount is for the 16th through the 31st, or 16 days, since the closing day belongs to the buyer. Therefore, credit the buyer and debit the seller ($44.52 x 16),or $712.26.

22.48 (d) $86,372
First calculate the transfer tax: ($322,600 / 500) = 645.2 units of $500. Round this up to 646, then multiply times $1.00 to get $646 transfer tax cost. Next figure the commission @ ($322,600 x .07), or $22,582. Next, the seller's real estate tax proration charge will be $2,000.   Then, add up the expenses: ($646 transfer tax + 450 title + 550 attorney + 22,582 commission + 210,000 loan payoff + 2,000 tax proration) = $236,228. Subtracting this from the sale price = $86,372.

22.49 (d) $5,848.
Be careful here. Since the net price is $5,000, the taking price (TP) minus the commission must equal the net price. In other words, the net price is 90% of the taking price. Since TP x 90% = Net, TP = Net / 90%. So the taking price is $5,556 ($5,000 / .9).   Apply the same logic to deriving the asking price: the taking price is 95% of the list price, therefore the list price = (taking price / 95%), or $5,848. Now work backwards to prove your answer: (5,848 x 95% margin x .90 net of commission) = $5,000

22.50 (d) $468,750
Use the formula: (Percent of insurable property value carried / 80% replacement cost) x claim = recovery, where the insurable property value variable excludes the land value and is valued at replacement cost. Here, the insurable portion of the property is ($740,000 - 25% land value), or $555,000. The Wildes are carrying insurance to cover 75% of the replacement cost of the entire property. Their recovery amount is therefore (75% / 80%) x $500,000, or $468,750.

22.51 (c) $140,000
Use the formula: (Percent of insurable property value carried / 80% replacement cost) x claim = recovery. Thus, (75% / 80% x $150,000) = $140,625. However, the face value of the policy is the maximum they can receive, which is $140,000

NEW YORK LICENSE EXAMINATION SAMPLE TEST
ANSWER KEY

S 1. (b) 75
The broker pre-license course consists of the 77-hour salesperson course plus the 75-hour broker course for a total of 152 hours. This requirement changed on 12/21/22.

S 2. (b) 2 years.
NY licensure terms are for 2 years. Consequently, licensees are required to complete continuing education requirements and renewal requirements every 2 years to maintain the license.

S 3. (d) prior to entering into a purchase contract.
New York's Real Property Law requires property sellers to disclose the existence of uncapped natural gas wells to purchasers prior to entering into a purchase contract.

S 4. (a) collect rents.
Individuals who collect rent payments must hold a NY real estate license.

S 5. (c) receive a monetary credit against the purchase.
The seller's failure to provide a property condition disclosure to the buyer results in the buyer receiving a $500 credit towards the purchase price of the property.

S 6. (c) allows clients to give advanced consent to dual agency.
Agency disclosures must be in writing and presented to prospective clients or customers at the first substantive meeting. All parties must be presented with the disclosure which allows clients to give advanced consent for a dual agency relationship.

S 7. (a) Open listing
Open listings allow sellers to contract with multiple brokers, and only the broker who procures a ready, willing, and able buyer is paid commission.

S 8. (b) single agent.
Within a dual agency, the broker may assign one sales agent to the seller and another sales agent to the buyer. The broker remains the dual agent, but the designated sales agents are single agents, each with the duty of undivided loyalty to their clients.

S 9. (a) universal agency.
In a universal agency, the principal uses a power of attorney to empower the agent to perform any and all actions that may legally be delegated to an agency representative.

S 10. (b) Trade fixtures that are personal property.
Trade fixtures are items of a tenant's personal property that the tenant has temporarily affixed to a landlord's real property in order to conduct business. Trade fixtures may be detached and removed before or upon surrender of the leased premises. Should the tenant fail to remove a trade fixture, it may become the property of the landlord through accession. Thereafter, the fixture is considered real property.

S 11. (c) Severance and affixing.
Severance is the conversion of real property to personal property by detaching it from the real estate; affixing, or attachment, is the act of converting personal property to real property by attaching it to the real estate, such as by assembling a pile of bricks into a barbecue pit, or constructing a boat dock from wood planks.

S 12. (d) absolute fee simple estate.
The fee simple freehold estate is the highest form of ownership interest one can acquire in real estate. It includes the complete bundle of rights, and the tenancy is unlimited, with certain exceptions. The fee simple absolute estate is a perpetual estate that is not conditioned by stipulated or restricted uses.

271

S 13. (d) Trustor, trustee and beneficiary.
In an estate in trust, a fee owner-- the grantor or trustor-- transfers legal title to a fiduciary-- the trustee-- who holds and manages the estate for the benefit of another party, the beneficiary.

S 14. (a) an encroachment.
Encroachments are unauthorized intrusions on an owner's property that may diminish the property's value. The owner may sue to have the encroachment removed or to receive compensation for damages.

S 15. (c) Power of eminent domain
An easement onto a property owner's land can be created by a government utilizing the power of eminent domain.

S 16. (b) subordination.
Subordination occurs when a lienor changes the priority of a junior lien by voluntarily agreeing to lower the lien's position.

S 17. (d) Voluntary/specific/junior
Liens are either voluntary or involuntary, general or specific, superior or junior. Mortgage liens are voluntary, specific, and junior in that they are specific to a house and inferior or junior as to the order in which they are satisfied.

S 18. (d) actual notice.
A notice is the means in which land ownership is evidenced to the public. An actual notice is knowledge acquired directly through demonstrable evidence, e.g., presenting or inspecting a deed, visiting a party in possession.

S 19. (b) Public grant
Voluntary title transfers are accomplished through deeds, wills, and public grants.

S 20. (c) show claim of right as the reason.
The use of adverse possession for an involuntary title transfer requires the possessor to show claim of right as the reason, to have unconcealed possession, to have hostile possession, and to have continuous possession for a statutory period of time.

S 21. (a) warrant of seisin.
A deed's covenant or warrant clauses include the warrant of seisin which provides the grantor's assurance that he/she actually owns the property.

S 22. (c) clarify and disclose costs associated with mortgage loans.
The Real Estate Settlement Procedures Act (RESPA) was created to protect the public by clarifying and disclosing costs associated with mortgage loans.

S 23. (b) settlement process.
During the settlement process, selling terms and costs are identified, including the determination of prorated and non-prorated debits and credits, and amount and responsibility of prorated debits and credits are figured.

S 24. (d) $2383.44
$3000 annual ÷ 12 = $250 monthly
$250 monthly ÷ 30 days = $8.34 daily
$250 monthly x 9 months (April – December) = $2250
$8.34 daily x 16 days (March 16 – March 31) = $133.44
$2250 + $133.44 = $2383.44 Charlie's debit

S 25. (c) title plant.
A chain of title shows the successive property owners from the original grant to the present. Unrecorded claims result in a cloud on the title; and an abstract of title is a written chronology of recorded owners, transfers, and encumbrances. However, a title plant is a duplicate set of property records that are maintained by a private company.

S 26. (a) estate for years.
There are four types of leasehold estates, with an estate for years being one with a specific lease term.

S 27. (c) shorter lease terms.
Commercial leases tend to have longer lease terms and negotiable lease clauses, while residential leases have shorter lease terms and non-negotiable lease clauses.

S 28. (d) voidable
Voidable contracts may be initially valid, but subsequently rescinded as a result of subsequent discoveries that were not known when the contract was executed.

S 29. (d) a seller accepting a purchaser's offer to purchase the seller's property.
A buyer's offer to purchase a seller's property may be considered as the first step in creating a sales contract, but the contract itself is not created until the seller provides an unqualified acceptance of the offer by signing the offer and returning it to the buyer with no changes.

S 30. (d) when the buyer pays the balance owed on the purchase price.
When an offer is accepted, the purchase price for the property is typically paid over time in installments. Although the buyer takes possession of the property, the seller retains the title until the buyer pays the balance of the purchase price at the end of the payment period. When the balance is paid, the buyer is given the legal title to the property.

S 31. (b) 45 days of the request.
When a mortgage loan is paid in full, a document showing the mortgage has been satisfied must be filed in the county recorder's office. In New York, this must be done within 45 days of the request to do so.

S 32. (a) Investment firms
The secondary mortgage market buys existing loans to provide liquidity to primary lenders and includes Fannie Mae, Ginnie Mae, Freddie Mac, investment firms, life insurance companies, pension funds.

S 33. (c) Borrowers of "federally-related loans" must obtain flood insurance if the property is in a designated flood-hazard area.
The National Flood Insurance Act requires borrowers of federally related loans to obtain flood insurance if the property is located in a designated flood hazard area. Flood zone maps are available that indicate where flood hazard areas are located.

S 34. (c) Truth-in-Lending Simplification and Reform Act
Regulation Z implements the Truth-in-Lending Simplification and Reform Act and the Consumer Credit Protection Act and requires lenders to disclose finance charges and APR prior to closing.

S 35. (d) net worth.
The extent to which an applicant's assets exceed his/her liabilities is referred to as the applicant's net worth.

S 36. (c) Redemption clause
A redemption clause gives the borrower time to satisfy obligations and prevent a forced sale of the property. If the lender holds the borrower in default, the redemption clause gives the borrower the right to reinstatement by performing certain actions, usually paying overdue payments plus expenses to the lender.

S 37. (c) a special exception.
A special exception occurs when the use of a property is not consistent with the zoning ordinance for that area, but the use is allowed to continue if it is clearly beneficial or essential to the public welfare and does not materially impair other uses in the same zone. Examples would be a school built in a residential zone or a hospital build in an industrial zone.

S 38. (b) Justify property tax increases
The goals of land use control include preserving property values; promoting highest and best use; safeguarding public health, safety and welfare; controlling growth; and incorporating community consensus. Increasing property taxes is not a goal of land use control.

S 39. (a) Residential
Residential zones restrict land use to private, non-commercial dwellings and include sub-zones that stipulate the

types of residences allowed.

S 40. (d) The apartment building is an example of an illegal nonconforming use.
When John builds the apartment building in an area strictly zoned for single-family residential homes, the apartment building will be an illegal conforming use that conflicts with the single-family residence ordinance currently in place.

S 41. (c) achieve optimum space efficiency and maximize open space.
PUD zoning restricts use to development of whole tracts for residential, commercial, industrial, or any combination. In doing so, PUD's design purpose is to achieve optimum space efficiency and maximize open space.

S 42. (c) the construction conforms with applicable building codes.
Building inspectors inspect a new development or improvement for code compliance. If the work complies, the municipality or county issues a certificate of occupancy which officially clears the property for occupation and use.

S 43. (c) smoke alarms in new home construction to be hardwired with battery backup.
The New York Smoke Detector Law requires hardwired smoke alarms with battery backup to be installed in all newly constructed homes.

S 44. (d) Single-family houses
The New York New Home Warranty provides exclusive warranty for all new construction home sales and applies to single-family houses and units in multi-unit residential buildings of five stories or less.

S 45. (a) a blueprint.
A blueprint is a scaled drawing of a building and its components that contractors use when constructing a new house or building.

S 46. (c) requires contractors to provide a written contract for the home improvement work.
The New York Home Improvement Law applies to improvements, goods, services costing more than $500; requires contractor to deposit customer payments into an escrow account or bond to guarantee funds are used only for the contracted work; imposes penalties for non-compliance, but none as high as $10,000; and requires contractors to provide a written contract for home improvement work.

S 47. (d) an appropriately licensed professional.
Termite extermination and damage repair is to be done by a NY State Department of Environmental Conservation licensed professional.

S 48. (b) economic obsolescence.
Economic obsolescence occurs when an adverse change in the surroundings results in a loss of value to the subject property. Derrick's house is a victim of economic obsolescence because the drainage ditch right next to his property has had a negative impact on his home's value.

S 49. (a) Cost approach
Steps in the cost approach include estimating land value, replacement cost of improvements, and total depreciation.

S 50. (b) Income approach
The income approach is primarily based on the principle of anticipation wherein the expected future income stream of a property underlies what an investor will pay for the property.

S 51. (c) Construction stops
In the supply-demand cycle, when there is an unmet demand, construction begins and adds supply, which then results in market equilibrium. Then when construction adds more supply to the point there is an oversupply, construction stops which then allows another market equilibrium, after which the demand absorbs the supply, and the cycle begins again.

S 52. (d) conjoining adjacent properties create a combined value in excess of the values of the unassembled properties.
When adjacent properties create a combined value in excess of the values of the unassembled properties, the excess

value is called plottage value.

S 53. (d) the act never happened.
Ignorance of the law, freedom of speech, and lack of intention are no legitimate excuses or defenses for illegally discriminating against someone. The only acceptable defense for such discrimination is proof that the act simply never happened.

S 54. (b) Yes, within sex as a protected class under Federal and New York laws
The New York Human Rights Law includes sex as a protected class and includes sexual orientation within that class. New York City Human Rights Law also includes sex as a protected class with sexual orientation included within that class, as do Federal human rights and anti-discrimination laws.

S 55. (d) Fair Housing Amendments Act of 1988
The Fair Housing Amendments Act of 1988 added sex, handicap, and families with children as protected classes.

S 56. (d) No law because her two-unit home is exempt
Although the laws do protect gender and sex as protected classes, the New York Human Rights Law allows exemptions that include a two-unit home when the owner occupies one of the units. Therefore, Barbara can refuse any protected class she wishes, except race which is never exempt under Jones v. Mayer.

S 57. (a) race
The Jones v. Mayer ruling mandated that discrimination in selling or renting residential housing based on race is prohibited without exception or exemption. Any exemption allowed based on situations or protected class cannot include race.

S 58. (d) Both owner and agent
Unless the property being shown qualifies as a legal anti-discrimination exemption, both the owner and the agent will be liable for discrimination practices because both are violating the law, the owner by restricting the buyer's ethnicity and the agent by going along with it.

S 59. (c) requires lenders to report the locations of housing loans.
To enforce the law and monitor lenders' potential redlining, the Home Mortgage Disclosure Act requires lenders of federally guaranteed or insured loans to report the location of their loans.

S 60. (d) Department of Building
The Department of Building enforces building, electrical, and zoning codes and standards along with NY labor law and multiple dwelling law.

S 61. (b) Planning Board
Members of the Planning Board serve terms equal to number of members on the board (7 members, 7 years, etc.) or until appointing board removes or replaces them.

S 62. (c) Variance
Whether there is an alternative way to achieve the same benefit is a factor weighed by the Zoning Board of Appeals when looking at granting a variance for area land use. Unnecessary hardships, the land's ability to produce a reasonable return, and the uniqueness of the owner's situation are all considered when granting a structure use variance.

S 63. (d) all of the above.
Taxing districts adopt budgets and determine deficits and tax rates. The tax rates are based on the specific district, the amount of deficit identified through the budget, and whether the property is a homestead or not.

S 64. (d) Offering coverage from a company who only employs its own agents
Independent agents sell insurance for multiple companies, comparing pricing and terms for the customer. If a company only employs its own agents, the company would not allow an independent agent to offer coverage through that company.

S 65. (c) Package
Multiple types of coverages require different insurance policies. Consequently, this homeowner would need to obtain a package policy that includes coverages for the home, structures, and third-party injuries.

S 66. (c) exclusion.
Exclusions are perils not covered under policy unless specifically added, resulting in limitations of the policy's coverage.

S 67. (b) When the client is new
Agents should only meet new clients at the office and obtain as much of the client's personal information as possible.

S 68. (d) Have the office call the agent at a specified time.
Agents should keep an eye on all members of groups to prevent theft. They should also notify at least one neighbor of the open house and should not turn their backs on any visitors or clients. However, having the office call at a specified time serves to let the office know the agent is ok.

S 69. (a) Advertise when a house is vacant prior to showing it.
Agents should wear practical clothing, know self-defense strategies, and limit the personal information they share; but they should not advertise when a house is vacant.

S 70. (b) school taxes.
The School Tax Relief program (STaR) allows homeowners to apply for a permanent reduction in school taxes and allows homeowners 65 and older to apply for an enhanced reduction in school taxes.

S 71. (b) from September 1945 to December 1991.
Veterans who served from September 1945 to December 1991 are eligible for the cold war veterans tax exemption.

S 72. (d) the elderly.
The New York special exemptions and reductions include veteran homeowners, construction of low-income housing, agricultural land, the disabled, and others; however, it does not include the elderly.

S 73. (c) $7,500
The tax bill is determined by applying the tax rate to the property's assessed value. So a property assessed at $150,000 with a tax rate of 50 mills (5%) will result in a $7,500 tax bill ($150,000 x 0.05 = $7,500).

S 74. (c) 1/10 cent.
Tax rates may be stated in mills with each mill equaling 1 tenth of a cent (1/10).

S 75. (c) Condominium Owners Association By-laws
The Condominium Owners Association By-laws set the method and means for governing the condo association, property, and finances; provide rules and regulations for condo activities, set the method for obtaining board members and officers, and set up the covenants, conditions, and restrictions for condo residents.

S 76. (b) Disabled tenants
Non-purchasing tenants are exempt from eviction for 3 years, but disabled tenants and residents 62 years and older are exempt from eviction with no time limitation.

S 77. (c) Board of Directors
In co-ops, the board of directors determines who may occupy the units.

S 78. (b) the tenant's proportionate share of operational cost increases.
The tenant's proportionate share of increased operational costs is determined by dividing the tenant's rentable area by the building's gross rentable area.

S 79. (c) space's rentable area.
A space's rentable area is the square footage of floor or unit of space which is used to calculate the annual rent based on full floor tenancy and often includes non-income producing common areas.

S 80. (a) income – operating expenses ÷ investment price.
The return on investment is derived by subtracting the operating expenses from the income and then dividing that figure by the investment price, or income – operating expenses ÷ investment price.

S 81. (b) a tenant pays a fixed rent and the landlord pays operating expenses.
In a commercial gross lease, the tenant pays a fixed rent with the landlord paying the operating expenses.

S 82. (a) a property's adjusted basis.
An income property's gains are calculated based on the property's adjusted basis which is calculated by adding the purchase price and improvement value and then subtracting the depreciation.

S 83. (d) a property's depreciable basis.
A property's depreciable basis is used to calculate annual allowable deductions. The depreciable basis is calculated by subtracting the land value from the total purchase price (to include realtor commission, legal fees, appraisals, etc.).

S 84. (c) The entire capital gain will be taxed.
Under 1031, the replacement property must be designated within 45 days of the first property's sale and the closing on the purchase of the replacement property must take place within 180 days of the first property's sale. Failure to meet those time limits will result in the entire gain being taxable.

S 85. (c) provide letters of loan commitment.
Mortgage brokers solicit, process, place, or negotiate mortgage loans for others and handle the loan application paperwork, but mortgage bankers issue letters of loan commitment.

S 86. (b) Mortgage brokers are responsible for analyzing a borrower's creditworthiness.
Mortgage brokers do not service loans, but they do establish a borrower's preapproval by analyzing the borrower's creditworthiness. Lenders require 2 years of the borrower's tax returns, not 5 years.

S 87. (d) obtain a NY mortgage broker surety bond.
To qualify as a mortgage broker in NY, one must obtain a NY mortgage surety bond to guarantee legal compliance.

S 88. (c) fiduciary
The management agreement creates an agency relationship between the manager and the principal. This is a fiduciary relationship and, in general, the agent is charged with producing the greatest possible net return on the owner's investment while safeguarding the value of the investment for the owner/investor.

S 89. (b) financial reporting to the principal.
Financial reporting to the principal is a fundamental responsibility of the property manager. Reports may be required monthly, quarterly, and annually. Required reports typically include operating budget, cash flow, profit and loss, and budget comparison statements.

S 90. (b) Routine, preventive, and corrective
The foremost maintenance objective is generally to preserve the value of the physical asset for the owner over the long term. Three general types of maintenance are required to keep a property in serviceable condition: routine (day-to-day), preventive (scheduled), and corrective (repairs and replacements).

S 91. (c) Resident manager
Individual managers manage properties for multiple owners; building managers are employed to manage a single property without necessarily living on site. However, resident managers live and manage the property on site. Consequently, Mr. Ignacio is a resident manager.

S 92. (c) 3
The total area of the living room is (8' x 14' + 8' x 18' + 8' x 16' + 8' x 18') = 528 SF. They will therefore need 528 / 200 SF, or 3 whole gallons.

S 93. (d) 218'
Since the investor paid $100,000 total, and that equals $250 per frontage foot, there are 400 frontage feet (100,000 / 250). If the property is two acres, it totals 87,120 SF. Dividing this by 400 produces a lot depth of 217.8'.

S 94. (c) Yes with $360 left over.
The loan she can get amounts to ($240,000 x 80%), or $192,000. The points charge is ($192,000 x .02), or $3,840. Total closing costs are then $3,840 + 800, or $4640. Thus she has $360 to spare.

S 95. (c) $90,000
First, the sale price is 115% of the appraised value, so the appraised value is $230,000 / 115%, or $200,000. The lender will lend $140,000 (70% of appraised value), so the investor will have to come up with $90,000 ($230,000 – 140,000).

S 96. (c) $496,000.
Since the comparable has an extra half-bath, it is adjusted downward to equalize with the subject. Conversely, since it has no patio, the appraiser adds value to the comparable. Thus, $500,000 minus $5,000 plus $1,000 equals $496,000.

S 97. (c) $508
The total assessed value is ($84,550 + 235,000), or $319,550. The annual tax is based on ($319,550 / 100) = 3195.5 100's. Round up to 3196. To derive the annual tax, multiply 3,196 x 1.91, or $6,104.36. Divide this by 12 for the monthly escrow: ($6,104 / 12) = $508.

S 98. (d) $92,000
The formula for equity is (current value – indebtedness). The current value is ($180,000 + 25% x 180,000), or ($180,000 x 125%), or $225,000. The current debt is ($180,000 x 80%) - $11,000, or $133,000. Their equity is therefore $92,000.

S 99. (b) $166,150
Use the formula: Gain = (Net selling price – adjusted basis) where adjusted basis = (beginning cost – depreciation). The selling price is $240,000 x 5% annual appreciation x 10 years, or ($240,000 + 50% x 240,000), or $360,000. Since land cannot be depreciated, the depreciable basis is ($240,000 total cost – 60,000 land value), or $180,000 (land = 25% total value). Annual depreciation = ($180,000 / 39 years), or $4,615. Thus total depreciation is ($4,615 x 10 years), or $46,150. The adjusted basis is therefore ($240,000 – 46,150), or $193,850. The total gain is therefore ($360,000 – 193,850), or $166,150.

S 100. (c) $80,000
Applying the formula (percent of insurable property value carried / 80% replacement cost) x claim = recovery), divide the amount of coverage carried ($160,000) by 80% of the insurable property value ($250,000) to get the percent of the claim the company will pay (80%). Multiply this percentage by the claim amount to get $80,000, what the company will pay.

Appendix: Useful Websites

New York Real Estate License Law Handbook
https://dos.ny.gov/system/files/documents/2022/03/re-law.pdf

New York State Department of State - Division of Licensing Services
123 William St. 2nd Fl.
New York, NY 10038-3804
https://dos.ny.gov/real-estate-broker

New York State Association of REALTORS®
130 Washington Avenue
Albany, NY 12210
518.463.0300
https://www.nysar.com/

Real Estate Board of New York
570 Lexington Avenue, FL 2
New York, NY 10022
212-616-5200
Education@rebny.com
https://www.rebny.com/contact/

If you liked New York Real Estate License Exam Prep, check out the other titles of Performance Programs Company!

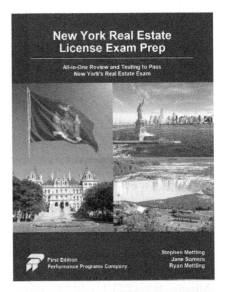

Cramming for your real estate exam? You need New York Real Estate License Exam Prep!

Where can you buy New York Real Estate License Exam Prep?
New York Real Estate License Exam Prep (NY-RELEP) is available as a printed book or e-book through nearly all online retailers.

Looking for a real estate principles textbook? Get what all the students love -- Principles of Real Estate Practice 6th Edition!

Principles of Real Estate Practice 6th Edition is invaluable reference material for real estate professionals. Its 485-pages contain the essentials of real estate law, principles, and practices taught in real estate schools and colleges across the United States.

Where can you buy Principles of Real Estate Practice 6th Edition?
Principles Real Estate Practice is available as a printed book or e-book through nearly all online retailers.

Struggling with real estate math? The solution to that equation is Real Estate Math Express!

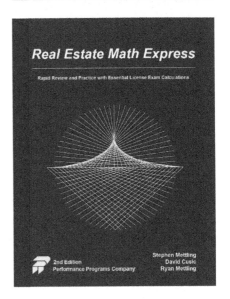

Real Estate Math Express is a concise, easy-to-study test preparation guide to help real estate students improve their real estate math scores to pass the state licensing test. The primary feature of Real Estate Math Express is that it contains all necessary formulas and practice questions in 70+ pages.

Where can you buy Real Estate Math Express?
Real Estate Math Express is available as a printed book or e-book through nearly all online retailers.

Publisher Contact
Ryan Mettling
Performance Programs Company
6810 190th Street East, Bradenton, FL 34211
ryan@performanceprogramscompany.com
www.performanceprogramscompany.com

Made in the USA
Middletown, DE
15 September 2023

38578711R00157